DOOMED FIRMS

To Matt

and to the memory of my dear mother

Doomed Firms

An Econometric Analysis of the Path to Failure

P.J. CYBINSKI
School of Economics
Faculty of Commerce and Administration
Griffith University,
Brisbane, Australia

Routledge
Taylor & Francis Group
LONDON AND NEW YORK

First published 2003 by Ashgate Publishing

Reissued 2018 by Routledge
2 Park Square, Milton Park, Abingdon, Oxon OX14 4RN
711 Third Avenue, New York, NY 10017, USA

Routledge is an imprint of the Taylor & Francis Group, an informa business

A Library of Congress record exists under LC control number: 2003056037

ISBN 13: 978-1-138-71197-6 (hbk)
ISBN 13: 978-1-315-19935-1 (ebk)

Contents

List of Figures

List of Tables

Preface

Never in the history of corporations has the subject of bankruptcy analysis been so pertinent to managers as it is today. The magnitude of recent corporate collapses and the economic losses suffered by the community has raised the issue of public confidence in corporate management, and in the auditing profession's ability to warn investors and the public about a firm's future viability. In the light of the current crisis facing the auditing profession, this book attempts to improve our understanding of enterprise failure by offering a method for bankruptcy modelling that emphasises process over the bankruptcy event.

Understanding bankruptcy presents an enormous theoretical challenge that still remains to be met, probably because past efforts were more concerned with prediction than with explanation. That such a theoretical challenge has largely gone unanswered is relatively easily understood. For practical and commercial reasons, predictive models that estimate risk of failure and/or give a warning of imminent bankruptcy (rather than theoretical explorations) have been the 'Holy Grail' of researchers. Not surprisingly lending institutions, investors, fund managers, credit insurers, auditors and others have backed such research aims. Consequently, financial distress as an area of research has been 'putting the cart before the horse', as a result of commercial pressures to produce the elusive reliable bankruptcy prediction model, when the field is still at a relatively formative stage of development. It has been concerned with prediction before proper explanations for the bankruptcy phenomenon have been tendered or hypothesised, then analysed and tested in a scientific manner.

Improved bankruptcy modelling will also, no doubt, engender greater public confidence in auditor objectivity with the professional use of quantitative decision support. Current audit procedures require the auditor to trust client management for information in an intensive, interactive relationship that has led to standards that focus on prescriptive behavioural parameters. Rather than introducing more of the same in the imminent revision of auditing standards, the inclusion of sophisticated and objective approaches to audit procedures such as statistical modelling should be seriously considered. This would allow for a more impartial analysis of the client firm and provide an opportunity for auditors to increase their professional decision-making expertise.

As a statistician, I have presented the problem of firm failure from a statistician's perspective rather than giving it an economics or an accounting focus. In this respect the reader who is well versed in the latter disciplines may be expecting more discussion and interpretation of the models tendered within the context of those disciplines. I leave it up to the experts in those fields to debate the meaning and implications of my statistical results and I offer only brief interpretations regarding the significant predictors in the various models. I make no apology for this, as the purpose of the book is not to influence corporate policy but rather to improve model building and estimation. The specific data and models are but vehicles to this end.

My intention is also to offer a manual for those graduate students and other researchers in the field of bankruptcy modelling who would like to apply the methods to their own data. To facilitate this I have included many of the SAS programs that I wrote, as appendices to the book. Alternatively, the SAS ASSIST application will automatically do much of the programming required for the straightforward logit models and descriptive statistics presented in the early chapters. Similar applications can also be found in various other major statistical packages.

It is important that I record my appreciation to a number of people without whom this book would not have reached publication stage.

Firstly, I am indebted to Dr. John Forster of the School of Economics at Griffith University. Without his support, encouragement, and patience, I would not have endured and completed the thesis on which this book is based. Many difficult issues were resolved due to his willingness to listen and his enthusiasm for the work. John was able to see the forest when I was focussing on the trees. I am particularly appreciative of the time he has spent reading and re-reading the various drafts of the chapters and for all the constructive criticism received. He read the drafts not only carefully, but also expeditiously, and I appreciate the latter almost as much as the former.

Secondly, I would like to thank the Faculty of Commerce and Administration, University of British Columbia, Vancouver, for allowing me to access the COMPUSTAT database, and especially to Dr. Joy Begley of that institution for her help and advice; also to Professor Keith Houghton of the University of Melbourne, Professor Peter Booth of the University of New South Wales, and Professor Scott Holmes, of the University of Newcastle, for the time and effort spent in thoroughly examining the final manuscript and offering their suggestions and advice. The book is much improved as a consequence. I am grateful to Professor Gordon Karels of the University of Nebraska, and the other (anonymous) reviewers of a sample chapter, for their very helpful comments.

I thank the editors of the *Journal of Business and Management*, *Managerial Finance,* and the *International Journal of Business and Economics* for their kind permission in allowing me to use some previously published material in this book.

Lastly, my most heartfelt thanks go to my son, Matthew, who, through no choice of his own has sacrificed many hours to this work that were rightfully his. Yet, just by being there, he gave me more support than he will ever know.

Patti Cybinski

PART I
THEORETICAL ISSUES

Part I of the book introduces the field of study; that of modelling failure in public firms as measured by various gauges, particularly that of bankruptcy. The first chapter suggests that this dichotomous gauge, i.e. bankrupt/not bankrupt, has determined the static and often simplistic modelling trap that much of the area has fallen into, with only a few researchers attempting to break away. This chapter outlines the rest of the book and its overall philosophy. It argues for a move towards explanation rather than prediction associated with a focus on the process of failure rather than upon purely static models.

The second chapter provides the evidence and background for this stance in the form of a highly critical review of the area. It indicates the major contributions of the past thirty years, concentrating on the weaknesses and challenges of these prior studies and especially their associated methodologies. It is argued that this work has massively over-emphasized method at the expense of methodology, as a consequence becoming blinded to new and alternative approaches. This discussion distils some of the concepts and methodologies of prior research that are relevant to the book's research and that will provide the basis for the new methodology and research design.

The third chapter follows through with an entirely new research agenda. A new modelling methodology is required, this chapter indicating the form of the new methodology. It raises a variety of issues by developing the new methodology for financial distress, which includes the role of explanation rather than prediction, and allowance for empirical testing of hypotheses that may be developed. It describes some of the statistical methods required. A specific family of models is then presented which allows individual models to be considered within an overall framework rather than in isolation.

Chapter 1

Introduction

A major impetus for writing this book arose from the conviction that our insight into the process of firm failure can be enhanced by making more extensive and appropriate use of the internal financial histories of failed firms, along with the data that describes the external economic environment in which these firms operated. However, these data are often artifactual in nature and the notion of 'failure' is itself, subjective. At best, it can be measured on a qualitative or categorical scale as an event rather than as a process, given that failure is preceded by degrees of financial distress.

Unfortunately, the data that we have are generally available for only a few discrete, and not completely regular, points in time and it is these data with which we are forced to work. We need new methodologies that better link our data with the realities of financial distress.

Despite the measurement problems referred to above, there has been strong and continued interest in the subject of bankruptcy prediction, because accurate instruments would benefit many interested parties, such as investors, lenders, auditors, management, employees and their unions. Using multivariate statistical techniques, bankruptcy models have had varying degrees of success in classifying firms *ex post*, as bankrupt/non-bankrupt.

These methods usually employ an estimation sample that consists of bankrupt and solvent, usually strong, firms as the basis for discrimination. Scott provides a summary of the process:

> Most bankruptcy-prediction models are derived using a paired-sample technique. Part of the sample contains data from firms that eventually failed; the other part contains contemporaneous data from firms that did not fail. A number of plausible and traditional financial ratios are calculated from financial statements that were published before failure. Next, the researcher searches for formula based either on a single ratio or a combination of ratios, that best discriminates between firms that eventually failed and firms that remained solvent. A careful researcher also tests the resulting formula both on the original sample and a holdout sample that was not used to derive the formula (Scott, 1981, p. 320).

Regarding this and other types of business research, Emory and Cooper suggest that:

> A rough measure of the development of science in any field is the degree to which explanation and prediction have replaced reporting and description as research objectives. By this standard business research is in a relatively formative stage of development (Emory and Cooper, 1991, p. 14).

Financial distress prediction, as an area of research, in its crude form as described by Scott, can be regarded as being at just such a relatively formative stage, since no rigorous theoretically derived hypotheses have yet been entirely satisfactorily formulated and tested within the existing methodology. On this topic, Ohlson states:

> Most of the analysis should simply be viewed as descriptive statistics – which may, to some extent, include estimated prediction error-rates – and no 'theories' of bankruptcy or usefulness of financial ratios are tested (Ohlson, 1980, p. 111).

With these comments in mind, this book develops a new methodology for the theoretical and empirical analysis of bankruptcy. It is intendedly *explanatory* rather than predictive. It concentrates on (disequilibrium) dynamics and not state comparisons, because it is more likely that bankers and other resource suppliers need to assess the likelihood of bankruptcy for *problem* companies, not financially strong ones. What is needed are models that can either discriminate between 'at risk' firms that survive and 'at risk' firms that fail or that give an indication of which factors are involved when a firm that was surviving becomes one that is failing. It is the latter, which is the central question of this book. A definitive solution to either objective is difficult, at best complex with currently available distressed firm data, again emphasizing the need to search for new methodologies.

This book makes no claims about being the final word in developing such a methodology, but rather, by addressing some of these challenges, it explores and opens up new areas of research rather than closing them off.

1.1 The Distress Continuum

The major problem in bankruptcy research to date is highlighted in the exposition that follows:- that the nature of the dependent variable, 'failure', is not a well-defined dichotomy as it should be for the types of modelling techniques that have been used to analyse it e.g. logit analysis[1] or discriminant analysis. This section examines the basic bankruptcy problem as now embedded in the literature.

Consider a model developed on n variables to distinguish between two groups of failed and non-failed firms. This can be represented graphically on some (n-1)-dimensional hyperplane. For instance, and for ease of exposition, Figure 1.1,

---

1 Although dichotomous input is used, logit analysis (logistic regression) is more useful in that it will give predictions on a continuum, which can be interpreted as the probability of an event (say, failure), conditional on the explanatory variables.

below, shows the cut-off for discrimination between the two populations on only one normally distributed variable that has historically been shown to influence firm failure, as a point on the X-axis. (Probability density shown on the vertical axis.)

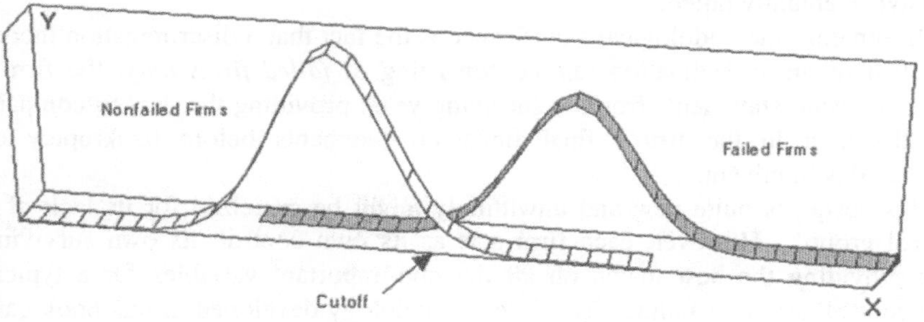

Figure 1.1 Discrimination on One Normally Distributed Variable

In many studies of bankruptcy the reported misclassification rates have been small, usually when the two groups of failed and nonfailed firms are already well separated in multidimensional space, as in the illustrative diagram, Figure 1.1, but we are often interested in a much finer distinction. It is the area of overlap, or indecisive area which is most difficult to classify but which is also of most interest.

The performance of a model is highly dependent on its potential to separate the groups in multidimensional space, i.e. to reduce this 'grey' area to a minimum, which is in turn dependent on the sophistication of the modelling technique, whether the model is complete i.e. it includes the important explanatory variables and, more importantly, where the sampled firms lie on the success-failure continuum. It is not surprising that these model formulations are most successful when the data conforms to the expectation that the two groups are already well separated on the success-failure continuum i.e. a bankrupt group and a non-risky surviving group. A study by Gilbert, Menon and Schwartz (1990) provides evidence that supports this logic.

With these inherent problems in the modelling procedure and with no firm grounding in theory, it is contended, with reference to the quote from Emory and Cooper above, that 'explanation' is the level of sophistication that researchers should now be aiming for rather than 'prediction'. This requires a complete review and an almost complete revision of the statistical and modelling methodology employed in studies of firm failure. This book attempts to do this in Chapters 2 and 3 and then attempts to take initial steps in formulating a generalized model for failure risk.

1.2 Study Methodology

As detailed in Chapter 3, this book investigates the distress continuum with a design that is an improvement over past studies in model specification for relevance over time, and for its ability to investigate the *pattern* of failure over time for firms that have eventually failed.

Of immense methodological significance is the fact that a discrimination model is built here on an estimation sample consisting of *failed firms only*; the firm's earlier financial statements from its surviving years providing the data to compare with the data in the firm's final financial statements before bankruptcy or liquidation is imminent.

This design is quite new and unwittingly might be criticized for its lack of a 'control group'. However, each firm acts as its own control; its own surviving years providing the best match on all the non-important variables for a typical 'case-control' study of failure risk. The methodology developed in this book can, in some ways, be regarded as linking these years together with a single explanatory model. Though, if a comparison is to be made with a survival study in the health field, here we are more interested in the progression mechanisms of the 'disease' once it is established rather than examining healthy versus diseased firms - or the probability of contraction.

In addition, because a purely ratio-based model may not show sufficient discrimination between the earlier 'at risk' or distressed firm-years and the final bankrupt year, external factors relating to the macro-economy were included to help properly model both the external environment of the firm as well as the time dimension of the model. As Johnson points out:

> Ratios to predict failure... do not contain information about the intervening economic conditions... the riskiness of a given value for (a) ratio changes with the business cycle... (Johnson, 1970, pp.1166-1167).

1.3 Background and Position of the Book

Numerous researchers have investigated the distress continuum. As early as 1968, Altman selected his non-bankrupt sample based on the fact that they had losses in at least two of the three previous years (matched on the year of bankruptcy). Hong (1983) developed a theoretical model to distinguish among three categories of financially distressed firms; firms that file for bankruptcy and then successfully reorganize, firms that file for bankruptcy but ultimately liquidate, and firms that continue operating without filing for bankruptcy. Casey, McGee and Stickney (1986) tested empirically a model proposed by White (1981, 1984) for distinguishing bankrupt firms that successfully reorganize from those that liquidate.[2]

More recent research by Gilbert, Menon, and Schwartz (1990), and Flagg, Giroux, and Wiggins (1991) has produced new insights into the finer distinction between distressed firms and failed firms. Gilbert *et al* (1990) excluded obviously strong firms from the nonbankrupt portion of their estimation sample to conclude that ratio-based models perform poorly in identifying likely bankruptcies from a pool of problem companies. Flagg *et al* (1991) considered failing firms exclusively and used four failure-related events in addition to standard financial ratios to predict which firms will ultimately go bankrupt. Both these studies used designs that represent a far more difficult predictive environment than previous studies but neither took into account the external influence of the macro-economy on the failure process. Neither did they veer from the traditional cross-sectional study, assuming stationarity of failure models over time. Models designed to examine failure risk (and many attempt to predict it) must incorporate appropriate lead-lag relationships among observed economic data series – a common feature of empirical economic research.

The decision in this book not to ignore the timed influence of the macro-economy on firm failure risk is a necessary and important modelling refinement that has been missing empirically until only very recently in the financial distress literature.[3] It can be properly argued, therefore, that the work described provides a first step in formulating a generalized model for failure risk with *an emphasis on the dynamics of failure* – one that may shed light on the patterns of financial health experienced by firms over time in the context of the prevailing economic conditions. As argued in the opening section of this chapter, the aim is for explanation rather than prediction of financial distress, though this work still has the potential to be applied to many of the areas to which bankruptcy prediction models aspire. With express knowledge of the failure mechanism acting upon firms that we know to be failing it still may be possible to curb failure with specific and timely intervention or even to recognize it's presence in a firm that is currently a going concern.

---

2 Note that publicly traded companies that fail either file Chapter X1 bankruptcy petitions, liquidate under Chapter 7 of the bankruptcy code, or merge with other firms. These studies included firms that choose bankruptcy voluntarily (Chapter XI) and are concerned with reorganisation under the new Bankruptcy Code of 1978 (the Bankruptcy Reform Act of 1978) where requirements were relaxed for debtor firms to enter bankruptcy.

3 Studies by Theodossiou (1993), and Hill, Perry, and Andes (1996) have included the time dimension in their respective models of firm failure.

1.4 Structure of the Book

This book is divided into three sections and eight chapters arranged as follows:

Section I Theoretical Issues

The first three chapters present an introduction to the field, the motivation for this book and a complete review and a new statistical and modelling methodology for studies of firm failure.

Chapter 1 establishes the motivation for this book. It provides an introduction to the field of financial distress prediction and gives evidence about the importance of explanation of the failure phenomenon rather than its prediction as an appropriate research goal if the long-term aim is to gain more useful, valid, and practical knowledge in this field. It argues that the focus of the research ought to be on the distress continuum, which requires the formulation of dynamic rather than static models of failure.

Chapter 2 reviews and loosely categorizes the different areas within the financial distress literature to date. It summarizes the major contributions of the past thirty years, concentrating in the main on the last decade and discusses the strengths, weaknesses, and challenges presented by these prior studies and their associated methodologies. This discussion distils some of the concepts and methodologies of prior research that are relevant to the book's research and that will provide the basis for the new methodology and research design.

Chapter 3 presents the initial steps in formulating a generalized model for failure risk based on a family of multi-equation models. A detailed discussion of the new methodology along with the modelling procedures and techniques necessary to implement the methodology are given.

Section II Empirical Issues: Towards a Dynamic Modelling of Financial Distress

Chapters 4 to 7 examine the quantitative issues arising in the modelling of failed firms and present specific empirical formulations of the different models of firm failure that were theorized in Chapter 3. It is recognized that both environments act simultaneously on the firm but initially, the two data sets, the internal financial data of the firms and the external macroeconomic data of the USA, were isolated, with separate and different data analyses performed on each set. Then a combined single-equation model of failure risk for the failed service industry firms is estimated based on both internal and external variables but that still treats the data from different years for each firm as independent observations. The assumption of independent observations as well as independent predictors of firm failure is abandoned in subsequent chapters when further, more complex multi-equation models are estimated from the family of generalized linear models presented in Chapter 3.

Chapter 4 describes the data collected from financial statements on failed US firms in the Service group of Standard Industry Codes for the 21 year period 1971-

1991 and examines any relevant data issues that apply to this data; for example the treatment of measurement errors. Using stepwise regression methods, a preliminary single-equation logit model of firm failure is estimated with only the internal financial variables as predictors, and which takes no account of the dependencies that exist between firm-years.

Chapter 5 discusses the Principal Components Analysis used to provide the raw macro-economic variables for the subsequent modelling of this aspect of failure risk and the naming of these orthogonal variables. Further, a discussion of the experimentation with different lag models is given. These transform the external variables in order to account for their possible delayed effects on firms at risk. Finally, a second preliminary model of failure risk is given similar to the first model presented in Chapter 4, but now modelled on only the external variables, again taking no account of the dependencies that exist within firms from year to year.

In Chapter 6, a combined failure risk model based on both the internal and external variables is estimated, assuming independence between firm-years within firms. The statistical probabilities yielded by the logit model are used to measure a firm's level of insolvency risk at each period prior to failure. These signals of a firm's deteriorating condition are produced sequentially for many years before failure and can be useful in predicting a firm's tendency towards failure.

Chapter 7 presents models that incorporate the data dependencies within each firm from year to year i.e. models that include lagged risk and multi-equation structures such as a seemingly unrelated regression model. Some of the predictors that were assumed independent but were actually highly correlated in the single-equation models of earlier chapters are now treated as endogenous to systems of simultaneous equation models.

Section III Discussion and Conclusions.

Chapter 8 summarizes and integrates the book. It also presents a discussion and the concluding remarks about the work conducted.

1.5 Publications

This book is being published with the kind permission of the editors of the journals in which the following papers already appear in relation to this work:

Cybinski, P.J., (2000), 'The Path to Failure: Where are Bankruptcy Studies at Now', *Journal of Business and Management*, 7(1) Spring, pp. 11-39.

Cybinski, P.J., (2001), 'Description, Explanation, Prediction - the Evolution of Bankruptcy Studies?', *Managerial Finance*, 27(4), Special Issue, 'Detection and Prediction of Financial Distress', ed. K.Kumar, pp. 29-44, MCB Press, UK.

Cybinski, P.J. and Forster, J., (2002), 'The Macroeconomic Environment and the Process of Business Failure: Explorations with U.S. Firms in an Economically Volatile Period, 1974-1988', *International Journal of Business and Economics*, Fall, pp.13-23.

Chapter 2

Precursors and Challenges in the Literature

2.0 Introduction

The literature of financial distress prediction is huge and broadly based in terms of publication outlets, e.g. banking, economics, finance, accounting, statistical, and lately, information systems journals. The review that follows is non-exhaustive, since excellent review literature already exists for the studies of the 1960s and the 1970s. I refer to the work of Scott (1981), Ball and Foster (1982), Altman (1983), Zavgren (1983) and Foster (1986). Also Taffler and Abassi (1984) offer an informative literature review in the related context of debt rescheduling among developing countries and Jones (1987) offers a comprehensive literature review of the 1980s publications.

The aim of this chapter is to extend those reviews into the 1990s to show the evolution of thought over the last decade in a number of new and exciting directions. This has been achieved by summarizing only the important papers in the area that are the precursors of the newer literature that builds upon those papers. For ease of exposition and in the absence of any theoretical underpinning to the area, 'importance' is usually defined here to mean 'an extension to technique', either statistical or by design, rather than 'an extension of the methodology'. This is because motivations for new research in the area have occurred when either a new technique or new database becomes available and usually not because of any new theory in the area. In the former case, attempts to use models to guide empirical research on distress have usually drawn on either the statistical or applied mathematical rather than economics literature. Possible exceptions are some of the studies in section 2.3 which are based on explicit economic theory.

So with the above intention in mind, this chapter attempts to systematically explore the state of the art. It is organized as a historical summary of those papers where a major extension in technique has occurred. These are broadly categorized for the reader to highlight what are believed to be the important areas where these extensions have been achieved in the last decade:

- Theories of bankruptcy influencing the choice of independent variables;
- The time dimension and dynamic models;
- Statistical methodology;

- The distress continuum; and
- New technology as the impetus for new methodology.

2.1 The Pioneering Models

Historically significant studies are those of Beaver (1966), univariate, and Altman (1968;1971) and Ohlson (1980), multivariate. The models of these three authors will be discussed at greater length since subsequent studies largely constitute modifications of their approaches.

2.1.1 Beaver (1966) – Univariate Models

Beaver (1966) applied a univariate approach in predicting corporate failure and used ratios selected on the basis of three criteria: popularity in the literature, performance of the ratios in previous studies, and adherence to a 'cash flow concept'. He applied a univariate ratio analysis for 30 ratios with up to 5 years lead time taken from 79 failed industrial firms matched by industry and asset size to nonfailed firms. Beaver defined 'failure' to mean 'any of the following events have occurred: bankruptcy, bond default, an overdrawn bank account, or non-payment of a preferred stock dividend' (p. 71). The data were selected from *Moody's Industrial Manual* and a list of bankrupt firms provided by Dun and Bradstreet.

His view of the firm as a 'reservoir of liquid assets, which is supplied by inflows and drained by outflows (and) the solvency of the firm can be defined in terms of the probability that the reservoir will be exhausted' (pp. 79-80) created widespread interest. His cash flow model was based on logical rather than theoretical propositions, that:

(1) The larger the reservoir, the smaller the probability of failure.
(2) The larger the net liquid-asset flow from operations (i.e. cash flow), the smaller the probability of failure.
(3) The larger the amount of debt held, the greater the probability of failure.
(4) The larger the fund expenditures for operations, the greater the probability of failure. (Beaver, 1966, p.80)

Beaver used the above four propositions in the empirical analysis of the predictive ability of the financial ratios. A comparison of mean values indicated that the means of the chosen ratios were different for the failed and nonfailed firms in the directions consistent with the four propositions. Then, using a dichotomous classification procedure that was validated against a holdout sample, the original set of ratios was reduced to a set of six ratios that were parsimoniously best in classifying firms as failed or nonfailed. The best performing ratio was cash flow to total debt with an overall error rate on the holdout sample of 13 percent for one year prior to failure and 22 percent for the fifth year before failure. The ratio of net income to total assets was the second best predictor, and the other ratios, in declining order of predictability, were total debt to total assets, working capital to total assets, current ratio, and no credit interval (ibid., p. 85). Since different costs are attached to each of the within group errors (Type I error = misclassifying a failed firm and Type II error = misclassifying a nonfailed firm), these have to be considered. These rates were 22 percent and 5 percent, respectively (ibid. p. 89) one year before failure with the Type II error remaining stable over the five year period but the Type I error increasing as the number of years prior to failure increased.

Nevertheless, Beaver's predictors perform well in the short term but classification can only occur for each ratio taken singly, which may give inconsistent results for different ratio classifications on the same firm. Also, most financial variables are highly correlated and it is problematic to assess the importance of any variables in isolation. Since the financial status of a firm is actually multidimensional and no single ratio is able to encapsulate the complexity of the interrelationships that exist, researchers found more promise in multidimensional techniques that could integrate the important ratios into a single measure.

2.1.2 Altman (1968) and Early Followers – Multiple Discriminant Analysis Models

Altman (1968) pioneered the use of multiple discriminant analysis (MDA) for predicting bankruptcy. His sample consisted of 33 'manufacturers that filed a bankruptcy petition under Chapter X of the National Bankruptcy Act during the period 1946-65' (ibid. p.593) paired with 33 nonbankrupt manufacturing firms randomly selected from a sample stratified on asset size. For one year prior to either bankruptcy or the study period, five variables provided the most efficient discriminant function from the original 22 variables. No cash flow variables were included. His discriminant function has been published extensively:

$$Z = 0.012\,X_1 + 0.0141\,X_2 + 0.033\,X_3 + 0.006\,X_4 + 0.999\,X_5$$

Where X_1=Working Capital/Total assets, X_2=Retained Earnings/Total assets, X_3=Earnings before interest and taxes/Total assets, X_4=Market value equity/Book value of total debt, X_5=Sales/Total assets, Z=Overall index.

On a strictly univariate level, all the ratios indicate higher values for the non-bankrupt firms, and since they all display positive coefficients in the equation one can assess any firm's likelihood of bankruptcy; the greater the firms bankruptcy potential, the lower the discriminant score.

On the original estimation sample the Type I and Type II errors were only 6 percent and 3 percent, respectively (cf. Beaver's 22 percent and 5 percent on one ratio). Using data for two years prior to bankruptcy, a second classification produced increased errors of 28 percent and 6 percent, respectively. For validation purposes, a secondary holdout sample of 25 bankrupt firms was classified and gave a Type I error of 4 percent but an additional sample of nonbankrupt though financially troubled firms gave a Type II error of 21 percent.

The accuracy of Altman's multivariate model was superior to Beaver's univariate model for data samples one year prior to bankruptcy but performed badly for data taken two to five years prior to failure where Beaver was able to predict bankruptcy more accurately.

Deakin (1972) modified Altman's model to include the fourteen ratios initially used in the Beaver model, because of its superior accuracy for two or more years prior to failure. He selected 32 firms failing between 1964 and 1970 and randomly selected his nonfailed firms. He extended Altman's definition to include insolvencies and liquidations (ibid. p. 168). Deakin retained all fourteen ratios for increased accuracy of his MDA model and assigned probabilities of group membership for classifying the cases rather than using a critical value. This technique improved the classification accuracy over those of both Altman and Beaver, especially for the first three years prior to failure. Nevertheless, a significant deterioration of accuracy for the model upon validation against a random sample of bankrupt and nonbankrupt firms suggests that the results might be sample specific.

Edmister (1972) applied a technique, similar to Altman's, to small business using applicants for Small Business Administration loans in his samples. He used ratios previously found to be significant predictors of bankruptcy but transformed them into dichotomous variables. For example the level of ratios compared to industry averages, three-year trends (either up or down, a dichotomous measure), and the interaction effect of industry relative level and industry relative trend were some of the variables included in a regression model used for discrimination. The result for MDA is the same as that for a regression with a 0-1 dependent variable. Stepwise inclusion of variables reduced multicollinearity and the potential for sample-specific results. The seven variable discriminant function produced was 97 percent accurate overall. Although consideration of the cost of errors was deemed important in selecting a cut-off point for classification, Edmister advocated a more practical approach – to leave a 'grey' area where classification is difficult.

Altman, Haldeman, and Narayan (1977) considered data from the period 1969 to 1975 and improved on Altman's model with several refinements to the statistical technique and adjustments to the data. The different cost of errors and the prior probability of failure were both considered in the classification process. The ZETA model so produced has high discriminatory power, is reasonably parsimonious, and includes accounting and stock market data as well as earnings and debt variables. As a consequence, many financial institutions have used this model.

2.2 The Research of the 1980s – The Logit Model

Ohlson (1980) pioneered the use of maximum likelihood methods or conditional probability models in modelling financial distress. This modelling is the most sophisticated in terms of statistical methods and methodology of those considered thus far. These models estimate the probability of an outcome (e.g. bankruptcy) conditional on the attribute vector of the individual and the outcome set. In addition, a regression-type technique, such as logit analysis avoids most (not all)[1] of the distributional problems associated with using MDA, and it has the added advantage of allowing qualitative variables, i.e. those with categories rather than continuous data, into its formulation. Many authors have argued for and provided evidence of the superiority of logit to discriminant analysis (DA) in their application to bankruptcy prediction studies, one of the first being Ohlson (1980).

Although DA and logit analysis are distinct, these two methods are closely related as McFadden (1976) had shown, though demonstrating that logit is applicable for a wider class of distributions than is normal DA. Lo (1986) compared and tested the DA estimator and the logit analysis estimator using an empirical example involving corporate bankruptcies. It should also be noted that a distinct and important advantage of the logit model over DA is that the coefficient on each variable may be interpreted individually as to its importance,[2] subject to the limitations imposed by multicollinearity.

The coefficients of the logit model are estimated by the method of maximum likelihood (ML). The key to its advantage lies in the *direct* estimation of the parameters in the logit function with an iterative technique, rather than substituting suspect estimates under suspect conditions into the discriminant analysis formulae.[3] Essentially the process iteratively improves the fit of the probability estimates of the outcomes for each firm so that those observations where failure occurred are assigned low ex ante probabilities of survival, and those that survived are assigned high probabilities. A 'good fit' is a set of coefficients for the linear predictor that best satisfies this objective.[4]

Two of the most important papers of the 1980s, both using the logit model, are next discussed in more detail.

2.2.1 Ohlson (1980)

Ohlson applied the econometric methodology of conditional logit analysis to avoid some of the well-known problems associated with MDA, which, until this time, was

---

1 See Palepu (1986) for a detailed discussion of the methodological issues relevant to research settings that involve binary state prediction models, and Press and Wilson (1979) for the reasons why the logistic regression model with maximum likelihood estimators is preferred for both classification and for relating qualitative variables to other variables under nonormality.

2 The statistical properties of the maximum-likelihood estimates, which are asymptotically unbiased and normally distributed, are discussed in detail in Bradley and Gart (1962).

3 Halperin et al (1971) compare the results of MDA and ML estimation of the coefficients when the logistic model holds but the normality assumptions of the independent variables are violated.

4 Martin (1977) gives a good explanation of ML estimation techniques in the context of bank failure predictions.

the most popular technique for bankruptcy studies. He used an improved data base (the 10-K financial statements from the Stanford University Business School Library rather than from *Moody's Manual*) from which 105 industrial firms were sampled that 'filed for bankruptcy in the sense of Chapter X, Chapter XI, or some other notification indicating bankruptcy proceedings (in the) period from 1970 to 1976' (ibid. p.114). The sample of nonbankrupt industrial firms was selected from the *COMPUSTAT* tape. Nine independent variables were used with no theoretical considerations. Firm size was included as a variable, calculated as log (total assets/ GNP price-level; index) (ibid. p. 118), and was the most significant predictor. Three ratios were scaled for total asset size, and two dummy variables were used: one as an indicator of negative owners' equity and the other as an indicator of negative net income. Ohlson gave four basic factors as being 'statistically significant in affecting the probability of failure (within one year)':

(i) The size of the company;
(ii) A measure(s) of the financial structure;
(iii) A measure(s) of performance;
(iv) A measure(s) of current liquidity. (Ohlson, 1980, p. 110)

Ohlson's examination of error rates on his large estimation samples was, nevertheless, disappointing (no holdout samples were used for validation), but he used no equal-sized matched samples to bias accuracy, as in past studies, nor any 'data dredging' to improve the accuracy of his models. He states:

> A logit analysis is not an econometric method which is designed to find an 'optimal' frontier, trading off one type of error against another. This is in contrast to MDA models, which satisfy optimality conditions under appropriate assumptions (Ohlson, 1980, p. 126).

The restrictive assumptions of MDA are not required under logit, and interpretation of individual coefficients is appropriate in the logit model, which therefore lends itself to broader research application than MDA.

2.2.2 Zavgren (1983)

Zavgren (1983) modified the application of the logit model using an extension of Ohlson's variables set, time period, and analysis. Both the logit and probit models were used and the focus was to provide a measure of the probability of failure and to analyze the significance of various financial attributes in distinguishing between failed and nonfailed firms. Factor analytic studies by Pinches (1975) was used to identify the main stable and orthogonal dimensions of financial variables and those ratios with the highest factor loadings were used by Zavgren. These were total income/total capital, sales/net plant, inventory/sales, debt/total capital, receivables/inventory, quick assets/current liabilities, cash/total assets and the current ratio. The current ratios was replaced by the acid test ratio, since the inclusion of inventories in the current ratio reduces its meaning as a measure of liquidity.

Firms were selected from the *Compustat* files, if they filed chapter X or chapter XI bankruptcy proceedings in the period 1972-78. The 45 industrial firms meeting the five-year data availability requirement were matched with nonfailed firms by industry and total asset size. The likelihood ratio test is an indicator of a model's ability to distinguish between the two populations of failed and nonfailed firms, and gave a significance value at the .005 level for all five years prior to bankruptcy. The model estimated the probability of failure for the failed firms to range between 0.9 and 0.7 for one to five years prior to failure, whereas the probabilities ranged from 0.2 to 0.4 for the nonfailed firms.

The classification error rates showed no improvement over those from previous studies. The error rates were similar to Ohlson's for one year prior to bankruptcy but better for longer lead times to five years – similar to MDA results.

The significance of the individual coefficients of the model was evaluated using the asymptotic t-statistic. A summary of the findings given in Zavgren, (1980, p.29) on the important distinguishing characteristics of failed and nonfailed firms is:

- The degree of leverage was found to be most important in all years.
- Liquidity and efficiency (turnover) ratios are important in the early years prior to failure.
- The acid test ratio is highly significant close to failure.
- The profitability measure is not significantly different for failing and nonfailing firms.

The main contributions of the logistic function technique applied by Ohlson (1980) and Zavgren (1983), then, are the strong significance of the models estimated, the pattern of significance of the financial variables, and the information content of the probabilities as a financial risk measure.

As the above-mentioned studies can testify, technique developments such as MDA and logit analysis by econometricians and statisticians are important to, and often the motivation for, undertaking research into distress prediction, but as Ball and Foster observed:

> Improvements in econometric and statistical techniques are a legitimate source of new accounting research. However, there is always the danger that the technique itself becomes the focus of attention. This danger is especially apparent in literatures such as time-series analysis and distress prediction, where the economic underpinning of the research can be minimal. (Ball and Foster, 1982, p.172)

The next section identifies and summarizes some studies that have used theory and not just empirical method as the impetus for undertaking their research.

2.3 The Choice of Independent Variables and Theories of Bankruptcy

Most bankruptcy prediction models put forward have been derived by a statistical search through a number of plausible financial indicators rather than by any economic theory of symptoms. The major thrust in this area, with some significant achievements to its name, has been to find empirically validated characteristics that distinguish financially distressed from nondistressed firms. Until 1980, the major studies in the area had identified four significant variables or type of variable that help discriminate between the two groups of firms:

(i) The size of the company;
(ii) A measure(s) of the financial structure;
(iii) A measure(s) of performance;
(iv) A measure(s) of current liquidity. (Ohlson, 1980, p. 110)

One could argue that the empirical successes in the literature have been gauged by optimistic accuracy rates often gained from multivariate approaches that suffer from statistical overfitting. The existence of many dissimilar prediction models is evidence of overfitting and sounds a warning that these models would not do well when applied to new data. To test this assertion, and since a variety of ratios had been used in the models developed across different research settings – Chen and Shimerda (1981) listed over 100 ratios cited in the literature[5] – Hamer (1983) tested to see if classification success was, indeed, sensitive to variable selection. She used four variable sets: from Altman (1968), Deakin (1972), Blum (1974) and Ohlson (1980), and tested these on a sample of 44 bankrupt and 44 nonbankrupt firms for classification accuracy using a method based on the Lachenbruch holdout method and pairwise chi-square tests. Although there was very little consistency in the variables selected for inclusion in the four sets, each set contained variables that measure profitability, liquidity, and leverage. Subsequent classification results showed no statistically significant difference between the results from the four sets for each of the five years before bankruptcy, regardless of whether the logit or the discriminant analysis technique was used.

Other studies have chosen independent variables not wholly motivated by their empirical performance, but rather, on the basis of theory. Scott wrote:

> Theory can serve several useful functions. (It) can provide logically consistent explanations for the existing empirical successes. Further, theory can organize the search for new empirical models. These new theoretically based models may be especially effective, since by suggesting variables and functional forms, explicit theoretical frameworks reduce the scope for statistical overfitting. (Scott, 1981, p. 325)

---

5 Dmitras *et al*, 1996 also did an extensive literature review on 158 articles concerning business failure and spanning the period 1932-1994 to find that 'there are no financial characteristics common to all predictive studies'.

The following is a brief summary of papers in this area that have been guided by theory.

2.3.1 Models from the Probability and Statistics Literature

The gambler's ruin model. Wilcox (1971, 1973, 1976), Santomero and Vinso (1977), and Vinso (1979) used the Gambler's Ruin Model (Feller, 1968), taken from probability theory, upon which to base their bankruptcy prediction models. The firm is viewed as a gambler, assumed to have an initial arbitrary amount of money and through a series of independent trials where he either wins a dollar with probability p, or loses a dollar with probability 1-p, the amount of money will either grow or be depleted to zero. The firm becomes bankrupt if it's worth ever falls to zero. In this model a firm meets losses by selling assets. The theory provides expressions for the firm's ultimate ruin, the expected ultimate gain or loss, the expected duration of the game, etc. Scott (1981) and Altman (1983) concluded that the results of these studies are difficult to assess in the absence of holdout samples, but nevertheless, Wilcox's work is notable as the first attempt to use explicit theory to predict bankruptcy.

The Perfect-Access Model. Scott (1976) presented a new theory based on the perfect-access model that appeared to fit the data well. This model assumes that while a firm can meet losses by selling assets, it can also sell either debt or equity in an efficient, frictionless security market. In both this theory and the gambler's ruin model, the mean and standard deviation of an earnings-type variable is important in predicting bankruptcy, only the gambler's ruin model includes a liquidation value of stockholder's equity, while the predictor from the perfect-access model includes the market value of equity. Since the empirical evidence supports both these models, only one assumes the firm has no access to the securities market while the other assumes that access is perfect, Scott (1976) considered a firm that has imperfect access. Thus, he presented examples from a class of bankruptcy theories that lies between the gambler's ruin and perfect-access models.

The CUSUM Model. Theodossiou (1996) used a sequential procedure for detecting a shift in the mean of a multivariate time series process and showed how the procedure can be used to predict a firm's tendency towards failure. This paper is discussed in 2.6.5. The procedure is based on Healy's (1988) CUSUM framework and Shumway's (1988) time series discriminant analysis framework. The paper can be viewed as an extension of the earlier works of Wecker (1979) and Neftci (1982,1985) on the prediction of turning points of economic time series.

2.3.2 The Cash Flow Model

Since financial distress is a solvency issue, some researchers have focussed on cash flow models, and these are notable in that they base their models on economic guidelines. With the works of Casey and Bartczak (1984), Karels and Prakash

(1987), Aziz *et al* (1988), and others, a controversy arose as to whether cash-flow variables added significant discriminating power over the benchmark accrual-based variables in the earlier models.

Research into assessing whether operating cash flow data can lead to more accurate predictions of bankrupt and nonbankrupt firms than accrual ratios has produced contradictory results.

Beaver (1966) pioneered the idea with his adherence to a 'cash flow concept' with positive results, and Gombola and Ketz (1983) found, using factor analysis, that cash flow ratios contain certain information not revealed in other financial ratios, but other researchers have shown that operating cash flow data does not provide incremental explanatory power over accrual-based measures.

Much of this variability may be explained by the construct validity of operating cash flows (Sharma, 1997). The definition of cash flow from operations, as used in many of the earlier studies[6] investigating the ability of cash flow information to predict failure, was 'net income plus depreciation, depletion and amortization' which Largay and Stickney (1980) pointed out is not an accurate measure of cash flow but rather, of working capital. The consequent evolution of measures of cash flow from operations into a more refined measure has led to the introduction of a cash flow accounting standard in the USA, Canada, U.K., Australia, and New Zealand.

Casey and Bartczak (1984, 1985). Based on their examination of 60 bankrupt and 230 nonbankrupt firms, Casey and Bartczak (1984, 1985) maintained that not only is operating cash flow a poor predictor of financial distress, but it also fails to even marginally improve a ratio-based model's predictive value. They also report that cash flow based models misclassify nonbankrupt firms at a higher rate than do ratio-based models. Gentry, Newbold, and Whitford (1985a), and Viscione (1985), confirmed Casey and Bartczak's findings. Other research has produced differing results. Studies that support the predictive ability of cash flow variables include Largay and Stickney (1980), Ketz and Kochanek (1982), Lee (1982), Gombola *et al* (1983), Gombola and Ketz (1983), Mensah (1984), Gentry *et al* (1985b),[7] Gahlon and Vigeland (1988), Aziz *et al* (1988), Gilbert *et al* (1990), Ward (1995).

Aziz, Emanuel, and Lawson (1988). Aziz *et al* (1988) developed logit models and discriminant analysis models to test a hypothesis about corporate bankruptcy in terms of cash flow variables. They used theoretical as well as empirical arguments as a rationale for formulating such a hypothesis in order to avoid what Ball and Foster termed a:

> Brute empiricism approach using stepwise discriminant/regression analysis as a result of which the selected variables tend to be sample-data specific and the empirical findings do not permit generalisation. (Ball and Foster, 1982, p. 419)

---

[6] Beaver (1966), Deakin (1972), Blum (1974) Norton and Smith (1979), Mensah (1983).

[7] Note the earlier study supported Casey and Bartczak.

The theoretical argument is based on Lawson's (1971) cash flow identity. Aziz *et al* derived both logit formulations and MDA functions with a jack-knifed classification as a validation technique. These were calculated for all years up to five years prior to bankruptcy on data obtained from Standard and Poor's *COMPUSTAT* Research File for firms failing in the period 1971-1982. These firms were paired with active companies on the basis of industry classification and asset size. Comparisons of the results of both logit and MDA models showed the logit model to be the superior technique with which to formulate the cash flow based model. Comparisons with Altman 's (1977) ZETA model for predictive accuracy showed that 'the CFB model is more likely to provide early warning three or more years before the event (whereas) the ZETA model is superior in the two years immediately preceding bankruptcy' (ibid. p., 435). More importantly, the Type I error for the CFB model was less than both their MDA model and the Zeta model for three or more years prior.

2.4 The Time Dimension and Macro-Economic Conditions

In the 1980s a great mass of work was conducted which followed the lead of the earlier papers by which it was informed. The great impetus for this work, however, was almost certainly the economic downturn of the seventies and the bankruptcies and closures it engendered, perhaps because investment decisions seem to be more difficult to make when recession is the reality rather than when the economy is healthy.

Empirical evidence shows that distressed firms often have financial ratios that are significantly different from those which prevail under more normal trading conditions (Houghton and Woodliff, 1987). Signals of a firm's deteriorating condition are produced sequentially for many years before failure and procedures that detect a shift, say, in the mean of a multivariate time series process would be useful in predicting a firm's tendency towards failure. Added to these internal influences are those that are acting from outside the firm, so procedures that are able to quantify changes in the economic environment need also to be incorporated in the modelling.

Following his 1968 work, Altman (1971) performed the earliest study using general economic conditions, i.e. measuring the firm's business environment, and attempting to explain the change in total bankruptcy from quarter to quarter, by using first difference regression in his model. This model included changes in GNP, money supply, the Standard and Poor's Index of Common Stock Prices but the results show very little correlation, with an R^2 of only 0.19, indicating relatively little explanatory power from economic factors.

Later Rose *et al* (1982) and Mensah (1984) re-examined these effects with more promising results, the former concluding that macroeconomic conditions are significant factors in the process of business failure. Levy and Bar-Niv (1987) found that the corporate failure rate in the USA is correlated specifically with the fluctuations of the GNP and the overall price level and Levy (1991) provided an aggregate econometric analysis of the effects of variations of macroeconomic factors on the rate of bankruptcy in the USA. He showed that the GNP and the GNP deflator affect this rate significantly.

Moore (1990) applied the work of Rose *et al* (1982) to develop a small business bankruptcy prediction for Texas by combining the financial variables from the Edmister (1972) model and the Altman (1983) Z-score model with national and state economic variables. He concluded that models containing macroeconomic data were better than models without the data, indicating 'that a company is not just an isolated entity; its existence is influenced by the economy of the state in which it resides and, on a bigger scale, by the economy of its nation' (p.29).

In this section, some of this work, as well as the most recent work of the 90's are examined in more detail showing how they each contributed significantly to the theory of bankruptcy by examining the external environment in which a firm operates.

2.4.1 Rose, Andrews and Giroux (1982)

The first major research after Altman (1971) to consider the external environment in the prediction of bankruptcy was a paper by Rose, Andrews, and Giroux (1982), They offered a macroeconomic perspective to business failure by analyzing which economic indicators might signal a critical climate for companies with higher exposure to business failure.

They tested the following linear model:

$$BFR_t = a_0 + a_1 I_{t-j} + a_2 C_{t-k} + e_t$$

where

BFR_t = index of the business failure rate (comprising the period 1970-1980 in the form of failures per 10,000 firms.)

I_{t-j} = leading and coincidental cyclical indicators

C_{t-k}= vector of variables reflecting monetary, cost, and savings-investment causal factors in the cycle; and

e_t = disturbance term reflecting exogenous shocks and other random influences on the business failure rate.

A bivariate simple correlation matrix was initially calculated in order to examine the relationships between 28 individual economic variables obtained from a number of data sources, including the Survey of Current Business Conditions Digest and other publications of the Bureau of Labor Statistics, the Federal Reserve Board, and the US Department of Commerce. Fifteen variables that were highly correlated ($p>0.8$) were eliminated before a forward stepwise selection regression technique was utilized to analyze the impact of the remaining macroeconomic factors on the failure index.

The ten variables entered with a resulting R^2 of 0.9 included the Dow Jones industrial average; unemployment rate; profits after tax/income originating in corporations; corporate AAA bond rate; free reserves; gross savings/GNP; gross private domestic investment/GNP; change in total business investment; output per hour; and new orders for durable goods/GNP. These preliminary results suggested the possibility of a complex relationship between business failure rates and business cycle indicators. The research results, however, say little about the form of the relationships.

2.4.2 Mensah (1984)

Although most models of failure in the literature are interested in the predictive value of the models derived, few examine the performance of their functions for periods outside of those on which the models were developed. In order to permit a detailed examination of the stationarity of bankruptcy prediction models over diverse economic environments and industries, Mensah (1984) created a parsimonious set of variables by performing a factor analysis on his original set of 38 ratios taken from 110 paired firms. The distributions of each factor were found to approximate normality much better than any of the original ratios. Subsequent logit analyzes were formulated on the orthogonal factor scores on ratios taken for the second year before bankruptcy of the failing partners.

Firstly, a model aggregated over all periods and industries, gave the following most important factors, all significant at an alpha level of 0.01 and identified as:

- Cash-flow Generation;
- Liquidity;
- Financial Leverage;
- Turnover of Equity. (Taken from Table 3, Mensah, 1984, p.388)

Secondly, to examine the stationarity of the models, logit models were derived for different levels of aggregation of the data by period and industry. The results were cross-validated using MDA on the raw ratios and the effect of multicollinearity between the ratios on the stationarity of the prediction models was also examined. A summary of Mensah's results was as follows:

- The accuracy and structure of models differ across different economic environments and for different industrial sectors;
- Models derived from homogeneous economic periods perform better than aggregate models;
- Different prediction models seem appropriate for companies in different industrial sectors even for the same economic environment;
- Failing firms may be easier to identify in the periods immediately preceding a recession than in periods followed by business expansion;
- Reducing collinearity increases the accuracy of the model;
- Contrary to the findings of Casey and Bartczak (1985) and others, cash flow variables add to predictive accuracy.

2.4.3 *Kane, Richardson and Graybeal (1996)*

The paper by Kane *et al* (1996) added much to what we know about *why* failure occurs, why accounting data are associated with the corporate failure event, and under what contexts better statistical prediction is possible. In particular, two stress processes resulting in corporate failure are discussed: macroeconomic stress processes induced by firms' exposure to events such as a recession: and microeconomic stress processes resulting from firm and industry-specific causes. The hypothesis tested is whether the occurrence of recession-induced stress is an incrementally informative factor that contributes to the predictive and explanatory power of accounting-based failure prediction models.

A number of studies are sited that document that accounting data have information content about stock returns that is conditional across varying stages of the business cycle. Kane *et al* argued:

> Because stock returns presumably reflect premiums investors demand for bearing nondiversifiable risk, and because recession-induced default risk (having a macroeconomic origin) is one form of risk that probably cannot fully be diversified away, it follows that the observed sensitivity may reflect contextual information contained in accounting numbers that is related to the increased risk of default during recessions. (Kane *et al*, 1996, p.632)

They further assert that 'the effect of recession-induced stress on the risk of corporate failure will vary as a function of firms' fundamental and stress-related characteristics – some companies may be better positioned than others to mitigate the default risk associated with recession-induced stress' (p. 635). For instance, the reduction in liquidity arising from an untimely expansionary strategy by some firms would increase their recession-induced stress and risk of default whereas other firms, anticipating recession, may take action such as building up cash, reducing capacity, and carefully managing inventory in order to mitigate the stress (p. 635).

Their findings supported the hypothesis that accounting-based statistical models conditioned on the occurrence of a recession will have incremental significant explanatory power over models not so controlled.

2.5 Statistical Methodology

This section is concerned with issues of statistical methodology in deriving bankruptcy prediction models. A variety of estimation procedures have been used in these models that differ in their underlying assumptions and in their computational complexity. Accounting data do not meet the specifications for most statistical models.[8] 'The numbers are typically bounded below by zero and exhibit various degrees of skewness and kurtosis' (Richardson and Davidson, 1983). Watson (1990) discussed methods that have been used when the denominator approaches zero and ratio values become extreme causing severe right skewness in the ratio distribution. Cybinski (1995) further discussed this problem and the additional measurement problem when ratio values are confounded by negative values in the numerator, denominator, or both. Kane, Richardson and Meade (1998) improved the predictive usefulness of standard failure prediction models by applying rank transformations, as they are then less sensitive to outliers and/or non-normal distributions.

Thus, researchers need to understand the sensitivity of their results to violations in the assumptions that underpin the empirical technique being used. Violations may preclude examination of the model coefficients but may not reduce the model's predictive ability. Joy and Tollefson (1975) and Eisenbeis (1977) gave comprehensive reviews of these issues, particularly outlining the pitfalls of the use of MDA in financial applications.

In addition, Zmijewski (1984) provided several insights into the effects of sampling bias on financial distress prediction models and Marais (1984) examined several issues in the experimental design and empirical testing of classification models,

With a keener understanding of methodology, researchers are better able to interpret the results of extant research and to develop new models.

2.5.1 Zmijewski (1984)

Zmijewski investigated the influence of sampling biases on the conclusions drawn in studies. Especially important is the bias that occurs when a non-random sampling method has been used such as matching nonbankrupt firms with bankrupt firms – common in bankruptcy studies. Zmijewski identifies the two types of bias as:

- Bias due to non-random sampling procedures. This bias falls within the topic of *choice-based sample biases*. Many studies tend to include bankrupt firms in the estimation samples beyond their relative frequency in the population of firms (since historically, bankrupt firms account for less than percent of firms, although this percentage is increasing). This leads to a bias in favour of bankrupt firms i.e. lower probability of misclassifying bankrupt firms (Type I error) at the expense of a higher probability of misclassifying surviving firms (Type II error).[9]

---

8 See Deakin (1976), Frecka and Hopwood (1983), and Lee (1985). In an applications study, Richardson and Davidson (1983) discuss the effect of accounting data on classification results from the linear discriminant model.

9 This can be beneficial as the cost of a Type I error is usually considered to be far greater than the cost of a Type II error.

- Bias due to missing data. This bias falls within the topic of *sample selection bias* and occurs because data for financially distressed firms are often unavailable. Firms that experience major financial difficulties are more likely to have incomplete data, and therefore are more likely to be excluded from the estimation sample. This leads to under-representation in the estimation sample of firms experiencing difficulty, and hence, a large error probability for misclassifying bankrupt firms in the resulting model (Type I error).

Zmijewski found that the choice-based sample bias 'does not, in general, affect the statistical inferences or the overall classification rates for the financial distress model and the samples tested' (Zmijewski, 1984, p. 77). Similarly, an examination of the sample selection bias showed that 'a bias is clearly shown to exist, but, in general, it does not appear to affect the statistical inferences or overall classification rates (p. 80).

2.5.2 Marais, Patell and Wolfson (1984)

Marais, Patell, and Wolfson (1984) examined several issues in the experimental design and empirical testing of classification models. They stress 'the importance of and the interactions among three elements: the loss function associated with classification errors, the algorithm used to discriminate among or predict classifications, and the method used to estimate the expected misclassification losses achieved by various algorithms' (ibid. p. 87). They used two nonparametric, computer-intensive statistical techniques – recursive partitioning and bootstrapping.

This paper centres on statistical issues applied to the classification of commercial bank loans but applies equally well to corporate bankruptcy prediction modelling. They compare the recursive partitioning and polytomous probit approaches to model estimation using misclassification error rates to compare the two procedures. In addition, four approaches designed to mitigate the effects of overfitting of the data in the estimation of error rates are discussed. Use of the bootstrap approach was recommended after a consideration of the problems associated with the other three, together with simulation results in the Efron (1979; 1982; 1983) studies that point to its superiority in small samples.

2.6 The Distress Continuum

Although there have been some successes in improving the discriminating power of bankruptcy models, the contention of Wood and Piesse (1987) is that *ex post* discrimination between risky companies that have failed and non-risky companies that have not, is 'neither surprising, nor evidence that any additional information is generated by (multivariate statistical) techniques' (ibid. p. 29). Indeed, such is the *ex post* nature of the models and methods used that it is pointed out by Taffler

(1984) that bankruptcy model scores should be interpreted as descriptions of financial distress rather than predictions of bankruptcy *per se*.

Levy (1991) contended that 'though financial distress is a necessary condition for bankruptcy it is not a sufficient one' (p. 1). This is pertinent when we consider the bankruptcy-liquidation decision since financial distress precedes both reorganization as well as bankruptcy/liquidation. Yet, in most bankruptcy studies the outcomes have a zero-one characteristic – either an immediate liquidation of the firm or a continuation of its operation. In other words, 'failure' is measured on a qualitative or categorical scale as an event rather than as a process. Notably, Hopwood (1994) document and analyze *two* primary failure processes: a relatively rapid and unexpected failure where financial distress is not evident in the accounting numbers; and a second process of relatively long duration in which financial distress is evident. They predicted that accounting-based statistical prediction models can significantly explain only the second type of corporate failure but also suggest that bankruptcy not preceded by financial distress is more likely to be driven by management fraud.

The notion of 'failure' as a distress continuum rather than a discrete event logically leads to two related areas of study for financially distressed firms:

- Analysis of the length of the continuation period and liquidation timing, i.e. of 'time to failure' or survival studies and
- The analysis of the distressed firm's financial characteristics and its external environment over time.

Note that both areas of research explore and attempt to understand *why* failure occurs – whether by identifying the characteristics that lengthen/shorten the period of time until the failure event or those that impact on the risk of occurrence of the failure event. Both are interested in the conditional probability of an organization failing in a time interval, given that it had survived up to the start of the interval. In survival analysis this probability is termed the 'hazard rate'. The papers by Crapp and Stevenson (1987), Eddey, Partington, and Stevenson (1989), Kassab, McLeay, and Shani (1991), and Partington, Peat, and Stevenson (1991), apply techniques drawn from survival analysis to the area of financial distress or one related to it. Other papers that develop formal models linking financial distress with corporate strategies for distressed financial restructuring are those of Bulow and Shoven (1977), White (1980; 1981; 1984; 1989; 1993), Levy (1991; 1994), and Chen, Weston, and Altman (1995).

An ongoing challenge for the second area of research is to produce a model that distinguishes characteristics of distressed firms filing bankruptcy from others, also at risk, but avoiding it. In other words the question of interest here is how do firms transform from surviving (or even moderately successful ones) into failed ones. Models that can accurately assess a firm's risk of failure at different periods can also be useful for adjustment purposes especially if the risk feeds back into the firm's already-distressed position and increases as a consequence.

In this second area, important extensions to previous corporate failure prediction models were made by:

- Lau (1987) who used five financial states instead of the conventional two, and estimated the probabilities that a firm will enter each of the five states;
- Zavgren (1985) and Hopwood (1989) who took a longitudinal approach in analyzing a firm's progression toward bankruptcy by estimating logit or probit models at one to five years prior to bankruptcy;
- Gilbert *et al* (1990) who found different statistically significant explanatory financial variables for financially distressed versus bankrupt groups and stable versus bankrupt groups;
- Hill *et al* (1996), discussed in section 2.6.6, who employed a dynamic event history methodology and three states – stable, financially distressed, and bankrupt, to distinguish between financially distressed firms that survive and those that become bankrupt; and
- Theodossiou (1993) who used the CUSUM model to detect the point at which a firm's financial variables shift from a 'good performance' distribution to a 'bad performance' distribution.

Note here that the research in this book belongs predominantly to the second area as the major focus is on an explanation of the failure process and not the timing of failure. Nevertheless, it has an affinity with the first area in that an estimation of failure risk is sought, though not via a proportional hazard model. Some of the papers from both areas are discussed in more detail in the following sections.

2.6.1 Survival Analysis

As discussed in Ogg (1988), financial distress models need to use the statistical techniques drawn from survival analysis, knowing that the potential to fail always exists *ex ante* – for both non-failed firms as well in the period leading up to the *ex post* failures. Since these techniques require no specification of the distributions of the data set, models based on them overcome the problems of bias outlined by Zmijewski (1984). For instance, many use the Cox (1972) proportional hazards model incorporating regression-like arguments into life-table analysis. Studies of financial distress incorporating these techniques include those of Crapp and Stevenson (1987), Kassab, McLeay, and Shani (1991), and Partington, Peat, and Stevenson (1991) and Luoma and Laitinen (1991). In a related area of research, Eddey, Partington, and Stevenson (1989) predict the timing and probability of takeover bid success using survival analysis.

Crapp and Stevenson (1987). Crapp and Stevenson (1987) provide estimates of failure probabilities of organizations at a point in time, drawing on established methodology from other disciplines that requires no specification of the distributions of the data set. The authors claim that their model also overcomes the variable-selection problem due to lack of guidance by theory that has often been discussed in the literature. Part of this claim is to ensure that all variables that are thought to be potentially relevant predictors of financial distress are included in the ratio set before the stepwise analysis. Included is an exhaustive set of variables from many different general areas of relevance including those related to macro-economic conditions, managerial efficiency, asset quality, firm growth, as well as the usual financial ratios.

The method follows closely the model suggested by Cox (1972) who incorporated regression-like arguments into life-table analysis. A life table is a method of summarizing the results of a study by grouping the times to failure into time intervals. For each time interval the table records the number of firms that are still in the study at the start of the interval, and the number censored. The ability to use censored data (the time to failure is greater than the predetermined time horizon of the study) distinguishes this technique from other statistical methodology. The probability of interest is the conditional probability of an organization failing in the time interval i.e. the probability of failure in the next period given survival to that period (the hazard rate or age-specific failure rate).

The methodology also provides the opportunity to test for structural change by examining the movement of conditional failure probabilities between three sub-periods in:

- The type of explanatory variables fitted in the hazard function; and
- The order of fit of variables forced into the model.

The authors developed the procedures for estimating the probability of failure and the stepwise regression procedure for the selection of variables, and then applied the model to the analysis of failure of a group of Australian credit unions with encouraging results.

An area of research related to bankruptcy prediction is that of firm takeover. Using methods similar to the above study, Eddey, Partington, and Stevenson (1989) estimate a survivor function, specifying the probability that the time to takeover of a firm, after a takeover bid has been announced, will be greater than or equal to any one of a range of possible time horizons of interest. They use this function to examine the probability that the firm will be taken over and when. The model provided a good fit to the overall distribution of survivor times as observed in a holdout sample and achieved reasonable prediction accuracy of the success of the takeover bid. Some interesting insights into the effects of the different covariates on the hazard rate were also gained from this study.

2.6.2 Formal Models

A separate but related area of research is concerned with the survival of the firm once it is financially distressed, in the context of reorganization strategies aimed at warding off bankruptcy, or liquidation once Chapter 11 has been petitioned. In recent years the literature of financial distress has been enriched by the development of these formal models investigating the circumstances under which a firm will be forced into bankruptcy. These models can be viewed as part of a larger framework which would be necessary to address the question of optimal financial policy in a world of taxation, bankruptcy costs, investment and depreciation, uncertainty, etc. (Bulow and Shoven, 1978).

Important contributions in this area are the papers by Bulow and Shoven (1978), White (1980; 1981; 1984; 1989; 1994), Casey *et al* (1986), Levy (1991; 1994) and in the Australian context with regard to the performance of reorganized companies, Routledge and Gadenne (2000). This area deals with questions like: can the distress be removed and a positive going-concern value re-established, or will liquidation result in a higher value? Chen, Weston, and Altman (1995) developed a synthesis of these formal models linking the related finance literature and corporate strategies for distressed financial restructuring.

Central to these strategies are the re-contracting arrangements proposed between owners, creditors, and other relevant stakeholders. The work of Bulow and Shoven (1978) demonstrated how financial distress decisions could be parsimoniously modelled by examining coalition behaviour. The coalition behaviour approach, and particularly White's discussion of its application to firm reorganization decisions, has since been used in development of reorganization prediction models. Other papers that discuss the modelling of investment decisions by distressed firms are Ang and Chua (1980), Gertner and Scharfstein (1991), Fisher and Martel (1995), and Hotchkiss (1995).

Levy (1991, 1994). Levy's analyzes follow Altman (1971), and Levy and Bar-Niv (1987) who found that the corporate failure rate in the U.S. is correlated with the fluctuations of the GNP and the overall price level. Levy (1991) states 'though financial distress is a necessary condition for bankruptcy it is not a sufficient one' and that his purpose was 'to develop a sufficient condition for bankruptcy within a framework which takes into account the nexus of interactions among financial, industrial and macroeconomic factors characterizing the environment in which firms operate' (p. 1).

Levy (1991, 1994) presents an analysis of the length of the continuation period and liquidation timing of the financially distressed firm. He extends the work of Bulow and Shoven (1978) who argue that the criterion for bankruptcy is a positive gain to the coalition of the firm's claimants from immediate liquidation of the firm, by also considering certain industrial structure and stochastic macroeconomic conditions affecting the firm's operation. White (1980) also used a similar analytical framework to examine the social efficiency properties of alternative priority rules in liquidation.

The analysis of the optimal continuation of an insolvent firm's operation was conducted within a framework in which the firm's managers are sheer profit maximizers. The Pareto optimal period of continuation of the firm's operation was found by maximizing the stockholder's utility level equal to that under immediate liquidation with an adequate compensation payment. Levy (1991) derives the Pareto optimal collaboration period and presents the condition for immediate liquidation of the financially distressed firm. The subsequent econometric analysis focuses on the effects of variations of macroeconomic factors on the rate of bankruptcy in the USA.

2.6.3 Gilbert, Menon and Schwartz (1990)

Gilbert, Menon and Schwartz (1990) gave us a landmark paper with a different study design to provide some evidence that a bankruptcy prediction model developed along traditional lines would not be able to distinguish firms that fail from other financially distressed firms. They therefore further question whether such models have the capacity to influence bankers and other resource suppliers. I will discuss this paper in detail, as I believe this is an important extension to the literature to date.

Two stepwise logistic regression models were developed on firms taken from the *COMPUSTAT* files. The first estimation sample was comprised of 52 bankrupt firms and 208 randomly selected nonbankrupt firms. The second estimation sample consisted of the 52 bankrupt firms and 208 distressed firms i.e. firms that were financially weak but avoiding bankruptcy. The latter were screened to exclude obviously strong firms by the condition that they had negative cumulative earnings (income from continuing operations) for any consecutive three-year period. Two types of holdout samples were used; the first consisting of 24 bankrupt and 96 randomly drawn firms and the second, of financially distressed firms, combining the 24 bankrupt firms with 96 distressed firms. All samples had a four-to-one ratio of nonbankrupt/bankrupt firms after Zmijewski's (1984) suggestion to use unequal proportions more like prior population proportions. The independent variables were drawn from two prior studies: Casey and Bartczak (1985), and Altman (1968).

The first logistic model using the bankrupt/random estimation sample was significant at the 0.0001 alpha level and three independent variables entered the stepwise model at a 5 percent level of significance. They were: earnings before interest and tax/total assets, cash flow from operations/total liabilities, and stockholders' equity/total liabilities. The overall accuracy of 88.5 percent for the estimation sample and 90.8 percent for the bankrupt/random holdout was lower than for earlier studies and the Type I error rates were as high as 37.5 percent; a reason given being the unequal proportions of bankrupt and nonbankrupt firms. The overall classification results obtained when the model was used to predict the status of firms in the bankrupt/distressed holdout was much reduced with a misclassification rate of 33.3 percent.

Since the financial characteristics of the distressed firms can be expected, *a priori*, to be similar to those of the bankrupt firms, when the model was re-estimated using the bankrupt/distressed estimation sample it was expected that discrimination would be more difficult than for the bankrupt/random model. This was indeed the case and although the overall fit was good, the Type I error rates were about 70 percent both in the estimation and holdout samples! The significant variables to enter this model were: cash flow from operations/current liabilities, cash/total assets, retained earnings/total assets and the only one common to both models – stockholders' equity/total liabilities. The important findings of this study were as follows:

Contrary to the findings of Casey and Bartczak (1985) and others, cash flow variables add to predictive accuracy. The financial variables that show any ability to distinguish between bankrupt and randomly selected nonbankrupt firms are different from those that discriminate between bankrupt and distressed firms. Most importantly, 'the findings of this study demonstrate that if the objective is to identify likely bankruptcies from a pool of problem companies, these bankruptcy models perform poorly' (ibid. p. 169). The authors suggest that the choice of an alternative strategy to bankruptcy for companies in financial distress, such as merger, restructuring of debt or voluntary liquidation, 'is affected by factors not reflected in the financial statements' (ibid. p. 170). They reiterate Taffler's (1984) contention that bankruptcy model scores should be interpreted as descriptions of financial distress rather than predictions of bankruptcy *per se*.

2.6.4 Flagg, Giroux and Wiggins (1991) – A Failing Company Model

Because most distressed firms do not become bankrupt, a critical examination of those that do may provide additional insights into the failure process. Flagg *et al* (1991) examined only firms experiencing financial distress in order to distinguish those which go bankrupt from those that eventually recover.

The three specific objectives in this study were to define the failure process for those firms experiencing financial distress, to postulate events that signal that a firm is experiencing financial distress, and to combine the postulated events with traditional financial ratios in a stochastic model for classifying bankrupt and non-bankrupt firms.

The firms examined were all dividend-paying COMPUSTAT firms in the manufacturing and service industries during the years 1975-1981 that were considered to have entered the failure process i.e. during that period they must have had an initial net operating loss following at least three consecutive years of profitability (income greater than zero).

The financial ratios included in a logistic regression model were those most often found to be significant in prior studies, reflecting a firm's liquidity, cash flow problems, leverage position, and profitability. They were: current ratio, cash flows to total assets, total debt to total assets, net earnings to total assets, retained earnings to total assets, and log of total assets. To improve the model, four potential failure 'events' were also investigated. They were: reductions in dividends, 'going concern' qualified opinions, troubled debt restructurings, and violations of debt covenants.[10] The modelling approach focussed on the presence or absence of these specific failure events at any time during the six-year period after a firm's first net loss and investigated both their association with bankruptcy and their predictive ability, along with the financial ratios.

The results suggested a successful model. Two events (a change in a company's dividend policy, and a qualified opinion) and four ratios (current ratio, net earnings to total assets, retained earnings to total assets, and total debt to total assets) were significant, and 94 percent of the firms were correctly classified. The significant events suggest that non-financial ratio indicators can be used to increase our understanding of the failure process and improve bankruptcy prediction.

2.6.5 Multivariate Time Series Process – Theodossiou (1993)

Theodossiou (1996) used a sequential procedure for detecting a shift in the mean of a multivariate time series process and showed how the procedure can be used to predict a firm's tendency towards failure. The procedure is based on Healy's (1988) CUSUM framework and Shumway's (1988) time series discriminant analysis framework.

The authors examined the distributions of the ratios, fixed assets to total assets, net working capital to total assets, earnings per share to price per share, inventory to sales, and operating income to total assets, using data from 197 healthy and 62 failed manufacturing and retail firms from the *COMPUSTAT* files for the years 1967-1986. Except for the ratio fixed assets to total assets, the means by year prior to bankruptcy (0, 1, ... 7) of the failed group approach the overall mean of the healthy group in the years moving backwards from the point of bankruptcy. The sequential (dynamic) business failure prediction model fitted to these data was used to detect the point at which a firm's financial variables shift from a 'good performance' distribution to a 'bad performance' distribution. The author shows the CUSUM model to be clearly superior in performance to a discriminant analysis model.

2.6.6 Hill, Perry and Andes (1996)

The study by Hill, Perry and Andes (1996) extends prior research on a number of fronts. After the work of Gilbert *et al* (1990) who provided the evidence that a bankruptcy prediction model developed along traditional lines would not be able to distinguish firms that fail from other financially distressed firms, Hill *et al* (1996) employed a dynamic event history methodology to model this distinction. The event history analysis looks at the transitions to and from stable and financially distressed states and from these states to the bankrupt state (using longitudinal data). This contrasts with cross sectional analysis which uses a snapshot focus

[10] The event data were obtained from the footnotes and auditor's reports provided by Form 10-K, Moody's Industrial Manuals, and the National Automated Accounting Research System.

assuming that each firm will remain in one state (since this type of analysis typically measures the financial state only once).

Secondly, the dynamic model also explicitly accounted for time-varying independent variables that may change over the observation period. Besides using ratios that measure liquidity, profitability, leverage and firm size, from prior research, the authors also included in their model a measure indicating whether a firm received a qualified account or unqualified audit opinion (one of the four events that Flagg *et al* (1991) used and postulated would signal that a firm is experiencing financial distress). The two macro-economic variables identified by Rose *et al* (1982) as leading business failure, the prime rate and the unemployment rate, were included in order to partly control for changes in the business environment.

An extra extension to the literature was afforded by an analysis by industry segment. Unlike other studies that attempt to control for industry differences by limiting the industries selected for the sample, or by matching failed and stable firms by industry classification, or by standardising firm specific financial ratios by industry ratios (Platt and Platt, 1991), the authors were thus able to test whether some variables have a statistically significant impact on bankruptcy or financial distress for some industries and not for others.

Since the model was successful in identifying significant explanatory variables that differ between financially distressed and bankrupt firms and also between industry classifications, the authors were able to conclude that the explanatory variables do, indeed, play a differential role in financial distress and bankruptcy as well as across industries.

2.7 Emerging Technologies

Papers using a purely technological breakthrough do not change basic methodology, only the method. Computer tools used by the financial community have undergone a fantastic revolution over the last decade. Neural networks, a technique from the artificial intelligence literature, has entered into the field of financial distress/bankruptcy prediction giving mostly superior prediction performance in comparisons with MDA models and logit models based on publicly listed firm data. The research described in this section has shown that the pattern recognition and generalization capabilities of neural networks can enhance decision making in cases where the dependent variable is binary and available data is limited. An emerging area that employs non-linear dynamic models and the chaos aspect of bankruptcy is also reviewed.

2.7.1 Neural Networks

Neural network technology is a form of parallel processing technique that attempts to mimic the human brain (Kohonen, 1988). The characteristics and capabilities of a neural network make the technology a promising tool for solving the classification problem: the problem of classifying an entity into one of a finite collection of groups based on the attributes of that entity.

Operation of a neural network occurs in two phases – learning and recall. The network is 'trained' in the learning phase with numerous examples of entities as input: their attributes and, in the case of bankruptcy studies, their binary group membership as output. The method used for neural network prediction is called generalization (Dutta and Hekhar, 1988) in that once the network has been trained, new data is input for the network to predict the output.

The growing popularity of applying the neural network approach to diverse fields of interest is due to the ease and power of the technique in finding patterns in data that need not conform to linearity or distributional assumptions. In addition, artificial neural networks can overcome the effect of autocorrelation, which is often present in time series data and the technique tolerates data errors and missing values; problems not accounted for in multiple regression models. Thus, their ability to model non-linear dynamics, to deal with noisy data, and their adaptability, make the approach a potentially useful one for a wide range of financial decision-making (Baestaens, 1994, p. 1). Some business areas already explored, with promising results, are applications in corporate bond rating prediction (Dutta and Hekhar, 1988; Utans and Moody, 1991; Garavaglia 1991), stock market prediction (Kimoto and Asakawa, 1990), emulating mortgage underwriting judgements (Collins *et al*, 1989), prediction of going-concern status (Lenard *et al*, 1995; Koh and Tan, 1999; Etheridge *et al*, 2000), as well as credit analysis, and fraud detection.

Instead of a linear function, any response surface can be used to map the data, in this case for discrimination purposes, allowing the model to represent the complex relationships inherent in the interpretation of financial ratios. Hence, without a linear restriction, the model can be made to fit the data 'like a glove'.

De-Bodt, Cottrell and Levasseur (1995) provide an introduction to these new tools along with thirty applications in finance, including some in the domain of bankruptcy prediction. The empirical studies in this area, some of which are described below, predominantly compare a neural network model with an MDA model using traditional financial ratios from earlier studies. Exceptions are:

- Fletcher and Goss (1993), and Udo (1993), who compare a neural network with a logit model of bankruptcy,
- Goss and Ramchandani (1995), who compare the classification accuracy of neural networks, binary logit regression and discriminant analysis and show how the alternative non-parametric methodology of neural networks predicts (in this case, insurer insolvency) more effectively than the parametric models, and
- Glorfield *et al* (1997), who compare four inductive decision models – discriminant analysis, logistic regression, neural networks, and pocket algorithm with ratchet – to evaluate the financial distress of stressed firms. Their results indicated that 'overall, neural networks and the pocket

algorithm tended to outperform discriminant analysis and logistic regression' (p. 358).

- O'Leary (1998) provides a 'meta analysis' of the use of neural networks to predict corporate failure. Fifteen papers are reviewed and compared in order to investigate 'what works and what doesn't work'.

Odom and Sharda (1990). Odom and Sharda (1990) built a neural network model for bankruptcy prediction and compared its performance with discriminant analysis models. As the input vector of the back-propagation neural network they used the same financial variables that Altman used in his 1968 study. Three experiments were performed with different ratios of non-bankrupt to bankrupt firms: respectively 50/50, 80/20, and 90/10 training sets. In all the experiments, neural networks performed significantly better in predicting the firms' failure in a holdout sample of 55 firms (28/27). However, the neural network misclassified non-bankrupt firms more often than discriminant analysis did.

Koster, Sandak and Bourbia (1990). Koster *et al* (1990) developed an artificial neural network (ANN) model based on only two ratios; the current ratio (current assets to current liabilities), and the debt ratio (total debts to total assets) which was superior to a MDA model based on the same data. Using a feed-forward ANN composed of three layers (input layer, hidden layer, output layer), the ANN was trained on data from 91 firms.

There is an optimum range for the number of neurons in the hidden layer; too few neurons cannot develop a sufficiently complex internal representation of the data and can produce many errors, yet too many neurons cause specialization effects, known as 'overestimation', that miss key points and also cause errors. In order to find this optimum range, the training regimen of Koster *et al* (1990) consisted of a number of trials in which about 20 of the 91 data vectors were randomly selected as training data sets. The remaining vectors were then used to test the effectiveness of the resulting ANN construct. The ANN was considered adequately trained when 200 iterations produced no difference between the output and the expected values. Using the proper number of neurons, the various ANN models based on different numbers of data vectors in the training sets, showed consistently better prediction results than the MDA model (86 percent vs. 78 percent) leading the authors to conclude that 'the ANN has clearly detected aspects of the data set space that were beyond the capability of the statistical model' (p.8).

Cadden (1991). Cadden (1991) compared a neural network and an MDA model based on data from 59 failed firms and 59 non-failed firms from the same time period using twelve ratios used in earlier studies. The data were collected for three years preceding failure. Ten firms from each group were held out for testing the model.

The results of the discriminant analysis follow the pattern in other studies, with the greatest accuracy in the year prior to failure and accuracy dropping off in the other years. The initial neural network model using raw data performed poorly in comparison to the MDA model, with a less-than 50 percent accuracy for the year prior to failure. This was due to extreme values in the data. On restructuring the data into dummy variables using interquartile values as boundaries, the resulting neural network model performed better than the MDA model for both failed and non-failed firms, for both the analysis and the test sample, and for all years preceding bankruptcy; at three years prior, the neural network still accurately classified 80 percent and 90 percent respectively, of failed and non-failed firms in the holdout sample.

Coats and Fant (1992). Coats and Fant (1992) demonstrated a perfect fit when they applied a neural network model to the five Altman (1968) ratio predictors, computed for three years prior. When classifying the estimation sample of 47 distressed and 47 healthy firms, they found the error rates *were all nil.* On the same sized holdout sample the Type I error rate was 9 percent and the Type II error rate was 4 percent. In all cases, the neural network's predictions were superior to the MDA results.

Fletcher and Goss (1993). Fletcher and Goss (1993) used the Back-Propagation Neural Network (BPNN). This is a particular case of ANN's, with a single hidden layer feed-forward network which implements an error back-propagation methodology. It is based on data from just 18 failed and 18 non-failed companies from an earlier study by Gentry (1985) and its performance was compared with that of a logit model of bankruptcy prediction. Only three explanatory variables were used: the current ratio (current assets to current liabilities), the quick ratio (cash and other near-cash assets to current liabilities), and the income ratio (net income to working capital).

Given such a small training set, a variation of the cross-validation technique known as *v-fold* cross-validation was selected to estimate prediction risk rather than direct training-to-test set validation. This method gave 18 subsets of six observations for each test set with three rotationally selected from the failed group and three from the non-failed group for a total of 108 observations in the test set. This also provided 18 training sets of 30 observations. (Each observation is represented three times in the test sets.)

Similar to earlier explorations by Koster *et al* (1990), the authors examined the number of hidden nodes of the BPNN structure in order to determine the optimal network architecture. They state that the recommendation of Kolmogorov's Mapping Neural Network Existence Theorem[11] (and of others) for the number of hidden nodes, 'in some cases, ... may lead to fitting (or memorising) the training set too well, resulting in poor generalisation capabilities' (Fletcher and Goss, 1993, p. 163), and give more practical ranges for optimal generalisation capability.

Their results correspond closely to other studies that have shown neural networks to be better at extracting information from attributes for forecasting bankruptcy. The BPNN predicted better than the logit model at 82.4 percent

[11] In Hecht-Nielsen (1989).

accuracy overall on the 108 test set (77 percent for the 54 bankrupt firms at the same rate as the logistic model, and a superior 89 percent for the 54 nonbankrupt firms).

Udo (1993). Using a much larger training set than Fletcher and Goss (1993), Udo (1993) also used a back-propagation method to train an artificial neural network (ANN) using data on 16 financial ratios previously used in bankruptcy studies, taken from 150 companies that failed in 1989-90 and from 150 corresponding healthy companies. In addition the ANN was tested on a holdout sample of 50 failed and 50 healthy firms. The regression model used to compare with the ANN from this study was adapted from the logit model of Platt and Platt (1990).

The accuracy of the ANN model, judged on the holdout sample, outperformed the regression model when they were both estimated on data taken at one year prior to bankruptcy, and performed equally well when based on data from two years prior. The prediction accuracy of ANN ranged between 82-92 percent compared with 72-80 percent for the regression models. The author makes the point that, typically, regression models need fewer predictors for good results, whereas ANN benefits from more information – adding that 'in this age of fast computers, it is not a major advantage for a model to use less information that results in a lower accuracy' (Udo, 1993, p. 380).

Lee, Han and Kwon (1996). Lee *et al* (1996) combine a back-propagation model with a SOFM (self organizing feature map)-assisted neural network. The performance of the resulting hybrid neural network model was promising when evaluated on Korean bankruptcy data against other benchmark models including an MDA-assisted neural network.

Final Remarks Regarding Neural Network Applications. As the above papers show, neural network technology may yet provide a powerful tool for early detection of company failures as evidenced by its application in many research settings. These papers have predominantly compared a neural net model with MDA models or logit models of failure prediction, with superior classification outcomes and have shown that, in essence, neural network models are easier to use, more robust, more flexible, and more responsive to change than a regression model. They appear, also, to be more robust on small sample sizes.

However, due to the problem of overfitting data with consequent declining generalizing ability of the ANN (as discussed by Koster *et al*, 1990, and Fletcher and Goss, 1993), these tools have generally been used to assist rather than become an alternative to traditional statistical and mathematical models. Yet, as their results verify, these authors have provided a principled mechanism for determining the optimal network architecture that mitigates against this problem.

Koster *et al* (1990) point out other problems with the use of this technology; *viz.* that of the confusing array of names and notations used by different disciplines for the same paradigms causing a 'Tower of Babel' effect in the (ANN) literature. There are also scaling problems – 'an application that works well with a given input situation can require extensive redesign if the length and scale of the input vector change' (Koster *et al*, 1990, p. 8).

The most important problem is the 'black box' nature of the ANN, i.e. there is a lack of understanding or knowledge regarding how it solves a particular problem. 'The theoretical foundations (of ANN) are highly mathematical and the application is essentially one of numerically solving sets of simultaneous equations' (Koster *et al*, 1990, p. 8), so no indications regarding theory are given to aid in the construction of hypotheses that can be tested to give meaning or explanation to the area of research to which ANN is applied.

So in spite of the optimistic results, one has to recognize the major limitations of ANN's. First, ANNs do not rely on formal theory for the purpose of determining the optimal network topology. Second ANN's do not provide explanations to the researcher about how inferences are made.

One method suggested here for further research into understanding process in neural networks is by investigating the discriminatory power of particular explanatory variables. This method is similar to forward and backward selection of variables in regression but without the statistical t-testing that accompanies that method's distributional underpinnings. Instead, one could compare, empirically, the prediction accuracy of the network when particular variables or sets of variables are successively excluded and included in the calculation of the network, thus providing some evidence of an important contribution or otherwise to discrimination.

With respect to bankruptcy prediction, further application of different neural network architectures and the use of different ratios from the traditional ones should lead to intensified research efforts and benefit from the implementation of this technology. The research described here 'shows neural networks to be a viable alternative to more traditional methods of estimating causal relationships in data, and offers a new paradigm of computational capabilities to the business practitioner' (Fletcher and Goss, 1993, p. 165).

2.7.2 *Chaos Theory*

Non-linear dynamic models have proven quite successful in the prediction of certain endogenously determined catastrophic system failures, such as myocardial infarction. Since a firm's principal investors and creditors would also consider firm bankruptcy to be a catastrophic event, then it should be possible to exploit the characteristics of chaotic behaviour in predicting this type of failure. Etheridge and Sriram (1993) argue that economics and finance researchers have already successfully used chaos theory to study systems such as the stock market (see Peters, 1991) and that it is time for accounting researchers to begin using the methodology. Though a complete introduction to chaos theory is beyond the scope of this book (see Yorke, 1976, and Gleick, 1987), a brief outline of its salient features and studies that have applied it to bankruptcy prediction follow.

Several forms of chaos have been identified mathematically that all share the common characteristic of identifying some order or element of predictability in seemingly disorganized phenomena. Chaotic systems, though, are deterministic and predictable only over short periods of time (Etheridge and Sriram, 1993; Goldberger, 1990). They are fractal, meaning that self-repetition exists on smaller and smaller scales; and they are extremely sensitive to initial conditions (Lorenz, 1963).

Cadden (1991) points out that bankruptcy is multi-causal, mostly attributable to management error; that these errors lead to financial losses, which in turn lead to financial difficulties.

> One can identify a series of mistakes on the part of management rather than a catastrophic error. This means that financial decline is generally gradual, although the actual event of bankruptcy is relatively sudden and abrupt (Cadden, 1991, p. 53).

Given that healthy systems exhibit more chaos than unhealthy ones (Goldberger, 1990), Lindsay and Campbell (1996) hypothesized that the returns of firms nearing bankruptcy would exhibit significantly less chaos. The amount of chaos was measured with Lyapunov exponents (Wolf, 1985) from which were constructed univariate and multivariate bankruptcy prediction models using industry match-paired data of 46 bankrupt and 46 non-bankrupt firms. For each firm in both samples, data were collected on the firms at an early two-year window of time; the period 7-5 years before filing for bankruptcy, and also at a late two-year window; from 3-1 years prior to filing. The study hypothesis led to the expectation that the early and late Lyapunov exponents would differ for bankrupt firms but not for others. A t-test of the differences between the Lyapunov exponents estimated for the early and late windows was calculated for the bankrupt and control samples with results consistent with the hypothesis.

A univariate bankruptcy prediction model that used a decision rule based on the size of the difference between the early and late Lyapunov exponents yielded a 65 percent accuracy rate on a 46 firm holdout sample (both Type I and Type II errors were 35 percent), comparing favourably to Beaver's (1966) best univariate predictor. Also, a comparison of a simple two factor discriminant analysis bankruptcy prediction model[12] and an expanded version with four chaos statistics added, yielded a much reduced Type I and Type II error on the holdout sample for the augmented model. Hence, the development of a full theoretical understanding of this chaos-derived model is a promising avenue for further research into the application of non-linear dynamics to the problem of bankruptcy prediction.

---

12 The DA model was based on the total debt to total assets ratio (recommended by Beaver, 1966) and the natural log of sales as a firm size variable (recommended by Foster, 1986).

2.7.3 *Latest Techniques*

Most of the early models that were used to 'predict' bankruptcy and that employed regression techniques (including MDA and logit analysis), numerical taxonomy and factor analysis, focussed on classifying objects into classes based on their multivariate characteristics. Newer research like recursive partitioning (Marais *et al*, 1984; Frydman *et al*, 1985), and research from the artificial intelligence field has turned to the modelling techniques of fuzzy logic (Alam *et al*, 2000, Ahn *et al*, 2000, Lenard *et al*, 2000), and rough sets (Pawlak, 1982; Siegel *et al*, 1995; McKee, 2000), which, like neural networks, provide extremely detailed models which are difficult to generalize or develop theory from. The very latest research, which is aimed at the long-overdue theory development aspect of bankruptcy research, uses the new technique of genetic programming (Koza, 1992), developed from genetic algorithms (Holland, 1975). This technique shows considerable promise in determining a general description characterizing a set of observations: a helpful step in theory building. For instance, the question of which ratio should represent a factor or conceptual pattern in bankruptcy has yet to be resolved (Chen and Shimerda, 1981, p. 59). See McKee and Lensberg (1999, 2002) for genetic algorithms applied to bankruptcy research.

2.8 Major Challenges and Future Directions

Major methodological problems in the literature are outlined in Chapter 3. Joy and Tollefson (1975) and Eisenbeis (1977) gave comprehensive reviews of the pitfalls of the use of MDA in financial applications and Zmijewski (1984) addressed the problems of sampling bias.

In addition, a major design problem that needs to be addressed involves the dichotomization of the failure-survival continuum. When both bankrupt and surviving firms make up the estimation sample, the second categorization is not fixed over time, and the distinction becomes blurred when surviving firms are, by most measures, financially distressed.

Also, the stationarity of the models is questionable across diverse economic environments over which the data were collected causing differences in classification rates between estimation and forecast periods. Inflation, interest rates, phases of the business cycle and availability of credit have been given as reasons for data instability in that they influence the vulnerability of the individual firm to failure. Richardson, Kane and Lobingier (1998) tested the hypothesis that recessionary business cycles can contribute to corporate failure and showed that accounting-based logistic regression models used to predict corporate failure are sensitive to the occurrence of a recession. Hence, adding measures of the external economic environment to the explanatory set can only improve the fit of the models.

Another area for improvement lies with the types of functions used to model the failure process. Most bankruptcy prediction models employ single equation models in their formulation e.g. a multiple discriminant analysis model or a logit/probit model as the primary statistical tool, which may not always be appropriate for the particular objectives, especially when the distributions of the ratios used as predictors are generally non-normal and multicollinear. The neural network approach looks promising in its flexibility in fitting models to data especially if macroeconomic variables are also included with the financial variables in the explanatory set, but may lead to overfitting and lack of generalization.

An ongoing challenge to researchers of corporate bankruptcy is to produce a model that distinguishes distressed firms filing bankruptcy from others, also at risk, but avoiding it. In other words the real question of interest is how do firms transform from surviving or even successful ones into failed ones. Financial distress models need to use the statistical techniques drawn from survival analysis, knowing that the potential to fail always exists *ex ante*. Other promising avenues for further analysis of the distress continuum that are described in this chapter are: the failing firm model of Flagg *et al* (1991) that includes postulated events signalling that a firm is experiencing financial distress; the sequential dynamic failure prediction model of Thoedossiou (1991) using multivariate time-series which can detect the critical point at which a firm's financial variables shift from a 'good performance' distribution to a 'bad performance' distribution; the event history methodology of Hill *et al* (1996); and the application of non-linear dynamics to the problem of bankruptcy prediction with the chaos-derived models of Lindsay and Campbell (1996). A new approach consists of the family of models described in Chapter 3 that allow for a comparison of each firm with itself over time – from when the firm was surviving, or avoiding bankruptcy, to when it failed.

Many of the above challenges can only be addressed by a totally new research design and modelling methodology as part of future research. The ad hoc specification of the model in the absence of any economic theory continues to be a problem and the predictive value of explanatory variables not yet utilized in the models needs to be evaluated. My introductory remarks concerning the level of sophistication reached in the field of financial distress are pertinent here. My interpretation of 'explanation' at this methodological level is based on antecedent causes. Until models can satisfactorily explain the internal dynamics of the firm, reliability in prediction will not be achieved.

Extra considerations not yet included in existing models are discussed be a number of authors, but by their very nature these may be too difficult to include as explanatory variables. Both McFadden (1973) and Martin (1977) discuss the issue of intangible influences on the outcome for each individual firm and Zavgren (1983) points out the need for company soundness criteria to be taken into account, as it varies over the business cycle. In periods when failures are relatively rare, the empirical link between certain otherwise-important indicators and the actual occurrence of failure will be weak. Consequently, a model estimated from such a period would always lead to questionable results no matter what specific form of modelling estimation technique were employed. For this reason, a theoretical component that accounts for this and a time series formulation that includes it is absolutely necessary with the inclusion of macroeconomic variables that affect the firm's vulnerability to failure.

2.9 Conclusion

This review has described the major research in this area, and has shown how they are linked, particularly in following a very narrow and static comparative (in the main, failed vs. non-failed) emphasis. It has also shown that since the important papers of the early 1980s, this paradigm has been accepted with (only recently) few detractors and research has been fine-tuning, mostly of method. In part, future progress in the field depends not so much on the further identification of relevant variables, but incorporating into the models a measure of the degree of economic adversity prevailing as well as other macroeconomic indicators. There is, even more, a need for an explicit dynamic formulation rather than the almost entirely static modelling indicated in this review.

The most recent literature has already revealed tentative new research methodologies that have produced some promising results in the field on the basis of more rigorous testing and theoretical reasoning than has been the case to date. New techniques such as those from the survival analysis field, from non-linear dynamics including chaos theory, and from the artificial intelligence field have had some success in discovering unique characteristics of bankrupt and financially distressed firms.

Nevertheless, despite a long research history, there is no bankrupt prediction model based primarily on a bankruptcy theory that is generally acceptable. As noted by Zavgren (1983), in prior financial distress studies, model development is characterized by a lack of theoretical underpinning and still more recently, by Dmitras (1996) 'a unifying theory of business failure has not been developed ...' (1996, p. 487). Hence most approaches that 'data dredge' in order to find unique characteristics that differentiate between bankrupt and non-distressed firms have been criticized. In the absence of theory, the results do not permit generalization, and a sustained correlation between variables and the event predicted cannot be expected (Blum, 1974; Ball and Foster, 1982).

To improve this situation, either greater research convergence or more theory building is needed. It is in the first area that the work outlined in this book is directed – toward more research convergence – in employing a family of models methodology. In addition, this book argues that a major methodological shift at the empirical level, from cross-sectional modelling to time series modelling with a multi-equation structure, is one of the changes required in achieving a greater degree of success in understanding the internal dynamics of firms at risk.

The suite of models outlined in Chapter 3 incorporates this shift as well as allowing for continuous dependent variables or jointly dependent variables to become the focus of research attention. Such developments coupled with an extension of the data base both cross-sectionally and over time, may yet yield more reliable models.

Chapter 3

Failure of Firms as Process: A New Modelling Methodology

3.0 Introduction

The methodological issues that are related to the analysis of company failures will be examined. The problems of past modelling methodologies are outlined and a new direction in modelling, a methodological shift, is offered as a possible solution to at least some of these problems. At its heart is the insight that failure of firms is a process, not a simple instantaneous state shift. This insight makes a new approach imperative, as well as throwing doubt on the usefulness of much of the prevailing work. The process approach has many implications but one is especially important. It is that although they are still alive, some firms are so far along the path to failure that they are already doomed, unless there is massive external intervention.

The shift involves expanding the failure model from a single-equation representation to a multi-equation structure that reflects the simultaneous nature of different forces (or variables) acting on the firm, both from within and without. Because there is an infinity of potential such models this book can be seen as a first step in that direction. It also involves an extension from a stationary time model (using cross-sectional data) to a representation of firm failure that is dynamic (using time-series panel data); one that can change with a changing economy and from feedback effects within the firm.

The last two decades have seen a post-war record number of business failures. Consequently, the topic of financial distress is a subject of international concern and analysis; the literature abounding with studies utilising statistical modelling applied to the financial ratios derived from publicly available financial statement information. Almost all claim to be useful to lending institutions, investors and shareholders, company directors and their auditors, as a warning signal to failure. For instance, by providing auditors with a model that is more objective in evaluating whether a firm is likely to continue as a going-concern, failure classification/prediction models may be able to complement the information contained in the financial statements. Such models should aid in presenting a more comprehensive picture of the firm's relative strengths and weaknesses and should also be useful for performance assessment.

Despite their avowed intent, few, if any, studies have any established and proven, let alone *predictive* ability measured in either statistical or commercial terms, though some significant achievements have been made finding empirically validated characteristics that distinguish financially distressed from non-distressed firms. Unfortunately, not enough attention has been paid to model specification, particularly in relation to theory and to the related problems of hypothesis testing when distress models are used for other than classification/discrimination purposes. As Blum (1974) points out, in the absence of either any general and/or generally accepted economic theory of financial distress, it is difficult to determine whether any observed correlation between independent variables and the variable financial distress, however measured, can be generalized. Ball and Foster (1982) note also that this problem will be especially severe if step-wise rules, essentially an ad hoc approach, are critical or central to the inclusion/exclusion of explanatory variables in the model being employed.

Partly as a consequence of this, and with the usually implicit assumption of time stationarity, discriminant functions or conditional probability (logit/probit) models used to forecast bankruptcy would generally show poor predictive power. This is particularly the case if tested against a holdout sample taken from a different time period to that of the sample used to estimate the model (though few researchers examine the performance of their functions under these conditions). Many show high Type I error probabilities – misclassifying bankrupt firms as healthy – which some authors[1] have deemed to cost between 20 to 30 times the cost of a Type II error – misclassifying healthy firms as bankrupt. Of course there are other reasons for the poor predictive power and high error probabilities that will, for example, lie in the techniques themselves as well as the nature of the data employed.[2]

3.1 Problems in Empirical Single-Equation Bankruptcy Analysis

This section shows why a reliable methodology for bankruptcy prediction using single equation empirical models has so far eluded researchers in the field. Ultimately this provides the impetus to construct a different modelling methodology, rather than merely using another data set or creating a new theory where others remain untested.

The multi-equation models are developed in this chapter as part of a family of models together forming a generalized model for failure risk. This generalized framework also embraces the single-equation models as special cases, with all the limitations that this engenders. A detailed discussion of this new methodology follows along with the modelling procedures and techniques necessary to implement the methodology.

---

1 See Altman *et al* (1977), Rose and Giroux (1984), and White *et al* (1994).

2 Zavgren (1983) compares past predictive bankruptcy studies in terms of their respective classification error rates.

3.1.1 Estimating Probabilities of Failure

One starting point for developing any new methodology is a reworking of the current modelling framework. Essentially the framework is that represented by the research considered in the previous chapter. This approach suggests a new methodology that retains significant bridges to the insights and forms of past work.

Bankruptcy prediction models to date offer a single equation empirical model that typically takes the following form where the probability of bankruptcy in the next period can be written:

$$\Pr(Y_i=1) = F(X_{i1}\, X_{i2} \dots X_{im},\, b_0, b_1, b_2, \dots b_m) \tag{3.1}$$

where:
Y_i represents the outcome or dependent variable, for the ith firm in the next period: either
$Y_i = 0$ for the population of surviving firms, or
$Y_i = 1$ for the population of failed firms,
X_{ij} is an element of the matrix of explanatory variables – the value of the jth characteristic for the ith firm,
$b_0, b_1, b_2, \dots b_m$ are constants of the model,
m = the number of explanatory variables, X_j, taken for each firm.

Which form of the probability function, F, is the most appropriate is decided by the researcher on the basis of interpretative and computational simplicity as well as the goals of the study – a point that Eisenbeis (1977) elaborates. One form is the cumulative normal distribution, which leads to a probit model. If this distribution is replaced by the logistic function, an approximation that is virtually indistinguishable from the cumulative normal except at the extreme 'tails', it leads to either the logit model or the discriminant analysis model. The difference lies in the method of estimation of the b_j's, the parametric coefficients of the function F. (Martin, 1977).

The independent variables, X_j, can be the firm's financial ratios or other variables that might be relevant to the firm's risk of failing. In the two-group MDA case, if the two populations of failed and non-failed firms are multivariate normal with respect to the independent variables and their covariance matrices are equal, the b_j's are estimated as:[3]

$$\begin{aligned} b_0 &= -1/2(\overline{X}_1 + \overline{X}_0)'S^{-1}(\overline{X}_1 - \overline{X}_0) + \ln(N_1/(N-N_1)), \\ (b_1, b_2, \dots b_m) &= S^{-1}(\overline{X}_1 - \overline{X}_0) \end{aligned} \tag{3.2}$$

where $\overline{X}_1$ and $\overline{X}_0$ are the group mean vectors of the ratios X_j with covariance matrices $S_1=S_0=S$, assumed equal, for the failed and non-failed firms respectively,

[3] from Lachenbruch (1975).

N is the total number of firms and N_1 is the number of failed firms. The probability of failure in the next period is given by the logistic function:

$$\Pr(Y_i = 1) = P_i = (1 + \exp\{-W_i\})^{-1} \quad (3.3)$$

where $$W_i = b_0 + \sum_{j=1}^{m} b_j X_{ij} \quad (3.4)$$

is the linear predictor – a combination of the ratios and the vector of coefficients, **B** = $(b_0, b_1, \ldots b_m)$.

Two important points to note regarding the logistic function are that P_i is increasing in W_i and that W_i is equal to log $(P_i/\{1 - P_i\})$, i.e. the linear predictor W_i in (3.3) can be represented as the logarithm of the conditional odds for $Y_i= 1$, the functional form of the logit model.[4] Thus the linear discriminant function is a special case of the logit model with the restrictions of multivariate normality imposed. The logit model does not imply that the independent variables are distributed multivariate normal[5] (Martin, 1977, p. 258).

The coefficients of the logit model are estimated by the method of maximum likelihood (ML). The key to its advantage lies in its *direct* estimation of the parametric coefficients in the logit function, employing an iterative technique, rather than substituting suspect estimates under suspect conditions into formulae (3.2).[6] Essentially the process iteratively improves the fit of the probability estimates of the outcomes for each firm so that those observations where failure occurred are assigned low ex ante probabilities of survival, and those that survived are assigned high probabilities. A 'good fit' is a set of coefficients for the linear predictor W_i that best satisfies this objective.[7]

3.1.2 *A Critical View*

It is important to mention here that authors using the models above frequently (almost invariably) report high classification accuracy for their single equation models. Nevertheless, the reliability of their reported error rates needs to be scrutinized. The estimation of the reliability of a model is subject to various types of overfitting bias, three levels of which are discussed by Marais *et al* (1984) as: (1) statistical overfitting – when the model is 'tailored' to the data, (2) overfitting in the choice of explanatory variables, and (3) sensitivity to a particular loss function. Methods to detect the problem in (1) include using holdout samples,

---

4 See McFadden (1973) for a comprehensive analysis of the logit model.

5 Cox (1970) and Jones (1975) expand on this distinction.

6 Halperin *et al* (1971) have compared the results of MDA and ML estimation of the coefficients when the logistic model holds but the normality assumptions of the independent variables are violated.

7 Martin (1977) gives a good explanation of ML estimation techniques in the context of bank failure predictions.

cross-validation, and jack-knife procedures. The overfitting problem in (2) is of particular importance when using stepwise regression procedures; finding the best fitting model from a hypothetical set of independent variables. This method can give spurious statistical significance to particular variables based on a purely coincidental relationship with the sample data set. Corporate failure prediction models are particularly sensitive to this problem. Palepu (1986) addressed the problem in (3) by using a Bayesian method of identifying the optimal cut-off point for classification.

An early stage in constructing a better methodology is to list the potential reasons for the poor performance of former models and then to investigate how a new research methodology might possibly address these problems. Subsequent sections of this chapter include a discussion of these possible solutions.

The problems are considered to be, among others:

(1) The inappropriateness of the estimation method usually employed given that accounting ratios as a group exhibit significant multicollinearity and measurement problems.
(2) Sampling bias in the data samples used in the empirical analysis.
(3) Incomplete model specification and the models' relevance in a dynamic economic climate.
(4) The intrinsic impurity of all public disclosure information.

Problems (1), (2) and (3) will be addressed individually and in detail in the next section by outlining the objectives that relate to each in the new modelling methodology.

Problem (4) refers to the use of alternative accounting methods e.g. different depreciation and asset valuation methods leading to inconsistencies across firms and years, failure to disclose complete information, biased reporting, among others. It is reasonable to assume, for instance, that distressed companies are more likely to engage in creative accounting, which distorts or suppresses unfavourable accounting information in order to mislead users of their financial reports (Schwartz, 1982; Lilien *et al*, 1988; Dharan and Lev, 1993). If the non-random 'noise' attributable to these causes proves to be a major problem across much of the data used to model distress, then no reliable model can be found; either in terms of model specification and completeness (see 3.2.3 and 3.2.5) nor repeatability of results. Zavgren and Friedman (1988) attributed lack of significance of two of their model variables to noisy measurements and the possibility that the profit figures were manipulated.

We would like to assume that the data will reveal a reasonably true account of the financial position of each firm despite these inherent data impurities. Some optimism in this respect, found from the studies examining the effect of accounting changes on the value of the ratios, include Fogelson (1978), and Norton and Smith (1979). For instance, with regard to alternative accounting methods in reporting asset value, the latter study concludes 'in spite of sizeable differences in magnitude that existed between general price level and historical cost financial statements, little difference was found in bankruptcy predictions.' Applying a discriminant function to a holdout sample, Mensah (1983) also found that the classification success of any single model, whether it utilized specific price-level restated financial statements, historical cost statements, or a combination of both, was not statistically different from another.

3.2 Emergent Research Objectives

The aim of this research is to address the first three problems outlined above on a theoretical as well as a practical basis such that a more reliable failure model can be produced. The inadequacies of the standard static, single-equation approach helped lead to the following five research objectives:

- Valid accommodation of the available data into appropriate models.
- Addressing the problem of sample selection bias.
- Improving model specification for relevance over time.
- Improving model specification to reflect dynamics.
- Improving model completeness.

3.2.1 Valid Accommodation of the Available Data into Appropriate Models

When analysing the available financial data of public companies, it is necessary to find either (a) a modelling technique that either explicitly allows skewed data into the model formulation or, if not, is robust to violations of data requirements, or (b) transformations of the data that reduce skewness and/or multicollinearity to allow the valid use of the financial ratios in the particular modelling technique being used.

If consistent estimators that are useful for prediction are required, and if misleading results regarding the significance of particular ratios entering the model are to be avoided, then estimation by the method of MDA requires that two assumptions be met. The ratios must be distributed jointly multivariate normal, and the group covariance matrices must be equal across both groups of failed and non-failed firms, or at least approximately so. If these distributional requirements are satisfied, then the multiple linear discriminant model will be an optimum classification procedure (Efron, 1975). Slight violations may cause little problem due to the robustness of the technique though empirical studies in economics have reported contradictory results (Amemiya, 1981).

Unfortunately, the use of accounting data, where the marginal distributions of the individual financial ratios are extremely skewed with some ratios taking on infinite values,[8] constitutes a gross violation of the MDA assumptions.

[8] Example are ratios with denominators that can be zero e.g. the ratio 'Interest Coverage after Tax' when no interest payments are due, or a ratio with Sales or Inventory in the denominator.

Deakin (1976) showed that 10 of 11 financial ratios analyzed for manufacturing firms were not normally distributed, and neither did standard transformation techniques result in normality. For instance, the cube root preserves sign and reduces the skewness by condensing the distribution, but transformations such as this necessarily distort the relative positions in the discriminant analysis space. Further, a comprehensive Australian study by Matolcsy *et al* (1993) found, on analyzing the distributions of 16 financial ratios, that not only are many resistant to conventional transformations to induce normality, but that deletion of outliers (by trimming or Winsorizing) often causes an unjustifiable loss of information (p. 12). Kennedy *et al* (1993) compared these procedures used to adjust for outliers in the data, as well as procedures that adjust for nonlinearities in the relationship between the dependent and independent variables in regression analysis. Their findings show that the choice of data accommodation procedure has a major impact on the predictive ability and coefficient estimates of the regression model (p. 161).

Regardless of the success of transformations to induce normality of the marginal distributions, they do not guarantee multivariate normality and will not typically induce equality of covariance matrices.[9] When only the first of the two distributional requirements for MDA is true, then quadratic discriminant analysis provides the optimum classification procedure, though Hamer (1983) found that the linear discriminant and logit models were found to give analogous results and were, in general, at least as accurate in prediction as the quadratic model.

When the normality assumption is violated in a model estimated by MDA, significance levels might be biased, leading to erroneous inclusion of ratios unrelated or not directly related to failure. Accordingly, the MDA approach can give misleading results that could inappropriately influence decisions. This is especially the case if managers, aware that investors, lenders and auditors are using these models, attempt to control these ratios although there is no direct link between them and failure.[10] Nor is MDA the correct approach if the probability of the outcome (bankruptcy or survival) is sought, because assignment of probability estimates to each firm is a different objective than classification into groups.

Many authors, among them Ohlson (1980), have provided evidence for their choice of the logit model over MDA in applications to bankruptcy prediction. The use of a regression-type technique, such as logit analysis, is more appropriate for the purposes outlined above, as it avoids most, though not all,[11] of the distributional

---

9 See Karels and Prakash (1987) and Watson(1990) for further discussion on multivariate distributional properties, outliers and transformation of financial ratios.

10 Joy and Tollefson (1975) provide an excellent summary of the applications of MDA in business and finance. Eisenbeis (1977) discusses the pitfalls associated with these applications, and Karels and Prakash (1987) provide valuable comparisons between predictions under suspect conditions for the different MDA models.

11 See Palepu (1986) for a detailed discussion of the methodological issues relevant to research settings that involve binary state prediction models, and Press and Wilson (1979) for the reasons why the logistic regression model with maximum likelihood estimators is preferred for both classification and for relating qualitative variables to other variables under nonnormality.

problems associated with using MDA. It has the added advantage of allowing qualitative variables, i.e. those with categories rather than continuous data, into its formulation.

Press and Wilson (1978) present theoretical arguments for using logistic regression with maximum likelihood estimation compared to using discriminant analysis in both the classification problem and the problem of relating qualitative (e.g. binary) to explanatory variables:

> Classifying an observation into one of several populations is discriminant analysis, or classification. Relating qualitative variables to other variables through a logistic conditional density function functional form is logistic regression. Estimates generated for one of these problems are often used in the other. If the populations are normal with identical covariance matrices, discriminant analysis estimators are preferred to logistic regression estimators for the discriminant analysis problem. --- Under nonnormality, we prefer the logistic regression model with maximum likelihood estimators for solving both problems. (Press and Wilson, 1978, p. 699)

So the logit model has a distinct advantage over MDA for assessing which ratios or other variables are important to failure risk in that the coefficient on each variable may be interpreted behaviourally and separately as to its importance,[12] subject to the limitations imposed by multicollinearity. Factor analysis or principal component analysis may be used to eliminate multicollinearity among the predictors and stepwise regression methods that reduce the variable set will reduce the amount of multicollinearity within the set.

As stated earlier, a problem with many accounting ratios is that their statistical distributions are generally highly skewed. This often happens because zero, or near zero denominators exist for many ratios. The transformations to overcome this may necessitate loss of information, as in the use of qualitative (dummy) variables to eliminate the effect that infinite-valued financial ratios have on any least squares or maximum-likelihood regression estimation technique. On the other hand, in some situations a better model can result from categorising a continuous data measurement if the response takes the form of a step function rather than a linear or higher order function (Cybinski, 1995).

Another consideration when dealing with financial ratios is when both the numerator and denominator of a ratio can take on negative values, as confounding can occur. For instance, the negative-divided-by-negative valued ratios need to be distinguished from their positive-over-positive counterparts and similarly for negative-over-positive and positive-over-negative ratio values. Any technique requiring only continuous variable measurement is precluded when such ratios are included in the model. Again, categorizing the variable can overcome this problem (Cybinski, 1995).

---

12 The statistical properties of the maximum-likelihood estimates, which are asymptotically unbiased and normally distributed, are discussed in detail in Bradley and Gart (1962).

3.2.2 Addressing the Problem of Sample Selection Bias

The problem of sample selection bias is a primary concern in past and current research. This bias can take two forms[13] from Zmijewski (1984) as outlined in *2.5.1*:

- Bias due to missing data, leading to under-representation in the estimation sample of firms experiencing difficulty, and hence, a large error probability for misclassifying bankrupt firms in the resulting model, and
- Bias due to non-random sampling procedures, leading to a bias in favour of bankrupt firms i.e. a lower probability of misclassifying bankrupt firms at the expense of a higher probability of misclassifying surviving firms.

A new and simple research design is proposed to address this sample selection bias – by using only failed firms in the estimation sample and analyzing how firms transform themselves from surviving entities into failed ones, much as a well person becomes diseased. No other study has been found which has used this approach in any systematic manner. This approach is entirely dependent on the proposed model having a dynamic nature as outlined in the next objective. Each firm is matched against itself over time, moving from its surviving years through to the final bankrupt year to capture the transitions through degrees of failure. The implications for modelling, empirical testing and interpretation, and for applied use are considerable.

By definition, the problem of bias under choice-based sampling (oversampling of failed firms) does not arise under such a design. The problem of bias due to incomplete data is also partly circumvented, since, by design, all firms have failed, and each firm has the same amount of information for its surviving years and failed year as every other firm in the sample. One highly significant advantage arising from the design is that there can be no confounding of successful firms with those surviving firms that are potential failures in the very near future.

Nevertheless, this methodology must have its costs. The major shortcoming of using only failed firms is that it may not be possible to directly generalize prediction of bankruptcy as there is a different type of bias in the sample. Since firms do not end up in distress for totally random reasons, the nature of the study is changed when using only bankrupt firms i.e. the method is directed towards explanatory power rather than prediction.

3.2.3 Improving Model Specification for Relevance over Time

Current approaches are highly deficient in the manner in which they treat, or do not treat, the external economic environment. The results of Rose *et al* (1982) suggest the possibility of a complex relationship between business failure rates and business cycle indicators. Mensah (1984) found that the accuracy and structure of predictive

---

[13] See also Manski and Lerman (1977) and Palepu (1986).

models of bankruptcy differ across both different economic environments and different industrial sectors. Yet the use of cross-sectional data in many studies implies that the external economic environment is held constant, whereas changes in it clearly influence company failure rates. Rising interest rates, a recessionary environment, the availability of credit, and other macroeconomic factors can all affect a firm's vulnerability to failure.

Consequently, there is a need to improve model specification and its relevance in a changing economic climate. This research addresses the problem of non-stationarity with a totally new research design and modelling methodology. The model needs to generalize the cross-sectional schema of past studies to a time series, which can incorporate the exogenous variables and, perhaps, their interaction with the financial variables. Fortunately, estimation of relationships that combine time series and cross-sectional data is a situation frequently encountered in economics and other social sciences and does not present a major methodological problem.[14] Typically, one may possess several years of data on a number of firms and the problem in trying to estimate a relationship, using these data, is to specify a model that will adequately allow for differences in behaviour between firms, as well as any differences in behaviour over time for a given firm. Of course, once a model has been specified there are the additional problems of the most efficient estimation procedure and how to test hypotheses about the parameters.

3.2.4 Improving Model Specification to Reflect Dynamics

The conceptual framework for the model must also reflect the fact that in any economic process, of which the financial dealings of a firm are a part, all variables are interdependent.

Hence, critically, a modelling procedure is proposed where a family of models is explored – from the most general simultaneous set with non-linear form through the least general recursive system to single equation models of the simplest form as described in 3.1. Only the last of these has, to date, been used exclusively in bankruptcy studies. As opposed to this, a model with simultaneity and timed variables may comprise a time series to predict a vector of values for several financial variables at time t from previous values, at time t-1, of the same variables and any important exogenous variables such as macroeconomic indicators. The results from various equations can feed the full set of explanatory variables into a logit model where the dependent variable is the outcome (survival=0, bankrupt=1) at time t. Each firm will provide a number of rows to the data matrix depending on the number of years, previous to bankruptcy, that its financial data are available. This will be an intrinsically non-linear, simultaneous equation system that is, in principle, testable.

---

[14] A standard references for pooled time-series, cross-section analysis is Judge *et al* (1985) 2nd ed. (Chapter 13).

Out of the analysis will come a model that is not static, and that will incorporate the 'ripple' effect due to failures feeding back into the economic system since each firm affects the health of other firms with which it does business. In this sense the model is dynamic rather than simply having a temporal element. More importantly, the temporal feedbacks within the firm can be dynamically modelled, as suggested below.

3.2.5 Improving Model Completeness

Closely related to an improved ability of the model to mirror the effects of the external environment on the firm is the quest for the optimal set of explanatory variables so that the model is also capable of reflecting the internal environment of the firm. This implies that the model is intrinsically dynamic in that the state of the firm at any point is dependent upon its previous states, as well as upon the levels of exogenous variables. In the literature, the ad hoc specification of the models continues to be a problem, and the predictive value of variables not yet studied needs to be evaluated. Without any theoretical guidance concerning the choice of variables there is often brute empiricism so the resultant model tends to be sample-data specific, and precludes ready generalization from the empirical findings.

In particular, as Zavgren (1983) points out, account needs to be taken of company soundness criteria, which will vary over the business cycle. In boom periods when failures are relatively rare, the empirical link between certain otherwise important indicators and the actual occurrence of failure will be weak. Hence, exogenous variables might include both firm specific variables, such as a measure of past performance of company directors, and macroeconomic variables such as a measure of prevailing economic adversity. Performance variables are difficult to obtain but inclusion of the recent-past and present macroeconomic indicators would be a desirable inclusion as a measure of economic adversity that would improve the explanatory power of the model.

3.3 A New Methodology

Future progress in the field depends upon incorporating measures of economic adversity and appropriate time effects. Only by such developments, coupled with an extension of the database both cross-sectionally and over time, will yield both more statistically reliable and readily interpretable models.

In summary, the proposed time series model will incorporate a subset of financial data (or transformations of raw data) accommodating the available data into appropriate models and taken over a given time period spanning both boom and slump periods of economic activity. This provides the temporal element allowing improved model specification for time. The time series model will fit into a family of appropriate model formulations including dynamic model specifications that are cross-sectional over the failed firms identified in the research design, thereby addressing the problem of sample bias and including variables that improve model completeness.

Methodologically, part of the new approach can be likened to a survival analysis in the health field. The analogy between a person's state of health and the firm's is a good one, insofar as the health of both entities today may deteriorate or even fail at short notice, and yet death or failure is but the final outcome of a chronic process where vital functions are progressively breaking down. While we are always alive before we are dead, the process of dying is gradual (traumatic events aside), and passes through *degrees* of failure whose symptoms are not always evident. Nor is the process necessarily irreversible if correct intervention (either internal or external) is timely before the final outcome. Beyond a certain point, however, the internal dynamics tell us resuscitation and recovery are impossible.

In survival studies it is usual to dichotomise the outcome at a particular point in time (because that is all we know) and, in the case of a conditional probability model, to formulate a model that will estimate the probability of survival to the next period conditional on the symptoms present. A similar situation occurs with bankruptcy studies using a model that is to discriminate between firms that have failed and firms that have not. It is usual, for the purpose of evaluating the success of the model, to predict the dichotomous outcome using a discriminant rule based on some cut-off value for the discriminant analysis score (usually zero) or the logit probability (usually 0.5). A count is taken for the number of correct and incorrect classifications for both the analysis sample and the holdout sample of firms and used to calculate the Type I and Type II error probabilities for the particular model. Also a firm is classified 'failed' or 'non-failed' regardless of *when* the data were collected; usually in the year prior to bankruptcy for the failed firm of a matched pair (one failed, one healthy), though some studies have estimated models using data to predict an outcome up to five years in the future (see Beaver, 1966; Altman, 1968; Deakin, 1972; Zavgren, 1983). Unfortunately, this black-and-white method lends itself easily to a naive model-validation purpose.

Naive, because a time lag is often acting until certain conditions affect the status of a firm, and a good model should give a high probability of failure to a presently surviving firm if the multivariate totality of its symptoms and environment indicate a deteriorating financial position. Yet the common method of evaluating a bankruptcy model in terms of a dichotomous classification of firm status would yield a misclassification for such a tenuously surviving firm. This would be regarded as a failure of the model to correctly classify, when the model is, in fact, performing sensibly. It is the timing that is crucial in deciding on whether a prediction is accurate, and hence, the common method of evaluating a model is inappropriate. Ohlson (1980) remarks on the modelling process that 'the dichotomy, bankruptcy versus no bankruptcy is, at most, a very crude approximation of the payoff space of some hypothetical decision problem' (p. 111).

Rather, it is preferable to view the number output from the bankruptcy model as an index of risk of failure or a direct estimate of it, depending on whether it is a discriminant analysis score or a logit probability. This can be meaningful for *both* types of firm, distressed and non-distressed. It can be viewed as an estimate of the degree of failure that the firm is experiencing at the time the data were collected or how close the firm is to bankruptcy (or some other instrument for the measurement of failure).

The contention of Wood and Piesse (1987) is that ex post discrimination between risky companies that have failed and non-risky companies that have not 'is neither surprising, nor evidence that any additional information is generated by (multivariate statistical) techniques' (p. 29). A model that distinguishes distressed firms filing bankruptcy from others, also at risk, but avoiding it would provide more information value. Gilbert *et al* (1990) contend that 'the factors that contribute to a financially distressed condition need not be the same ones that motivate bankruptcy filing' (p.162) given there are other strategies which are available to companies in financial distress, such as merger, restructuring of debt or voluntary liquidation (p.170).

The immediate real question of interest is how firms transform from surviving or even successful ones into failed ones. An equally valid and important question is how currently failing firms can be put back on the road to health. Although they are asymmetric, the answer to these two questions lies in comparing within firms at different time periods rather than between them in the analysis. As discussed in Ogg (1988), financial distress models need to use the statistical techniques drawn from survival analysis, knowing that the potential to fail always exists *ex ante* – for both non-failed firms as well in the period leading up to the *ex post* failures. Studies of financial distress incorporating such techniques include those of Eddey, Partington, and Stevenson (1989), who predict the timing and probability of take-over bid success, Kassab, McLeay, and Shani (1991), and Partington, Peat, and Stevenson (1991). The model presented here is one where the estimation sample used consists of *only failed firms,* treating the earlier data before failure as non-failures. In medical applications, where the probability of survival for x years after diagnosis is estimated conditional on the patient's lifestyle and the presence of other suspected causal factors, the records of only those patients who either have the particular disease of interest or have already died of it are analyzed with respect to the set of suspected causal factors or factors that accelerate the disease process. The model can then give some insight into the nature and influence of the causal factors on the progress of the disease.

Survival studies in epidemiology differ in their goal to case-control studies. Case-control studies match cases (diseased) with controls (non-diseased) controlling for as many other possible causal factors bar the one of interest to the study and then cross-tabulate disease status with the presence or not of a particular causal factor. It is therefore a univariate analysis that has as its goal the calculation of an odds-ratio for the disease with respect to the particular causal factor. The collection of the sample is analogous to the way most bankruptcy studies proceed, by using both surviving and bankrupt firms in the estimation sample. Finally, it is important to note that an analogy of processes is not being utilized in this treatise, but an adaptation of a methodology. One significant reason why the analogy breaks down, as discussed by White (1989) and others, is that bankruptcy can be a chosen avenue of action rather than imposed.

3.4 Constructing and Testing General Multi-Equation Models

A new bankruptcy modelling methodology is proposed here: generalizing the cross-sectional schema to a time series, which also incorporates cross-sectional data. Such a combined model is common in econometric investigations e.g. Forster and Ryan (1989). As indicated, the analysis incorporates logit estimation of probability from the solution of a multiple simultaneous equations framework that includes macroeconomic indicators as well as the financial variables of individual firms over several time periods for each firm. In other words the models will be dynamic (in disequilibrium since the firms will be in the process of failing until, of course, they have failed). Such non-linear simultaneous equation models are increasingly familiar and have even reached undergraduate texts such as Kelejian and Oates (1989) and Judge *et al* (1985). In explaining how these multi-equation systems can be applied to the area of financial distress modelling, it is first necessary to introduce their general form. Much of the following section is based upon Judge *et al* (1985), Kelejian and Oates (1989) and the SAS/ETS User's Guide Ver.6 2nd edition (1993).

Here we begin with the simplest general linear model. If, in model equation (3.1), F were the linear function, it could be represented by the general linear model:

$$\mathbf{y} = \mathrm{X}\,\beta + \mathbf{e} \tag{3.5}$$

for empirical purposes, where $\mathbf{y}$ is a (Tx1) vector of observations on the dependent variable, X a (TxK) nonstochastic design matrix, β a (Kx1) vector of unknown parameters, and $\mathbf{e}$ a (Tx1) unobservable random vector with $E(\mathbf{e}) = \mathbf{0}$ and $E(\mathbf{e}\,\mathbf{e}^T) = \sigma^2\,\Psi$, where Ψ is the disturbance covariance matrix. Autocorrelation exists if the disturbance terms corresponding to different observations are correlated; i.e. if Ψ is not diagonal.[15]

Equation (3.4) represents one firm in such a model after applying the logit transform. This model can be extended to the case where we have M such firms and hence, M such models, by considering a set of regression equations, where each member of the set is an equation of the form $\mathbf{y} = \mathrm{X}\,\beta + \mathbf{e}$, and where, because of the communalities between firms, there may be correlation between the

15 The off-diagonal elements are zero in a diagonal matrix.

disturbances in different equations. Such a specification is likely to be reasonable when estimating a number of related economic functions such as demand equations for a number of commodities or investment or risk functions for a number of firms. The disturbances for different functions, at a given point in time, are likely to reflect some common immeasurable or omitted factors, and so one would expect them to exhibit some correlation – known as contemporaneous correlation. If the observations on any one of the equations are observations over time, this leads to disturbances that are both contemporaneously and serially correlated.

Equation (3.5) can be extended to the case where we have M such models:

$$\mathbf{y}_i = X_i \beta_i + \mathbf{e}_i, \qquad i = 1, 2, \ldots, M \qquad (3.6)$$

where $\mathbf{y}_i$ and $\mathbf{e}_i$ are vectors of dimension (Tx1), X_i is a matrix of dimension (TxK_I) and β_I is (K_ix1).

All these equations can be combined and written conveniently as:

$$\mathbf{y} = X \beta + \mathbf{e}, \qquad (3.7)$$

where the new dimensions are, respectively, (Mtx1), (MTxK),(Kx1), and (Mtx1) with $K=\Sigma K_I$.

The matrix X now is a partitioned diagonal matrix with zeros on the off-diagonal partitions. It is usually assumed that $E(\mathbf{e}_i) = \mathbf{0}$ and $E(\mathbf{e}\ \mathbf{e}^T) = \sigma_{ij}\mathbf{I}_T$ and hence that the covariance matrix of the joint disturbance vector is given by

$$E(\mathbf{e}\ \mathbf{e}^T) = \Omega = \Sigma \otimes \mathbf{I} \qquad (3.8)$$

where Σ is the symmetric matrix containing the variance-covariances σ_{ij}.

In many applications $\mathbf{y}_i$ and X_i will contain observations on variables for T different time periods and the subscript i will correspond to a particular economic unit such as the firm. Hence the joint model equation (3.7) can be regarded as one way in which time series and cross-sectional data can be combined. If each observation in $\mathbf{y}_i$ and X_i represents a different point in time, the covariance assumption in equation (3.8) implies that the disturbances in different equations are correlated at a given point in time but are not correlated over time.[16]

When equation (3.7) is such a system of equations consisting of time series observations on a number of cross-sectional units, each cross-sectional unit being described by one equation from the system, and if the regression equations are not simultaneous so there are no dependent regressors, the term 'seemingly unrelated regressions' (SUR) is used since the system of equations still has correlated errors. When the system of equations (3.7) is viewed as a single equation for estimation via generalized least squares there can be gains in efficiency obtained.

---

16 Taken from Judge *et al* (1985), pp:465-468.

When simultaneity is present in sets of equations (i.e. when a dependent variable in one equation becomes a regressor in another) it is useful to define the terms. Judge *et al* (1985) classify the following types of variables in systems of equations:

> Endogenous or jointly determined variables have outcome values determined through joint interaction with other variables within the system. Exogenous, variables affect the outcome of the endogenous variables, but their values are determined outside the system. The exogenous variables are assumed to condition on the outcome values of the endogenous variables but are not reciprocally affected because no feedback relation is assumed. Lagged endogenous variables may be placed in the same category as the exogenous variables since for the current period the observed values are predetermined. The exogenous variables and any variables that may involve any length of lag are called predetermined variables. For statistical purposes the relevant distinction is between jointly dependent variables and predetermined variables (Judge *et al*, 1985, p. 564/5).

3.4.1 Techniques for Estimating the Parameters in a Linear Simultaneous System of Equations

While it has considerable theoretical advantages over the current modelling in bankruptcy studies, there is little advantage in building simultaneous equation models if they cannot be properly estimated (including tests of significance) in that form. Econometricians have developed a number of different techniques to deal with the estimation problems relating to systems of simultaneous equations.[17] The two fundamental methods of estimation are least squares and maximum likelihood. Within each category the two approaches are single equation methods and system estimation.

In the first category, two-stage least squares (2SLS) is a single-equation method that is often used because it is intuitively appealing and relatively easy to understand. In addition, one may estimate a given equation within a simultaneous framework by the 2SLS technique with only limited information about the other equations.

Two-way causation results in a non-zero covariance between the disturbance term and one (or more) of the independent variables in the model (represented in condition (3.8) above). In order to use the standard ordinary least squares (OLS) estimation procedure it is first necessary to get rid of the nonzero covariance so that the equation will satisfy the assumptions of the regression model. 2SLS is a two-step estimation procedure that eliminates, from the independent variable, that part which is correlated with the disturbance term in the first step. This involves generating a revised set of values for the suspect independent variables using instrumental variable methods. These 'revised' values are no longer correlated

---

[17] Advanced treatments can be found in Pindyck and Rubinfeld (1981), Kelejian and Oates (1989), Judge *et al* (1985), Johnston (1972), and Goldberger (1964).

with the disturbance term so that the second step is simply to estimate the parameters with the standard OLS technique.[18]

Thus, instrumental variable methods involve substituting a predicted variable for the endogenous variable Y when it appears as a regressor.[19] The predicted variables are linear functions of the instrumental variables and the endogenous variable. The 2SLS method substitutes $\hat{Y}$ for Y and the instrumental variables are used as regressors to obtain the projected value of $\hat{Y}$, which is then substituted for Y when the variable appears as a regressor. Normally, the predetermined variables of the system are used as the instruments. Other variables from the equations may not be as efficient. For consistent estimates, the instruments must be uncorrelated with the residual and correlated with the endogenous variable. Alternatives to 2SLS estimate the system of equations as a whole, and hence, are termed 'systems estimation'.

Unlike 2SLS, system estimation methods use information concerning the endogenous variables in the system and take into account error covariances across equations and hence are asymptotically efficient in the absence of specification error. (2SLS estimates are not asymptotically efficient.) The system methods are three-stage least squares (3SLS) and full information maximum likelihood (FIML) estimation. Additionally, the seemingly unrelated regressions technique (SUR) uses information about contemporaneous correlation among error terms across equations in an attempt to improve the efficiency of parameter estimates.

> The 3SLS method combines the ideas of the 2SLS and SUR methods. Like 2SLS, the 3SLS method uses $\hat{Y}$ instead of Y for endogenous regressors, which results in consistent estimates. Like SUR, the 3SLS method takes the cross-equation error correlations into account to improve large sample efficiency. For 3SLS, the 2SLS residuals are used to estimate the cross-equation error covariance matrix (SAS/ETS User's Guide, 1993, p. 847).

The contemporaneous correlation matrix is estimated using OLS and the SUR parameters will always be at least as efficient as OLS in large samples, providing the equations are correctly specified.

3.5 Applying Multi-Equation Models to the Area of Financial Distress

Having established (i) the general theoretical and methodological reasons for moving towards a dynamic and simultaneous equation form of bankruptcy models and (ii) the availability of appropriate linear and non-linear simultaneous equation estimation methods, we now look more specifically at modelling financial distress.

Consider the completely specified linear model which, using information from k prior years to failure, is specified as:

---

18 Taken from Kelejian and Oates (1989) p. 264.

19 Approach originated by Haavelmo (1944) and extended by Anderson and Rubin (1949).

$$\mathbf{X}_t = A_0\mathbf{X}_t + A_1\mathbf{X}_{t-1} + A_2\mathbf{X}_{t-2} + \text{------} + A_k\mathbf{X}_{t-k} + B\,\mathbf{Z}_t + \mathbf{e}_t \qquad (3.9)$$

where $\mathbf{X}_t$ is an mx1 vector of internal variables for the firm at time t, and $\mathbf{Z}_t$ is an nx1 vector of exogenous variables including macroeconomic indicators for the period (which may also be lagged). The matrices A_i and B are made up of the structural parameters for the model and $\mathbf{e}_t$ is the error vector. The A_i's are mxm order matrices and B is mxn. Here, for simplicity, these parameters are assumed to be fixed for all firms. The model is cast in a linear or log-linear form here purely for exposition but clearly it is more general for it to be non-linear form. Note that the internal variables in model equation (3.9) may include the outcome variable Y which is a 0/1 variable or, alternatively, the probability of failure in the next year, or the logit transformation of this probability. This is especially important as it has a significant impact upon model construction and upon the appropriateness (or lack thereof) of linear estimation techniques.

The reduced form of the structural model (3.9) is then:

$$\mathbf{X}_t = (I-A_0)^{-1} A_1\mathbf{X}_{t-1} + \text{------} + (I-A_0)^{-1} B\mathbf{Z}_t + (I-A_0)^{-1}\mathbf{e}_t \qquad (3.10)$$

or

$$\mathbf{X}_t = A^*_1\mathbf{X}_{t-1} + A^*_2\mathbf{X}_{t-2} + \text{------} + B^*\mathbf{Z}_t + \epsilon_t \qquad (3.11)$$

where $A^*_i = (I-A_0)^{-1} A_i$, $B^* = (I-A_0)^{-1} B$, and $\epsilon_t = (I-A_0)^{-1}\mathbf{e}_t$. The final model is a set of simultaneous equations that are linear in the parameters.

By ignoring the exogenous variables (assuming **Z** is constant) it is possible to reduce (3.11) to a first-order system in an augmented **X**-vector and examine the dynamic properties of the model, although this method has not yet been applied to financial distress models. The stability of the model can thus be determined by investigating the nature of the eigenvalues of the coefficient matrix of the reduced model. The theoretical aspects of the stability conditions can then be discussed in terms of the failed firm's internal dynamics.

Returning to the bankruptcy probability equation and its logit form, if it proves difficult to incorporate the 1/0 dichotomous outcome directly into a limited dependent simultaneous model, as one of the elements of **X**, then the model can be recast, at least as a starting point, as a single equation such that the ratios vector $\mathbf{X}_t$ feeds recursively into a logit model of failure risk as in equations (3.1) and (3.3). So for firm i:

$$\mathbf{p} = F(\mathbf{X}_t, \mathbf{X}_{t-1}, \ldots, \mathbf{Z}_t) \qquad (3.12)$$

or just

$\mathbf{p} = F(\mathbf{X}_t, \mathbf{Z}_t)$ if lagging **X** proves too cumbersome, or infeasible (3.13) where **p** is the vector of risks p_t for the firm's risk of failure in the next year at time t, t-1, t-2 and so on, but is actually input as the event Y_t taking on values of 1 or 0, depending on whether t is respectively the year of failure outcome, or some prior year and F is the logit link function.[20] In the complete non-linear model, the probability of failure is embedded in the simultaneous form rather than recursive form i.e. it occurs on both sides of the equation. This is important because financial distress can be expected to feed on itself, a form of positive feedback. An example would be the situation where the overall financial health of the firm, as measured by the probability of failure, will have an impact upon the ability to raise capital and so on.

The completely specified model may be empirically impractical to implement, e.g. through lack of appropriate data, and may need to be made less general, but the existence of the completely specified model gives a methodological basis for the more appropriate construction of smaller, more specific models. Thus, each smaller and less complete model can be fitted into an overall family of models. This also makes any weaknesses of the smaller, practical models more transparent.

3.5.1 A Family of Models for Estimating the Risk of Failure

This section specifies a family of models, all of them related, for which implementable examples are given. These models will be used for estimating the risk of failure in forthcoming chapters and are outlined here in order of increasing complexity and consequent difficulty of estimation technique. For ease of exposition, all error terms and residual terms have been omitted.

(A) Single Equation Logit (All Explanatory Variables are Exogenous)

$$\log (P_t / \{1 - P_t\}) = a_0 + a_1 X_{1t} + a_2 X_{2t} + a_3 X_{3t} \qquad (3.14)$$

where P_t is the relative frequency measure or other measure of risk of failure. The causal relationships can be represented as follows:

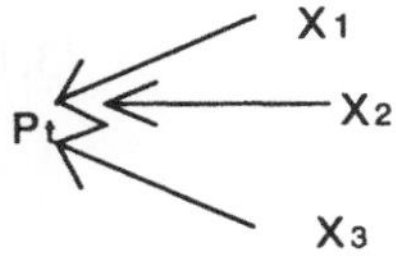

---

[20] There is a problem in estimating the parameters for this set of equations since the value of all the observed Y's when pooling the firms to estimate any one equation (for one lag time), is either '1' or '0'. It is well known that categorical variables cannot be properly used (without transformation) as dependent variables with current estimation techniques. Consequently some estimate of the 'true' probability of failure needs to be input instead. This can be achieved using a single equation logit model and pooling all the lag times as a first stage in the process.

$X_{1,2,3}$ are the exogenous variables – three are used for exposition only, any number may be included. This is the model tested in Chapter 5.4 where the exogenous variables are the first five principal component factors and their three-year lags for the US economy incorporating economic series over a twenty-one year period. The model was estimated using observations on firms from all four lag periods and matching the economic factors, X_{it}, on the appropriate year.

The same model (3.14) can be applied with the X's taking on the values of the internal financial ratios of the firm, assuming that these are all independent of each other and also independent of the risk of failure (i.e. exogenous with no causal feedback). This is the model tested in Chapter 4.6 using a stepwise logit estimation of risk regressed on 23 ratios, and again pooling observations for all four lag times. The combined model of Chapter 6.1.3 also falls into this category.

(B) Single Equation Logit (All Explanatory Variables are Exogenous or Lagged Endogenous)

$$\log (P_t / \{1 - P_t\}) = a_0 + a_1 X_{1t} + a_2 X_{2t} + a_3 X_{3t} + b_1 R_{t-1} \qquad (3.15)$$

R is an endogenous variable that could be, for example, the risk of failure or a financial ratio which is influenced by risk of failure. All the X variables are assumed exogenous. This is the model estimated in Chapter **7.1**. The causal relationships can be represented as follows:

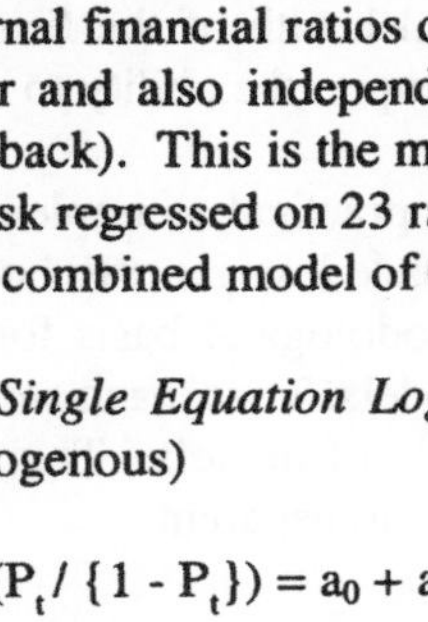

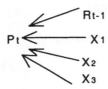

(C) Simultaneous Equations (All Explanatory Variables are Exogenous, Lagged Endogenous and Current Endogenous Variables)

$$\text{(i)} \log (P_t / \{1 - P_t\}) = a_0 + a_1 X_{1t} + a_2 X_{2t} + a_3 X_{3t} + b_1 R_{t-1} + b_0 Q_t \qquad (3.16)$$

where, in addition, the following relationships exist:

$$\text{(ii)}\ Q_t = \alpha_0 + \alpha_1 \log (P_t / \{1 - P_t\}) + \sum_{j=1}^{m} a_j X_{jt} \qquad (3.17)$$

or with a different functional relationship between Q_t and P_t.

$$\text{(iia)}\ Q_t = \alpha_0 + \alpha_1 P_t + \sum_{j=1}^{m} a_j X_{jt} \qquad (3.17a)$$

Q_t and P_t are current endogenous variables and the X_{jt} are exogenous (may be some in common with equation (i)). Q_t may be one of the internal ratios that has a two-way (feedback) relationship with failure risk as in the diagram below. This model is linear in form as a simultaneous equation system. Equations (i) and (ii) cannot be estimated independently of each other. 2SLS cannot be used directly because equation (i) has to be estimated from original binary data so a logit form is required. This is the type of modelling used in Chapter 7.2.2. The causal relationships can be represented as follows:

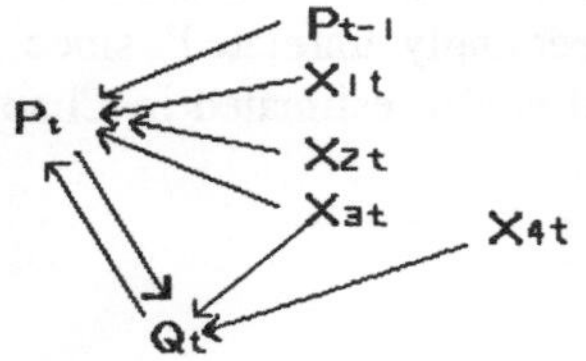

To perform the proper estimation of this simultaneous equation model firstly requires an estimation of the unrestricted reduced form equation for (i) providing a first-stage estimates of log $(P_t / \{1 - P_t\})$, or P_t as its inverse, using logit analysis, and secondly an estimation of Q_t from the structural form equation for (ii) based upon the reduced form estimates. This eliminates the non-linearity of log $(P_t / \{1 - P_t\})$ in (ii). Then estimate the unrestricted reduced form for Q_t, which can then be substituted into (i) and so on, as in 2SLS estimation.

(D) Seemingly Unrelated Regressions (SUR)

Consider the following equations, one for each lag time, one to four periods before failure:

$$\text{(i)} \log (P_t / \{1 - P_t\}) = \alpha_t + \sum_{j=1}^{m} a_{t,j} X_{j,t} \quad (3.18a)$$

$$\text{(ii)} \log (P_{t-1} / \{1 - P_{t-1}\}) = \alpha_{t-1} + \sum_{j=1}^{m} a_{t-1,j} X_{j,t-1} \quad (3.18b)$$

$$\text{(iii)} \log (P_{t-2} / \{1 - P_{t-2}\}) = \alpha_{t-2} + \sum_{j=1}^{m} a_{t-2,j} X_{j,t-2} \quad (3.18c)$$

$$\text{(iv)} \log (P_{t-3} / \{1 - P_{t-3}\}) = \alpha_{t-3} + \sum_{j=1}^{m} a_{t-3,j} X_{j,t-3} \quad (3.18d)$$

These equations are not simultaneous; each equation represents the same firms over different time periods but, as outlined in 3.5.1,[21] since they are a combination

[21] In Chapter 3.5 the equations each represented a time series for one firm. Here the focus is on estimating the parameters for different time lags in order to try to understand the time-varying nature, if any, of the parameters. The economic units, the firms, are the replicates.

of cross-sectional and time-series data for the same firms – a reasonable assumption is that the disturbances or error terms in different equations are correlated.[22] Providing the initial estimates[23] of the logit component are input into the algorithm to eliminate non-linearity, this set can be analysed together using SUR estimation (incorporating generalized least squares as for model (3.7)). This type of model is estimated for the service industry dataset in Chapter 7.2.1.[24]

The $X_{j,t}$ may also include lagged endogenous (which are deemed to be predetermined) variables and still be treated as 'seemingly unrelated' since no simultaneity is present. Such a model with P_t lagged is also estimated in Chapter 7.2.1.

3.6 Conclusion

As long ago as 1950, Marschak commented that 'economic data are generated by systems of relations that are in general stochastic, dynamic and simultaneous'. Thus far bankruptcy prediction models have avoided coming to grips with this methodological problem. This translates into the realisation that economic data, as the direct outcomes of an existing economic system, should be modelled as a system of simultaneous relations among the random economic variables, both current and lagged, internal and external to the firm. Marschak further noted that, although these properties of the data give rise to many unsolved problems in statistical inference, they constitute the basic ingredients underlying economic theory, and quantitative knowledge of them is needed for sound economic practice. It is striking that while these comments were written over half a century ago, the failure of firms has not yet been fully analyzed in any way approaching this manner.

The proposed failure-as-process methodology outlined in this chapter, with corresponding procedures for implementation, has several advantages:

- At this stage of the development of the methodology, using only failed firms and making comparisons within failed firms in a panel design rather than between going-concerns and failed firms avoids the problem of overrepresentation of failed companies that has led to bias in past models of public company failure.

---

22 Note that in the four equations, the constant terms are allowed to differ. If this were not made explicit in the model and as SUR is the equivalent of bringing the four equations into one regression, only one constant would have been estimated, or alternatively, three dummy variables relating to deviations from the fourth time period's base average value.

23 These first-stage estimates come from a 'full' single equation model, where all lag years are pooled. It would not be possible to get the estimates for failure risk from these four equations analysed separately as the Y values are constant for each; either 0 or 1.

24 Actually, the SAS/ETS statistical package provides the procedure MODEL, which is able to fit these directly when they are written in their logistic function form.

- Similarly, using only failed firms avoids confounding truly healthy surviving firms with those that are potential failures in the short term.
- In the proposed methodology, each firm is essentially matched with its previous states as information from its final failed year is used together with information from its earlier surviving years. In addition a time series formulation allows us to incorporate changes in macroeconomic conditions, and many allow us to translate vague statements such as: 'A company which may have been able to survive during a boom period may not be able to survive in a slump', into more precise and useful forms.
- Without exception, past models have used a single equation model that must necessarily be mis-specified, since the failures feed back into the firm itself causing a ripple effect.

At this stage of development, the disadvantages of the proposed modelling procedure are that it will not be possible to directly *predict* bankruptcy risk from a model whose analysis sample comprises only failed firms. However, prediction is not the purpose of this research. It may, however, provide an index that can be related to the risk of bankruptcy as a by-product of the explanatory modelling.

Also, as in other modelling schema, if bankruptcy is influenced to a great extent by other, perhaps nonfinancial and non-economic, factors that either cannot be ascertained or are not included in the set of explanatory variables, then the model will perform poorly.

A new sampling scheme, itself associated with the methodology of survival analysis, and a new modelling methodology, will no doubt have new problems still to become evident, exchanged for the old ones. The simultaneous equations framework is more complex than the single equation model and will generally necessitate the use of non-linear estimation techniques that may not readily be available (in the common statistical packages) because of the 0/1 problem. Useful exploratory work can nevertheless still be done using linear estimation techniques with suitable functional transformations. In other words, a large array of new avenues of development is opened up under the proposed methodological framework.

PART II
EMPIRICAL ISSUES: TOWARDS A DYNAMIC MODELLING OF FINANCIAL DISTRESS

As indicated in the previous chapter, a goal of this research is to formulate a generalized methodological model for failure risk – one that may shed light on the *patterns* of financial health experienced by firms over time in the context of the prevailing economic conditions. This involves a shift from the usual cross-sectional modelling framework used to directly predict bankruptcy risk, to time-series modelling where the emphasis is on the *dynamics* of failure.

It is known that the rate of corporate failures rises sharply during economic recessions (Lev, 1974, pp. 134-139). This fact helps to explain the lack of consistency both in the values of the coefficients reported and the relative importance of various financial ratios across different bankruptcy prediction studies. Besides using different sets of ratios in their models, in order to increase their sample size of bankrupt companies researchers typically pool data across different years without considering the underlying economic events in those years. Eisenbeis (1977) infers that such models are predictive only under the additional assumption that the models are stationary over time.

Mensah (1984) suggests that 'multivariate models of bankruptcy correctly identify the more common characteristics of failing companies, which make them *susceptible* to bankruptcy. The actual occurrence and its timing depend on the coupling of these characteristics with certain economic events (external to the firm) which exacerbate the situation' (p. 381). Wood and Piesse (1987) have also suggested that data instability due to changes in inflation, interest rates, and/or phases of the business cycle may be responsible for the differences in the classification rates from estimation (ex post) to forecast (ex ante) time periods in past models used to discriminate failed and non- failed firms.

The next three chapters examine the quantitative issues arising in the modelling of failed firms in the US over a twenty-year period (1971-1990) using internal firm data from financial statements on failed US firms in the Service group of Standard Industry Codes and linking that data to the corresponding macro-economic data of the external environment of the USA.

The four years prior to the last audited statements of each failed firm were examined with respect to the financial ratios deemed important in the financial accounting literature, as well as to the various economic series taken from the *Abstracts of the USA*. It is recognized that both environments act simultaneously on the firm but the two data sets, the internal data of the firms and the external macroeconomic data of the USA, were initially isolated, with separate and different data analyses performed on each set. These separate analyses are described and their outcomes discussed in Chapters 4 and 5 respectively. In Chapter 6, a combined failure risk model based on both the internal and external variables is estimated, assuming independence within firm years. In this way, when the important variables in the combined set were identified, they could then be analyzed together either in a simultaneous equation framework or as a recursive set of four equations: each estimating failure risk at successive years prior to bankruptcy as outlined in Chapter 3. This final analysis is described in Chapter 7.

In essence then, the previous chapters moved towards developing a new methodology while the following chapters move towards specific empirical modelling using that methodology.

Chapter 4

The Internal Environment: The Financial Ratios

4.0 Introduction

This chapter identifies and explains the sources, terms, definitions, time periods, and magnitudes of the internal variables used in subsequent models, as well as the firms that comprise the database with their industry classifications and any other relevant data issues. A preliminary failure model of the form given in Chapter 3, equations (3.3) and (3.4), is presented with only the internal financial variables as predictors which takes no account of the dependencies that exist between firm-years.

4.1 The Relationship Between the Financial Variables and Financial Distress

In the absence of an articulated economic theory of financial distress it is not a straightforward choice as to what variables to include in models that attempt to explain it. Even the term, 'financial distress', is a vague entity: one that often uses the operational criterion of bankruptcy, only because it is easily defined (as the dichotomous outcome of '1', where nonbankrupt is '0'). But the criterion of bankruptcy does not always reflect the implicit definition of financial distress; that of a 'long term severe cash flow problem', nor does nonbankruptcy imply the absence of such a problem.

As discussed in chapter 2.3, most research into finding new empirical models draws on the results of past studies to seek empirically validated characteristics that distinguish bankrupt from nonbankrupt firms, whereas only a few have been guided by theory. Until 1980, the major studies in the area had identified four significant variables that had been consistently successful at discriminating between the two groups of firms (within one year):

(i) the size of the company;
(ii) a measure(s) of the financial structure;
(iii) a measure(s) of performance;
(iv) a measure(s) of current liquidity. (Ohlson, 1980, p. 110)

Later, researchers were divided on whether to also include the controversial cash- flow variables in their formulations. Of late, the weight of research is in favour of cash flow variables adding significant discriminating power over the benchmark accrual-based variables as long as they are calculated in a way that considers changes in current assets and current liabilities other than cash (Gombola and Ketz, 1983).

Unfortunately, a weakness of many models employing a confusing array of variables that were chosen on an arbitrary or purely empirical basis is that the results become difficult to interpret because of the many redundancies in the accounting data. This problem can be remedied by the use of data reduction techniques such as factor analysis or stepwise regression analysis. Pinches *et al* (1973) identified the main stable and orthogonal dimensions of financial variables using factor analysis, and Zavgren (1985) used the ratios from this technique with the highest factor loadings: total income/total capital, sales/net plant, inventory/sales, debt/total capital, receivables/inventory, quick assets/current liabilities, cash/total assets and the current ratio. Zavgren replaced the current ratio by the 'acid test' ratio, since the inclusion of inventories in the current ratio reduces its meaning as a measure of liquidity.

The above findings influenced the choice of ratios used for the service industry failure model presented here but it needs to be emphasized that the correctness of any individual theory about which ratios to use is not a primary focus in this book. Hamer (1983) goes so far as to suggest, on the evidence from her attempts in assessing the relative accuracies of different variable selection techniques, that the prediction of business failure is insensitive to the selection of accounting variables and this finding is confirmed by Nash *et al* (1989). The crucial aspect in this research, then, is to provide a modelling framework that can be used to test various different theories rather than to provide a particular predictive model or a test for specific theories of bankruptcy. We therefore begin by using a single equation logit modelling framework but, in terms of an overall methodology as described in chapter 3, it is used as a stepping stone to fuller, better models.

4.1.1 Modelling Bankruptcy

Much has been written about the methodological issues surrounding the use of the logit model and the multiple discriminant analysis (MDA) model for binary state prediction and their relative performance under various conditions.[1] A regression-type technique, such as logit analysis avoids most (not all) of the distributional problems associated with using MDA, and it has the added advantage of allowing qualitative variables, *i.e.* those with categories rather than continuous data, into its

1 See Cox (1970), Halperin *et al* (1971), Martin (1977), Eisenbeis (1977), Press and Wilson (1978), Ohlson (1980), Taffler and Abassi (1984), Lo (1986), Karels and Prakash (1987), among others.

formulation;[2] a necessity when there exist measurement problems such as those described in Section 4.3.2 from Cybinski (1995). Many authors have argued for and provided evidence of the superiority of logit over MDA in their application to bankruptcy prediction studies, one of the first being Ohlson (1980).

A distinct advantage of the logit model over MDA is that the coefficient on each variable may be interpreted individually as to its importance,[3] subject to the limitations imposed by multicollinearity. When multicollinearity exists between the predictors in the model, inflated standard errors of the coefficients of the model often result, making it difficult to isolate any variables that are statistically important in distinguishing failing and nonfailing firms. Hence there are advantages in initially choosing an economical set of predictors; one that is less likely to have a great deal of codependence among them. One may then reduce the set even further by eliminating those ratios that do not add significantly to the model before embarking on the second stage of the modelling process, whether that be an iterative analysis based on the lagged risk of failure, or the estimation of a multi-equation model. In both cases, the second stage will be more manageable with a parsimonious explanatory set. Again, it is important to note that theoretical views about which particular modelling technique is more appropriate for the data-type are not the crucial aspect of this work but rather, a methodological framework that can contain them.

4.2 The Ratios

The initial set of explanatory variables, based on those ratios selected by Altman (1968), Ohlson (1980) and Zavgren (1983), and on the work of Pinches *et al* (1973) – all marked as • – were refined and tested in the model. Some cash flow variables (marked) as recommended by Aziz *et al* (1988) and other ratios that are pre-calculated on the COMPUSTAT files (marked o), were also tested. This initial set comprised:

- Log (Total Assets/CPI price level index)
- Working Capital/Total Assets

2 See Palepu (1986) for a detailed discussion of the methodological issues relevant to research settings that involve binary state prediction models, and Press and Wilson (1978) for the reasons why the logistic regression model with maximum likelihood estimators is preferred for both classification and for relating qualitative variables to other variables under nonnormality.

3 The statistical properties of the maximum-likelihood estimates, which are asymptotically unbiased and normally distributed, are discussed in detail in Bradley and Gart (1962), whereas Halperin *et al* (1971), in a careful and extensive study, prove that discriminant function estimators of the slope coefficients in the logistic regression will not be consistent.

- Cash and Marketable Securities/Total Assets
- Current ratio
- (Current Assets - Inventory)/Current Liabilities
- Retained Earnings/Total Assets
- Net Income/Total Assets
- Total Liabilities/Total Assets
- Sales/Total Assets
- Sales/Net Plant
- Sales/Inventory
- Receivables/Inventory

❑ Cash flow[4] from operations/Sales
❑ Cash flow from operations/Total Assets
❑ Cash flow from operations/Total Current Liability
o Long term debt/Shareholders' Equity (%)
o Net profit margin (%)
o Operating margin before depreciation (%)
o Pre-tax profit margin (%)
o Total Debt/Total Assets (%)

Definitions and a more detailed explanation of how these ratios are calculated can be found in Appendix B.

4.3 The Data

Data from firms that were either bankrupt or liquidated in the period 1971 to 1991[5] from the Research Companies[6] set were retrieved from Standard and Poor's COMPUSTAT 1991 database. A detailed account of how the internal financial data was retrieved from COMPUSTAT database using PC PLUS software for data screening and access, can be found in Appendix A, as well as the common screening variables. The Service Industry dataset was used for the analysis (the estimation sample) and the Trade Industry dataset for comparisons with one other

---

4 Note that the cash flow ratios were not calculated as merely 'Net income plus Depreciation' after concerns by Gombola and Ketz (1983) that they should be calculated in a way that considers changes in current assets and current liabilities other than cash. Cash Flow is defined here as Funds from Operations, Total plus Working Capital Changes – taken from the Statement of Changes/Statement of Cash Flows (see Appendix B).

5 I would expect that the 1991 failures would not have yet been recorded onto the Research File by October-November 1991 when the data were collected. The latest year recorded for a failed Service industry firm, for instance, was 1988.

6 Data for companies in the Research Companies dataset is no longer collected for the COMPUSTAT Industrial Files due to a merger, acquisition, bankruptcy, liquidation, etc. There are approximately 6100 Research companies in PC Plus.

industry, using the same failure risk model. Later research is planned utilizing some or all of the other industry groupings sampled from the COMPUSTAT files.

Problems occurring in the failed firm datasets are that of missing data, and measurement problems. These problems were investigated fully and for each ratio, a decision was made whether to replace problem values with a mean or to categorize the ratio so as to preserve some of the characteristics of each particular case when data techniques requiring continuous measurement were precluded. These data problems are not restricted to this work and consequently, this method has a greater area of applicability.

4.3.1 Missing Values

Missing values occurred in the Service Industry firms dataset for every ratio calculated at the rate of 31 to 47 cases out of 240, depending on the ratio. Since the SAS software deletes the whole case when any modelled ratio is missing, the analysis set can be drastically reduced, especially if different cases have different ratios missing. To counteract this problem, at least initially when all ratios were fitted into a stepwise model, missing values were replaced with the arithmetic mean of all non-missing cases in the data set for that ratio within the same lag year. The global mean was not used as significant differences ($p<0.05$) consistently occurred between means for each lag year.

In addition to missing values the original dataset included many ratio values that show up as an 'error' because a division by zero was attempted in the calculation of the ratio. These had to be dealt with and rather than simply make them 'missing' and replace them as described above, these values were further investigated for categorization as discussed in the next section. A more sinister error occurs when a numerator and denominator can both take on either positive or negative values as these are easily ignored, with no error flagged by the software. These measurement errors are discussed next.

4.3.2 Measurement Problems: Extreme Values and Confounded Ratios

There has been a tendency for researchers in the area of financial distress modelling to either ignore the measurement problems that exist in firm accounting data or to use some ad hoc method of dealing with them (Watson, 1990). These measurement problems consist of ratios with zero (not just close-to-zero) denominators[7] and ratios that can take on either a positive or a negative value for the numerator and the denominator. Whenever this happens, confounding occurs in two different ways: +/- with -/+ and +/+ with -/-. Firms with these data may be far from similar in their patterns of failure, so the data analysis must be designed to distinguish between members of such pairs.

---

7 Note that these so-called 'outliers' in the literature will be called 'extreme values' here since they are not strictly outliers in a statistical sense.

Simply removing firms exhibiting measurement problems from the data set is clearly not a valid solution if there are more than a few in the data set. This and other ad hoc methods drastically reduce the importance of the contribution these extreme values and confounded ratios may need to make in predicting the outcome state of interest. Ignoring them overlooks the serious effects they may have on parameter estimates and estimated variances in the resulting models. In terms of ad hoc procedures, Watson (1990) advises caution in using either Winsorizing (where extreme values for some ratios are replaced by substitute values) or trimming procedures to estimate correlation or covariance matrices, because the usual statistical properties of the estimators of location are not necessarily retained. An earlier study by Bowen, Burgstahler and Daly (1987) also demonstrated that these techniques have a significant impact on the regression results and can distort the conclusions reached concerning the presence or absence of the incremental information content in cash flow data. They used the statistical technique known as Cook's distance (Weisberg, 1985) to determine the extent of the influence that extreme observations make on regression parameters.

In this analysis, when very large absolute values and/or confounded ratios abound for a particular ratio, the probability of the binary outcome, 'fails in the next year' and 'survives the next year', is estimated by a logit model which uses a mixed explanatory set: a categorized form for such problem ratios, based on their empirical distributions from the sample of companies[8] and the continuous form of other ratios where no measurement problems occurred. This eliminates the need to substitute values or delete cases that would either bias the dataset or reduce its size.[9] Confounded values were given separate categories and the positive and negative extreme values were included in the highest and lowest percentile group respectively.

Categorization allows the inclusion of extreme values without unreasonably distorting the analysis by their accommodation.[10] Thus, on the one hand, we have a loss of information resulting from categorizing a continuous measurement while, on the other hand, using the discrete version of the data allowed information provided by the extreme cases to be retained in the estimation sample – and it is often the firms exhibiting measurement problems that offer the most information about patterns of failure. Categorization implies a weighting of all the cases in the

---

8 In the first instance, breakpoints for categorizing the empirical distribution of each ratio were taken as the 5th and 95th percentile and the first and third quartiles as used by Cybinski (1995). Depending on the significance of the dummy coefficients in subsequent models, these categories may be combined.

9 Since the SAS logistic procedure eliminates whole cases with any missing values.

10 Cybinski (1995) examined the information loss arising from categorizing predictors as a means of overcoming the quantitative pitfalls inherent in the analysis of accounting data in modelling financial distress. She used only categorized ratios in the estimation of a logit model that gave overall accuracy rates comparable to those of a discriminant analysis model using only continuous-valued ratios for a dataset of Australian small business firms.

analysis that does not allow those with extreme values to dominate the estimation technique. Essentially this is a form of averaging.

4.3.3 Ratios where Measurement Problems Existed

For the Service industry group, any ratio with Sales, Inventory or Net Plant in the denominator was problematic, as these items were often recorded as zero. This reflects a feature of Service Industry firms where there is often little 'bricks and mortar' in favour of leasing arrangements and where little or no inventory is kept. Also, income is often derived from a service and not recorded as 'Sales'. These peculiarities to a particular industry are reasons for some of the inconsistencies in the results when comparing distress models based on sample data taken from different industries.

Ratios affected by measurement problems include R10, R11, R12, R13, R19, R20, R21, and R22. Also categorized were: R18 with Interest Expense in the denominator often zero, and R5, R7,[11] R16, R17 with many outliers. (Refer to Appendix B for the ratio definitions.) Five categories were created from boundaries initially taken as the 5th and 95th percentiles and the first and third quartiles taken from their respective empirical distributions. These boundaries can be obtained by running the SAS procedure UNIVARIATE, which gives the various percentile point values.

Confounded values were given separate categories and the positive and negative extreme values were included in the highest and lowest percentile group respectively. Appendix C contains the SAS code used to categorize the variables into these five levels, or into binary variables. The categorized ratio names were denoted with prefix 'RC'.

4.3.4 Descriptive Statistics: Mean Values for the Ratios by Lag Year

Much understanding of the patterns of failure among firms can be learned from examining the averages and other descriptive statistics of the different ratios. This was the basis of the earliest methods used in understanding bankruptcy; e.g. the univariate approach of Beaver (1966). Movements in the ratio averages over the years before bankruptcy or liquidation can give an indication of the expected direction of the coefficients in subsequent multivariate models and a better 'feel' for the data.

Appendix D gives the descriptive statistics of the 23 internal ratios showing the output from the SAS procedure SUMMARY using 'Lag' (lag year) as the class variable. Also shown are the minimum and maximum values of each ratio taken from the SAS procedure UNIVARIATE.

---

[11] R7 had many outliers and was tested in the models as both continuous and categorized.

4.4 The Binary Dependent or Outcome Variable – A Definition of Failure

A diverse set of definitions are used to denote failure. Among them are: negative net worth, non-payment of creditors, bond defaults, inability to pay debts, overdrawn bank accounts, omission of preferred dividends, receivership etc. Karels and Prakash (1987) provide several definitions of Bankruptcy/Failure used by researchers in empirical studies of bankruptcy (p. 576).

> The literature has emphasized legal criteria when defining the term 'bankruptcy'. Generally the liquidation process under Chapter VII of the Federal Bankruptcy Code or the reorganization provisions of Chapter XI are used as the standard. The Bankruptcy Code of 1978 does not expressly provide a definition or financial criteria for bankruptcy. Each case is determined by the court on an individual basis. This may explain why a uniform definition has not been established. (Karels and Prakash, 1987, p. 575).

In this study, a one (1) recorded for the dependent variable in the dataset means that the data came from a final submission of financial statements before bankruptcy/liquidation. In other words, the firm's failure was imminent at the time the accounting figures were compiled. (See footnote in Appendix A explaining 'date of deletion'.) A zero (0) means that the data came from financial statements that, although they were submitted near the end of the firm's life, were not to be the final submission. At that point in time the firm-year was deemed a surviving year. This dichotomy can be but a crude representation of the true health of the firm, because the actual process of failing is sometimes a gradual one, as discussed in Chapter 3, but we only know that it failed after the COMPUSTAT-defined Current Period (CPD), with hindsight. The reliance on the occurrence or non-occurrence of an event (the submission of next year's financial statements) as a representation of failure risk in cross-sectional studies using failed and non-failed firms when it is really just a discriminant group tag, has been the reason for following the gradual failure of the firm here. So the same code, '0', is used for the outcome for all the failing firms in all of the three years previous to the final one, just as we would had we chosen to sample firms at that time in a normal cross-sectional study and we had no knowledge that they were to fail in the future. We then let a multivariate technique such as logit analysis use the pattern of the explanatory variables to discriminate between the two sets of surviving and failing firm-years and, in the process, output a new estimate of failure risk which now can fall anywhere on the 0-1 number scale. From an event-based variable, the technique provides a useful measure that can be interpreted as a propensity-to-fail estimate.

The average time in months between a Service Industry firm filing their last financial statements and filing for bankruptcy or entering liquidation proceedings can only be ascertained accurately from the Capital Changes Reporter. An estimate of this average can be calculated from limited data on the COMPUSTAT files by using the variables, Date of Deletion (DLDTE), and Current Period (CPD), plus

YR.[12] DLDTE is the month and year that the company was moved from the Active Companies set to the Research Companies set but may not be an accurate indication of when liquidation/bankruptcy took place. For instance, the average time period between Current Period and Date of Deletion is calculated at about two years for this dataset of companies in the Service industry group.[13] One would expect that actual liquidation/bankruptcy took place some time in the intervening period between CPD and DLDTE.

In the Service Industry dataset used in this research, there were three surviving years for every failing year, i.e. 60 observations with a '1' and 180 with a '0' for the dependent variable, Y_{ij}, the risk of failure in the next year. In this and the next chapter no account is taken of the dependencies between the years for the same firm, so the data set can be compared to that of a cross-sectional study using 180 non-failing firms and 60 failing ones.

Figure 4.1 shows the histogram of just the final year for the population of 60 failed service industry firms used in the analysis. Figure 4.2 shows the histogram of all 240 firm-years (60 firms for four years), which were treated as independent cases in the preliminary data analysis of this and the next chapter, although, clearly, they are dependent cases, being panel data of four continuous years of data taken from the same 60 firms.

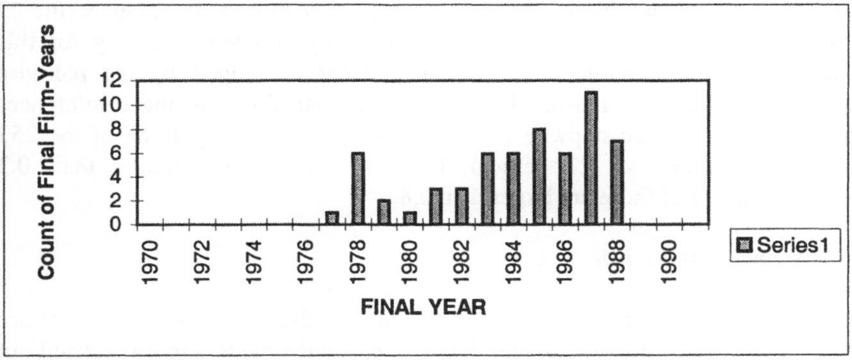

Figure 4.1 Histogram of Final Firm-Years (N=60)

12 FYR gives the month-end for each company's accounting year.

13 'A company is deleted approximately 27 months after receipt of the last annual source document' (from page 190 of the COMPUSTAT PC-PLUS manual, 1991).

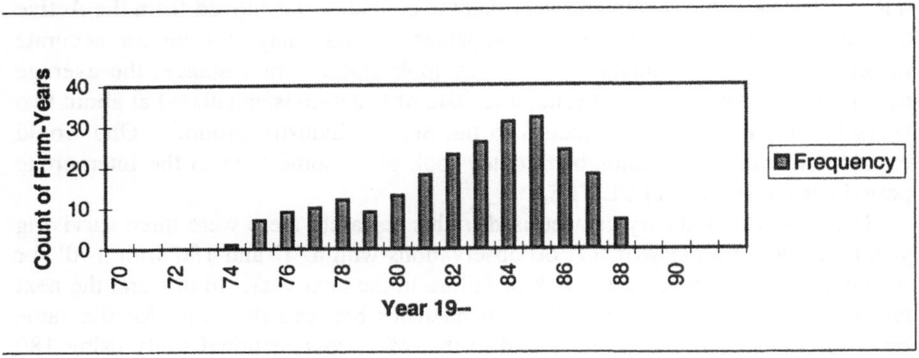

Figure 4.2 Histogram of Firm-Year Occurrences (N=240)

4.5 A Logit Analysis of Bankruptcy Risk Related to the Internal Variables of the Firm

When modelling failure risk for the service industry failing firms, a stepwise procedure was used because of the large number of independent variables (the 23 financial ratios) included in the model without any compelling theory for this group. In addition, multicollinearity was present as judged by the pairwise correlations between the ratios. This could limit our ability to make inferences from the model if a non-stepwise procedure is used. As many as 68 of the 253 pairwise correlations, or 27 percent, have absolute values greater than 0.3 ($p<0.0001$) and 11 of those are larger than 0.8.

4.5.1 Stepwise Analysis in Stages

The more variables that are included in the model, the more missing cases[14] are excluded from the estimation sample. For this reason the modelling was carried out in stages; firstly using all the ratios in their continuous measurement form and eliminating variables that show little, if any, discriminatory behaviour for failure risk (0-1). Initially the significance level to enter or leave the model was set relatively high at $p>0.25$. At the next stage, the more important variables (with $p<0.25$) were examined to see which had many extreme cases and these were categorized (see 4.3.3). This new mixed group of categorised and continuous measure ratios were then re-examined for significance to failure risk. SAS

[14] If a case has a missing or extreme value for *any* of the variables that are included in a particular modelling procedure and these values are not replaced in some way (see 4.3.2) then that case would be excluded by the SAS procedure from the estimation set, even if that variable is subsequently dropped in a stepwise procedure.

INSIGHT was used at this stage since this software automatically creates dummy variables from categorized ratios, making it an efficient procedure for eliminating variables and combining categories that show no significant difference to failure risk. The final set was then included in the more detailed stepwise logistic procedure, after creating the necessary dummy variables (see Appendix C) since it is not automatic for this SAS procedure. Regression diagnostics[15] at this point identified one firm as a major outlier on a number of criteria. Consequently, this firm was excluded from the estimation sample leaving 59 firms in the dataset for any further analysis.

4.5.2 The Significant Financial Variables to Failure Risk

With the logit model, it is possible to obtain a measure of goodness-of-fit analogous to the linear regression.[16] To compare different models for the same data, say the full model with s explanatory variables of interest, with a reduced model with t explanatory variables, we compute the residual chi-square, which has an asymptotic chi-squared distribution with (s-t) degrees of freedom. If this statistic is not significant at some pre-specified level, then the extra variables can be dropped. In this way the stepwise procedure can build the model, one variable at a time by testing for the most promising (significant) variable not yet included in the model at each step. Comparing the corresponding residual chi-square with a chi-square distribution with one degree of freedom does this. The procedure stops when no new variables reach the required significance level for entry or when an intermediate model is adequate i.e. the residual chi-square for the set of variables not yet included in the model is not significant. In other words, the model has a non-significant lack-of-fit to the data.

Within any model, the significance of each of the explanatory variables is assessed by a test that is parallel to the standard regression procedure. The ratio of the estimated regression coefficient to its standard error is computed and this statistic follows a chi-square distribution. Thus the usual hypotheses can be tested.

The logistic regression model included the following ratios in the stepwise logit model of failure consequent upon using a significance level of 0.15 for a variable to either enter or be removed from the model at each stage. The overall significance of the final model was $p<0.0001$ for the '- 2 Log Likelihood' statistic, which has a Chi-square distribution under the null hypothesis that all the explanatory variables in the model are zero. (The model Chi-Square value was 81.5 with 7 degrees of

---

15 Regression diagnostics developed by Pregibon (1981), including index plots of the Pearson residuals and deviance residuals, indicate that the firm, Advanced Drilling Systems Inc., is poorly accounted for by the model. The index plot of the the diagonal elements of the hat matrix suggests that all four years of this case are extreme points in the sample space.

16 See Amemiya (1981).

freedom.[17]) Details of these statistics can be found in the extract of the SAS output in Appendix E.

Bracketed values are the significance level of each ratio, when the others are already fitted, i.e. Pr > Observed Chi-Square, in the final model.

R2:	Working Capital/Total Assets, (p<0.0001)
RC21_1:[18]	Sales/Net Plant, 1st (lowest value) category, (p<0.0001)
R7:	Total Liabilities/Total Assets, (p=0.002)
RCD18:[19]	Interest Coverage After Tax, 2nd (highest value) category (p<0.02)
RCD13:[20]	Cash Flow From Operations/Sales, 1st (lowest value) category (p<0.04)
RC21_4:	Sales/Net Plant 4th (highest value) category, (p<0.05)
R6:	Return on Assets (p= 0.12)

The following ratios were not included in the final model but had shown more significance individually with failure risk than when the others were already fitted:

R15:	Cash Flow From Operations/Total Current Liabilities, (p=0.25) with a negative coefficient,
R14:	Cash Flow From Operations/Total Assets, (p=0.30) with a positive coefficient,
R5:	Retained Earnings/Total Assets (p=0.48),[21] also with a positive coefficient.

When comparing models, one needs a criterion for determining how well they perform. It is usual to set a single criterion to determine a ranking of 'goodness' by comparing the number of correct and incorrect classifications that result when the

---

17 The model Chi-Squared is computed as twice the difference between the log-likelihood of the model and the log-likelihood based only on the intercept alone. It is one of the criteria for assessing model fit and can also be used to compare different models for the same data.

18 R21 categorized as four dummy variables for five categories (see Appendix C): RC21_1=1 if R21 < 5th percentile, the mid-range or base level combines with the intercept term, and RC21_4 =1 if R21 > 95th percentile or Net Plant is zero.

19 Since INTEREST was often zero, R18 was categorised as a dummy binary variable with value: Category 1: 0 (baseline category) if R18<0: Category 2: 1 if R18 >=0.

20 R13 was first categorized into five categories (four dummy variables), RC13, as SALES was often zero, and then a binary variable RCD13 with value: Category 1: 1 if R13= -ve Cash Flow divided by zero Sales or R13<1st quartile (-0.26). Category 2: 0 (baseline category included in the intercept term) if R13 >1st quartile or R13 = +ve Cash Flow divided by zero Sales. (See Appendix C.)

21 R5, a profitability ratio, adds little to the model when another profitability ratio, R6–Return on Assets, is already fitted and vice versa. This has as much to do with the high negative correlation between R5 and both the variables R2 and R7, which are always fitted first as it has with the significant correlation between R5 and R6, and that R6 is not correlated with R7.

model is applied to either (a) the analysis sample from which the model was estimated, or even better, if available (b) a holdout sample not used in estimating the model. From the value of W in equation (3.4), the inverse logit of W can be calculated as the logistic function: $P = (1 + \exp\{-W\})^{-1}$, where P is the estimated risk of failure in the next year. In this way a value of failure risk can be estimated from the model for each firm-year and compared with the '1' or '0' that was input, i.e. whether it was, respectively, a failing or surviving year. (See 4.5.3 for more on classification).

The following model, a specific case of equation (3.4), has overall classification accuracy of 70.6 percent for the estimation sample,[22] with ratios presented in decreasing order of significance to failure risk. (See Appendix E for the full classification table and section 4.5.3 for a note on classification). The Somers' D index of rank correlation was 0.52.[23] The model is accurate at classifying surviving firm-years 72.9 percent of the time, i.e. a Type II error rate of 27.1 percent, but the accuracy rate for classifying failing firm-years was only 63.8 percent, i.e. a Type I error rate of 36.2 percent. This situation is expected to improve with the inclusion of variables that represent the macro economy into the model formulation.

$$W = \text{logit } P = 1.0507 - 0.0150\,R2 - 2.5360\,RC21\_1 - 0.00981\,R7 - 0.7032\,RCD18 + 0.6972\,RCD13 + 0.9033\,RC21\_4 + 0.00478\,R6 \quad (4.1)$$

The residual Chi-Square for this model has significance $p = 0.1178$ which indicates a non-significant lack-of-fit, so the model is adequate.[24]

A weighting of 3:1 for failed: surviving firm-years was used in the analysis in order to equalize the influence of failed and surviving years in the model estimations and consequently reduce the Type I error. A sensitivity analysis comparing a number of models based on an equal weighting of all the firm-years against a 3:1 weighting was conducted to check if this were indeed the case. The model based on a 3:1 weighting always gave better accuracy rates overall and lower Type I errors at the expense of the Type II errors (misclassifying surviving firm-years). This is as expected since the comparative weighting on surviving firm data is reduced in the equally-weighted models.

---

22 No holdout sample was used as prediction is not the focus of this work.

23 Somers' D is in some ways superior to a classification table for assessing the correlation between the predicted risks and the actual value of the dependent variable. This statistic is computed by considering all pairs of observations as having different values for the dependent variable and comparing the predicted probabilities of the observations in the pair. The index is the difference between the fraction of concordant and the fraction of discordant pairs.

24 Care is needed, particularly with binary data, in expressing the goodness-of-fit of a single model on the basis of absolute deviance. See Aitkin (1974) and Feinberg (1977) for a discussion of adequate models, minimum adequate models, and the principle of parsimony.

Note that this method falls prey to the general criticism by Zmijewski (1984) of sample weightings that do not reflect the nationwide probability of bankruptcy, which is estimated at less than 1 percent. He found that most studies consequently report misleading high classification accuracy rates for the bankrupt firms (by so reducing the Type I error). In defence of the above weighting I will reiterate that this work is not aiming for a prediction instrument to be used in the population of firms at large, unbiased or otherwise. Rather, an instrument is sought that can make the very fine distinction between a failed firm's ultimate year before failure and its prior years, and highlight the patterns of significance that occur among the predictors at this crucial time. It may be necessary initially, to err on the side of inflated accuracy rates for this exploratory work. The fine-tuning of such a model can be attempted later.

4.5.3 A Note on Classification

It is well known that a model will generally fit the data from which it was derived better than any other data. For rigorous validation of model performance one must either use a holdout sample, or if this is not feasible, some form of bootstrapping.[25] Here, for the purposes of comparison only, a classification table, applied only to the original dataset, was calculated for each model. A 0.5 cut-off risk was used for classifying a firm-year as either a surviving (not a final) year ($p<0.5$) or failing, i.e. a final year ($p>0.5$).

This is a crude method that recognizes the trade-off between the Type I and Type II errors. At one extreme, if the cut-off risk were set at 1, then all firm-years would be classified as surviving; the overall accuracy rate would be 75 percent, since three out of the four lag years are surviving years, and the probability of a Type II error (misclassifying a surviving firm) would be zero. At the other extreme, if the cut-off risk were set at 0, all firms would be classified as failing; the overall accuracy would be just 25 percent, but the probability of a Type I error (misclassifying a failing year)[26] would be zero. This means that a higher cut-off value improves the Type II error and a lower one improves the Type I error. Since both errors have to be considered, a value of 0.5 is a logical compromise[27] although it is easy to increase overall accuracy by merely improving the Type II error (since there are three times the number of surviving firm-years than failing firm-years in the sample). Alternatively, one could follow a cost minimising rule if the expected

---

25 Using either the method of Lachenbruch (1975) or those of Efron (1979,1982, 1983). See also Marais *et al* (1984) in chapter 2.5.2.

26 Many authors hold that a Type I error (misclassifying a bankrupt firm or a failing year in this case) is more costly to all concerned. See White, Sondhi, and Fried (1994), and Altman, Haldeman, and Narayan (1977).

27 The 0.5 cut-off point translates into using the group mean centroid in the discriminant space. See Palepu (1986) for a Bayesian derivation of optimal cut-off probability.

costs associated with each error were known, but the total classificatory efficiency would be expected to decrease.[28]

It deserves reiteration that this method is a very crude classification with a cut-off point of 0.5 for failing/surviving firm-years. This is especially so since it does not have the same meaning for the time series panel data of failed firms analyzed here as when it is used in studies involving cross-sectional samples of failed and surviving firms, though it suffers the same drawbacks under both study designs. In the former studies the classification is either 'failed firm' or 'surviving firm' whereas the classification here is either 'final year' or 'prior year' before inevitable failure. In the latter situation, one would expect, for instance, that even given a 'good' model of failure risk, it would be quite common for a failing firm to have an actual risk of failure in the penultimate year (lag 1) that is greater than 0.5 and yet it still survived that year. If the model correctly estimates the failure risk at greater than 0.5, then an incorrect classification of 'final year' would be recorded for this firm under the criterion used above. Of course, the same situation can arise in a cross-sectional study for a surviving firm that has all the indicators of a failing firm and somehow beats the odds against its survival.

For this reason, the classification data are presented only for comparisons with the models in Chapters 5, 6, and 7.

4.5.4 The Signs of the Coefficients

Since the logit (or log-odds) function of failure risk is monotonic increasing with risk, a positive coefficient in the logit model implies that the risk estimate increases with the ratio and vice-versa if the coefficient is negative. In the model represented by equation (4.1), the ratio that entered first and remained statistically the most significant ratio to failure risk was the liquidity ratio, R2 – Working Capital/Total Assets, which moves in the expected direction, opposite to failure risk. In other words, as this ratio increases and a greater proportion of the firm's assets are liquid, the expected failure risk decreases. This result is consistent with Altman's (1968) and most other studies[29] that rated this ratio as the best indicator of ultimate discontinuance. This ratio measures liquid assets in relation to the firm's size. Altman also mentions that the most widely used current and acid ratios were not as good predictors as this measure.

R18 – Interest Coverage After Tax or 'Times Interest Charges Earned' is a safety ratio telling us the amount of shrinkage allowable in net income before the firm has difficulty paying its interest debt. If the firm cannot pay this debt it is mandatory that it restructure debt, borrow money from elsewhere or sell off assets. Measured as a dummy variable, it has its highest values when RCD18=1 and failure probability is then decreased (negative coefficient) as expected. Similarly when

---

28 See Eisenbeis and Avery (1972, and Palepu (1986).

29 Ohlson's (1980) models all include 'Size' as a significant predictor but this may be due to a COMPUSTAT bias as only his nonbankrupt firms were taken from COMPUSTAT in that study (see Ohlson, 1980, p.122 and Lo, 1986, p.161).

R13, Cash Flow from Operations/Sales has its lowest values then the dummy variable RCD13=1 and failure probability increases (positive coefficient) as expected.

Sales/Net Plant is an interesting ratio since it moves in the same direction as the probability of failure. This means when Sales are a small proportion of Net Plant, the firm is more protected from failure than when Sales are multiples of Net Plant or Net Plant is zero. This could be because service firms often do not own their fixed assets but rather lease them, making the denominator of this ratio small and their financial viability also in doubt.

The coefficients whose signs are the opposite to that expected are R7, Total Liabilities/Total Assets (-ve) and R6, Return on Assets (+ve), though these coefficients are almost zero.[30, 31] In the case of R7, which ranges, in the Service Industry group, from a value of 6 to 1712, with an average of 92 and a median value of 69, one would expect that if the total liability of the firm were a greater multiple of total assets, the risk of failure would be greater.[32] Indeed, the correlation between R7 and R2 is negative, and R2 moves in the opposite direction to failure risk, so this fact would corroborate that R7 should move in the same direction as failure risk. But in the model it doesn't.

These anomalies can be partly explained by the statistically significant correlations between R2 and both R6 and R7, whereas there are no high correlations between any other paired internal variables (in their continuous measurement form) from the model.[33]

---

30 Zavgren and Friedman (1988) found that Return on Invested Capital was not very significant although the signs on this ratio in their logit models were also positive at three and four years prior to failure (p=0.2 and 0.1 respectively). They note that Ohlson (1980) found that many of his failing firms had profits at least as high as his healthy firms; many even showed a profit during their year of failure (p.130). These findings led them to conclude that the profitability of failing and healthy firms really do not differ.

31 Note that another profitability ratio, R5, Retained Earnings/Total Assets, vied for inclusion in the minimum adequate model with R6. (See the heading 'Analysis of Variables not in the Model' in Appendix E.). Had R5 been included in the model, it would also have a positive coefficient, opposite to expectations. Gilbert *et al* (1990, p.171) also found that retained earnings/total assets had a positive coefficient. They offer a plausible explanation that smaller retained earnings/total assets ratios (i.e. larger negatives) are associated with a greater accumulation of tax loss carry-forward benefits, which may be an incentive for merger or other non-bankruptcy strategies.

32 This ratio indicates the level of borrowings in relation to the total funds used by the organization: the higher the level of borrowings, the greater the insolvency risk. Firms that rely more on debt finance are more susceptible to financial difficulties in times of a downturn in profits (Lincoln, 1984).

33 Although R13 does have a statistically significant correlation with both R2 and R7, but only of magnitude 0.2.

Paired Correlations	**Pearson's r**	**Significance under $H_0: \rho = 0$**
R2 - R7	- 0.968	0.0001
R2 - R6	+ 0.45	0.0001

These correlations between the so-called 'independent' variables in the regression model are the main reason for using a stepwise regression analysis. This method eliminates variables already accounted for by virtue of their correlations with other variables already fitted. But anomalies still arise when there is still some valuable explanation to be gained from the inclusion of variables such as R7 and R6, although some of it has already been explained by R2 (see explanation with diagrams below). For this reason, some authors such as Pinches *et al* (1975) firstly apply a factor analysis to create new orthogonal variables for input into the regression analysis. This works well if the created variables are easily interpreted.[34] In our model the ratios are standard ones used in bankruptcy studies and also have well-established meanings. There are, therefore, strong reasons for using the standard ratios despite the statistical weakening of the model that is implied.

Following is an explanation of the anomalies encountered with the signs on the coefficients of certain ratios in terms of their interdependencies. Suppose we have the model for failure risk, P:

$$W_i = \text{logit}\, P_i = \alpha_0 + \Sigma\, \alpha_k R_{ik} + \Sigma\, \beta_m Q_{im} + e_i \qquad (4.2)$$

for each firm-year i = 1 to n, where α_0 is the intercept term, e is the error term, α_k and β_m are, respectively, the coefficients of the ratios R_k, k=1 to K, and the ratios Q_m, m =1 to M. The K ratios, R, have the correct coefficient signs in the estimated model and the M ratios, Q, have incorrect signs.

A simplified diagram illustrating the relationships between P, R, and Q, as represented by the above model equation (4.2), is:

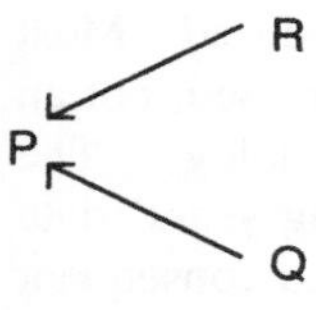

But the relationships, in fact, follow the scheme of dependencies as shown below:

[34] In Chapter 5 this method is used before regressing failure risk on the external macro-economic variables. The first five principal components, together accounting for 92 percent of the variation that existed in the economy, were, fortunately, relatively easy to interpret.

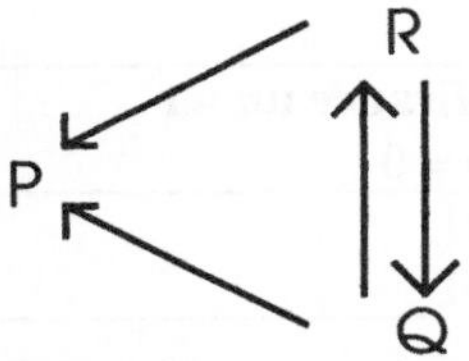

This simultaneity between R and Q causes high collinearity between R and Q and can be one reason behind the incorrect coefficient signs. Not surprisingly, these relationship diagrams become even more complex when the time factor (dependencies within firms) and the exogenous variables are also recognized in the model structure.

Note that the question of model specification begins to emerge at this point. Many of the internal variables could more legitimately be treated as endogenous. Consequently, with a temporally defined model we might well expect to see a feedback from probability of failure to some (not necessarily all) of the internal financial ratios. Model formulation (4.1) is therefore incompletely specified and is used as only one stage in empirical model development.

4.6 Conclusion

Estimation in this chapter has been via a standard logit model as found in the literature (see Chapter 2.2), but using only failed or failing firms. It has at least three failings as I have shown:

- It ignores simultaneity,
- It ignores dynamic effects, and
- It ignores macroeconomic conditions.

Nevertheless it remains a potentially useful exploratory tool, as in its use here.

Many of the data problems outlined in this chapter are left unaltered in either existence or severity by the new methodology, although some are reduced. Most importantly, on the basis of the evidence presented here, few are increased, but an understanding of these data problems is required for the new methodology. The methodology as used in this chapter compares each firm's surviving years' data with its failing year's data without any regard to the dependencies and consequent correlations that exist between firm-years within firms. In other words, we are comparing 'sick' cases with 'dying' cases and one would expect the discrimination cues for this distinction to be blurred. Because this design represents a far more difficult predictive environment than previous studies using cross-sectionally designed analyses of failing and nonfailing (often financially very strong) firms, it would be expected to give inferior results for a classification tool that aims to separate the two groups.[35] But this is not the case. Despite its acknowledged

35 Refer here to the comments made regarding the distress continuum in Chapter 1.1.

technical limitations the preliminary model gives surprisingly good results with regard to classification accuracy, logic, and consistency with the expectations from former literature. This is an early indication of potential robustness if a successful and more general model can be formulated and tested.

The present model yields some interesting insights into the effects of the explanatory variables on the failure process in terms of what can be deduced from the signs and significance of their coefficients in the model.

Nevertheless, a word of caution is advisable: generalizations stemming from and comparisons with the existing literature are hazardous because each study contains some unique features; and those of this study and the service industry have already been mentioned in 3.2.2, 3.3, and 4.3.3 respectively. Variations in industries and firms represented, the time periods used, sizes of sampled firms, statistical methodologies and design, and the constitution of the financial variables set give conflicting results, but the two ratios consistently displaying predictive ability across several major research studies are working capital/total assets and cash flow/total liabilities.[36] Despite the very different design of this study (with no going-concern comparison firms) and the careful treatment of existing measurement errors necessitating discrete variables, these two variables also figure in the best set with working capital/total assets the most significant ratio with a p-value of 0.0001 and, to a lesser extent, cash flow/total liabilities, with a p-value of 0.25.[37] The latter variable improves its standing as a predictor of risk (p-value<0.13) in a set also containing the macro-economic factors (in Chapter 6). It also proves (in Chapter 7) to be the ratio from this set that changes the most in the final four years before failure where it shows the most significance to failure risk in the final year when the inability to cover short-term commitments with cash flow has become most crucial.

Based on empirical fit, the preliminary failure model offered in this chapter for the bankrupt service industry data is a successful model: overall, it is correct 70 percent of the time in classifying whether data is taken from a firm's final set of financial statements before bankruptcy/liquidation, or from an earlier set. This, of itself, need not be very encouraging when it is known that three out of every four years (75 percent of cases) in this special data set are surviving years, so a simple rule classifying all cases as surviving would fare better if overall classification accuracy were the only criterion![38] But the model is also accurate, approximately two thirds of the time, at classifying the group of failing cases (admittedly from the original data set). Although based on bankrupt firms only, the model could be used as an unsophisticated (both in theory and testing) predictive model for service industry firms, including going-concerns, as an indicator of the firm's propensity to fail.

---

36 See the review articles of Chen and Shimerda (1981), Zavgren (1983) and Jones (1987) for details of these studies and the significance of the ratios used.

37 Gombola *et al* (1987) caution conductors of time series analyses using cash flow information because in early years cash flow data and accrual data were highly correlated. This can therefore mask the significance of cash flow within such models.

38 As explained in 4.5.3, this classification rule would have a cut-off risk, p, equal to 1.

Chapter 5

The External Environment: The Impact of the Macroeconomy

5.0 Introduction

As discussed in 3.2.3 and 3.2.4, both internal and external influences are important to a firm's risk of failure. Previous studies, in the main, have concentrated on only firm-specific (micro) information as explanatory variables of failure risk. Macroeconomic indicators may also be helpful in understanding the complex chain of events that leads to a firm's demise, since it would seem reasonable to suspect that propensity to fail is affected by whether the economy is in recession or a time of prosperity.

5.0.1 The Failing Firm in the Macroeconomy

It has long been established that the rate of corporate failures rises sharply during economic recessions (Lev 1974, 134-139), with Rose, Andrews and Giroux (1982) suggesting the possibility of a complex relationship between overall business failure rates and business cycle indicators. This means any temporal modelling of firm failure risk calls for the inclusion of an array of macroeconomic variables, yet this remains a relatively unexplored dimension to financial distress modelling. Among the relatively few contributions analysing this in the failure literature are Mensah (1984), Levy and Bar-Niv (1987), Levy (1991), Theodossiou (1993), Hill, Perry, and Andes (1996), Kane, Richardson and Graybeal (1996), and Cybinski (1996, 2000).[1] While the bankruptcies and closures engendered by the economic downturn of the seventies and eighties led to a surge in the numbers of studies concerned with business failure, few of those studies took explicit account of business cycles in their modelling.

During the post-war economic boom in the USA that lasted into the early 1970s, failures of established public corporations were relatively unusual events, often explicable by circumstances peculiar to the organization rather than to the state of the economy (Geisst, 1997, 273-298). It can be argued that one reason for the absence of large failures was the ability of successful firms to purchase financially troubled firms before failure. During downturns this behaviour is far less likely as there are less available funds and the prospects of turning around a

---

1 See Chapter 2 sections 2.4 and 2.6

troubled company are also much lower. These sorts of issues have rarely been considered. Even in periods of prosperity, companies in declining industries can be expected to experience higher than average failure rates. While the roots of these failures are not those to be attributed to macroeconomic conditions, they are intensified by downturns. The overall point is that macroeconomic conditions have complex interactions with failure that are still largely ignored in the failure literature.

Given that susceptibility to failure is affected by the state of the macro-economy, the volatile and recession-prone environments of the United States in the seventies and eighties makes them fruitful periods for the analysis of corporate failures, while, for the opposite reason, the more stable periods of the fifties and sixties and the decade long expansion of the nineties were not utilized.

Rose *et al* (1982) examined which economic variables signalled a critical climate for companies with higher exposure to business failure. During their study period governments were attempting to control inflation, with considerable impacts upon corporate debt and interest rates. Their results suggested a complex relationship between business failure rates and business cycle indicators. Similarly, Kane *et al* (1996) suggested that empirical accounting-based models specifically conditioned on the occurrence of a recession would have greater explanatory power over non-conditioned models. Zavgren (1983) noted that in boom periods, when failures are relatively rare, the empirical link between some otherwise important indicators and the occurrence of failure would be weak. Supporting this is evidence that distressed firms frequently have financial ratios that are significantly different from those which prevail under more normal trading conditions (Houghton and Woodliff, 1987). And, not surprisingly, failure studies examining macroeconomic conditions distinguish between the asymmetric impacts of the expansion and contraction stages of the cycle upon failure rates (Lev, 1974; Mensah, 1984; Kane *et al*, 1996). Other relevant work includes Scott (1981), Ball and Foster (1982), Altman (1983), Foster (1986) and Jones (1987).

5.0.2 Some Methodological Issues

The picture that emerges may go a long way to explaining the lack of empirical consistency among studies that rely solely on firm-specific information as explanations of failure risk. Inconsistencies between studies arise in relation to widely differing estimates of otherwise similarly defined internal parameters and also to the relative contributions of various financial ratios to failure. While individual failure studies may report very good empirical results, between study inconsistencies cast enormous doubt on the their overall methodological framework.

As part of this framework, most failure studies still rely on static comparisons of failed and non-failed firms. The dominant means of attempting this is by examination of the chosen sample of firms utilizing pairwise matching of each failed firm with a non-failed firm at the same point in time. This facilitates

cannot be either readily generalized (for explanatory purposes) or utilized in another time period (for predictive purposes). Fundamentally, this methodology ignores the reality that 'business failure' is a temporal process rather than a dichotomous (failed/non-failed) state, and that during the process business conditions will change, modifying, hastening, slowing or even halting the process.

Consequently, an important part of the data analysis necessitated modelling the external environment of the firms for the 21-year term of the study. The inclusion of macroeconomic variables gives a relatively new dimension to financial distress modelling that incorporates time, the business cycle – essentially government policy – and notably the effect of monetary tightness on failure risk.

This chapter discusses the Principal Components Analysis used to provide the raw macroeconomic variables for the subsequent modelling of this aspect of failure risk. This includes the difficult interpretation and naming of these orthogonal variables – based on the weightings of each published economic series and the significance level of the correlation between each series and the principal component in question.

The value of each factor for each year is matched to the respective lag years for each firm in the database as a measure of the external influence of the economy on failure risk. Further, a discussion of the experimentation with different lag models is given. These transform the external variables in order to account for their possible delayed effects on firms at risk. Finally, a second preliminary model of failure risk is estimated similar to the first model presented in Chapter 4, but now modelled on only the external variables, again taking no account of the dependencies that exist within firms from year to year.

5.1 Principal Components Analysis of the External Economic Variables of the USA

The annual US government publications entitled *Abstracts of the USA* were the source of the data used to model the external environment of the bankrupt firms. Data were collected over the 21 years from 1971 to 1991, inclusive, from publications dated 1971 to 1992, on 76 economic series, deemed relevant to this study. The series names and table numbers can be found in Appendix G.

The *Abstracts of the USA* contain a large number of time series but there exists high levels of collinearity between many of the series. They are statistically related as well as economically related since their economic definitions are similar, so the next challenge was to incorporate them into the analysis retaining as much as possible of the information within the set of time series without being too cumbersome a dataset. Without expert advice it was difficult to choose which of the series should go into the failure model except by data mining e.g. stepwise regression analysis. Instead, the choice was theory driven and advice was sought from economists to help with the decision as to which series should be retained as having an important relationship to bankruptcy rates. These consultations resulted

having an important relationship to bankruptcy rates. These consultations resulted in the use of 76 economic series, deemed relevant to this study. Information on these series is given in Appendix G.[2]

Principal Components Analysis was used both to maximize the use of the data available, yet at the same time, to reduce the number of variables in the model which represent the economy's influence on the firms' risk of failure. Principal Components Analysis creates a set of orthogonal (uncorrelated) variables that, together, account for most of the variation that exists in the economy. The orthogonality is a distinct advantage when using maximum likelihood methods for model estimation as multicollinearity among explanatory variables interferes with decisions about the statistical importance of individual variables and specific subsets of variables (since the estimators are not consistent).

Using a Principal Components analysis of these 76 series, five orthogonal factors, called PC1 to PC5, were identified. Between them they accounted for 92 percent of the variation in the economy over that time. See Figure 5.1 for a graphic representation of the five principal component values for each year of the study, where the series number in the legend corresponds to the principal component number.

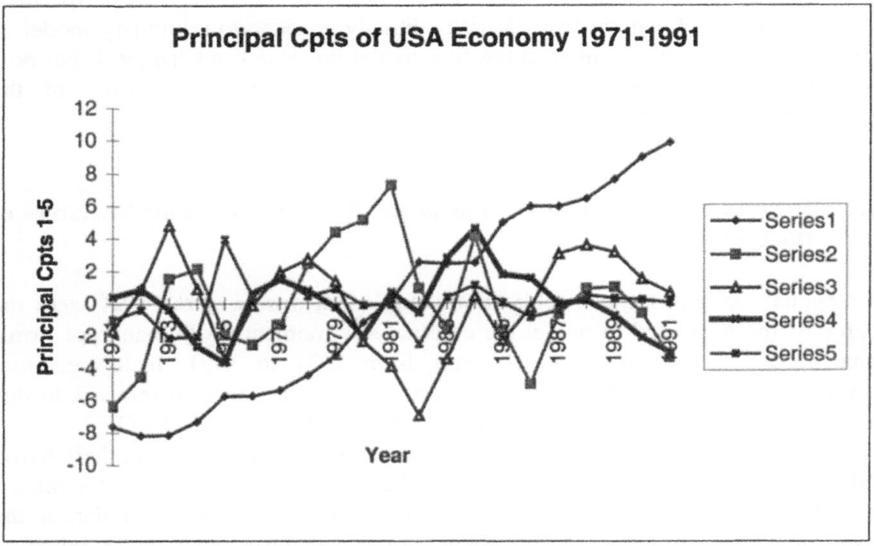

Figure 5.1 Principal Components of the USA Economy 1971-1991
(See enlarged figure in Appendix G)

2 See Chapter 2 for details of the paper by Rose *et al* (1982), who used a bivariate simple correlation matrix to eliminate 15 highly correlated economic variables from a total of 28 initially, and regressed an aggregate index of business failure rate in the form of failures per 10,000 firms on these variables.

An interpretation of the composite external variables is made on the basis of those series having strong loading patterns shown in Appendix G. The five principal components were identified as:

- Economy Growth
- Cost of Capital and Borrowing
- Labour Market Tightness
- Construction Activities
- Expenditures (Private, Public, Business)

It cannot be overemphasized that the five labels are necessarily subjective and are not intended as definitive (see Kim and Mueller, 1978). Indeed, the principal components show several unexpected features in their contributory variables given their titles (Appendix G gives details). Nevertheless, the use of principal components allows the overall incorporation of the business cycles into the failure process modelling, as it is the temporal patterns that are important rather than the specific interpretation of each individual variable.

The relevant values of these five factors were calculated for each year – the values can be found in Appendix G – and these numbers were then added to each of the firm's data by relevant year, and then exported into SAS for model testing.

5.1.1 The Five External Factors

1st Principal Component, PC1: Economy Growth factor (Level of Activity / Demand in the Economy)

This factor explains 54 percent of the variation accounted for in the macroeconomic dataset and loads most highly ($p<=0.0001$, $r > 0.985$) on the following top ten in descending order of correlation magnitude.

Positively:
Federal Budget Outlays Total, ($r = 0.995$, $p = 0.0001$)
Consumer Price Indexes,
Manufacturing and Trade Inventories,
Money Stock and Liquid Assets M3 Total,
Money Stock and Liquid Assets M2 Total,
GDP - all in current $,
Personal Consumption Expenditures,
Manufacturing and Trade-Sales,
Producer Price Indexes – Capital Equipment,
Business Expenditure for New Plant and Equipment All Industries ($r = 0.986$, $p = 0.0001$).

Negatively:
Federal Budget Surplus or Deficit (r = - 0.945, p = 0.0001),
US International Transactions–Balance on Current Account (r = -0.72, p = 0.0002).

Figure 5.2 shows this factor against the sampled firm-years and time.

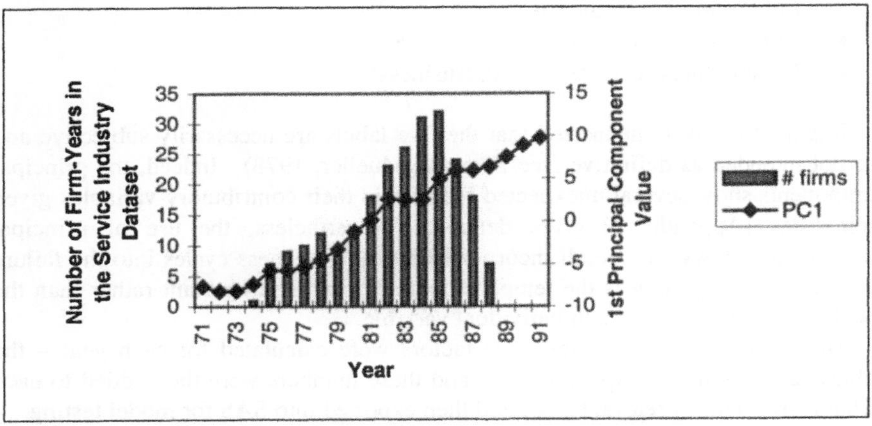

Figure 5.2 Economy Growth Factor (Level of Activity/Demand) and Number of Firm-Years by Year

2nd Principal Component, PC2: Short-Term Cost of Capital Borrowing factor

This factor accounts for 17.6 percent of the variation and loads most highly ($p <= 0.0002$, $r > 0.72$) on the following top ten in descending order of correlation magnitude, all positively. Note that 'Δ' stands for the percentage change from one year to the next.

Money Market Interest Rates Commercial paper 3 mth (r = 0.87, p = 0.0001),
Δ(Bond and Stock Yields (%)-US Treasury constant maturities 5-yr),
Money Market Interest Rates US Govt Securities 1yr Treasury bill,
Δ(Bond and Stock Yields (%)-US Treasury constant maturities 3-yr),
Δ(Net Interest Payments),
Δ(Bond and Stock Yields (%)-US Treasury constant maturities 10-yr),
Money Market Interest Rates Prime Rate charged by banks,
Δ(Money Market Interest Rates Prime Rate charged by banks),
Bond and Stock Yields (%)-US Treasury constant maturities 3-yr,
Δ(Money Market Interest Rates US Govt Securities 1yr Treasury bill)
(r = 0.72, p = 0.0002).

Figure 5.3 shows this factor against the sampled firm-years and time.

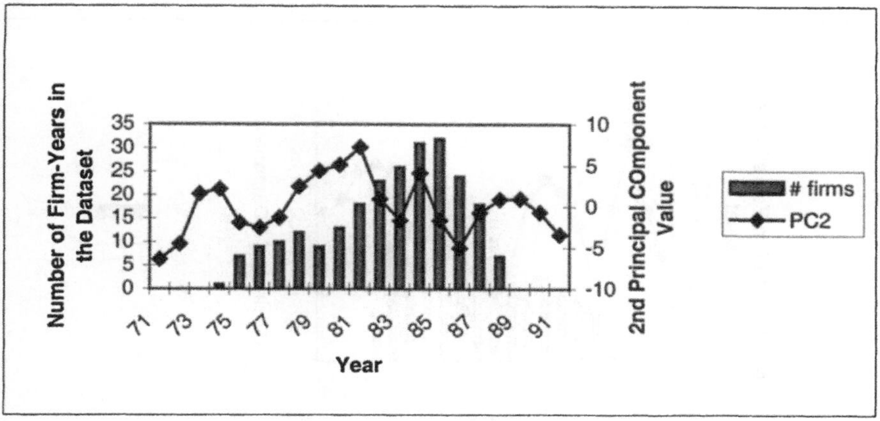

Figure 5.3 Cost of Capital Borrowing and Number of Firm-Years by Year

3rd Principal Component, PC3: Labour Market Tightness factor

This factor accounts for 12.4% of the variation and loads most highly ($p <= 0.01$, $|r| > 0.55$) on the following top ten in descending order of correlation magnitude, both positively and negatively (shown as -ve). Note that 'Δ' stands for the percentage change from one year to the next.

(-ve) Labour Force - Total Unemployed, ($r = -0.68$, $p = 0.0007$),
Security Prices -Standard and Poor's Municipal ($r = 0.63$, $p = 0.002$),
Δ(Labour Force - Total employed),
Bond and Stock Yields (%)-US Treasury constant maturities 10-year,
Bond and Stock Yields (%)-US Treasury constant maturities 5-year,
Δ(Money Market Interest Rates Commercial paper 3 mth),
Bond and Stock Yields (%)-US Treasury constant maturities 3-year,
Δ (Gross Investment),
Δ(Money Market Interest Rates Prime Rate charged by banks),
Δ(Money Market Interest Rates US Govt Securities 1yr Treasury bill)
($r = 0.55$, $p = 0.0096$).

Figure 5.4 shows this factor against the sampled firm-years and time.

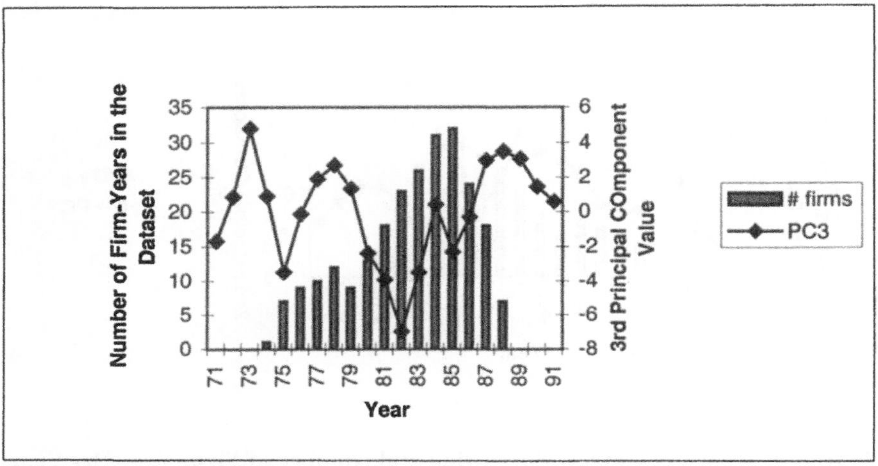

Figure 5.4 Labour Market Tightness and Number of Firm-Years by Year

4th Principal component, PC4: Construction Activity factor

This factor accounts for 5.6 percent of the variation, and loads most highly ($p < 0.04$, $|r| > 0.46$) on the following *in descending order of correlation magnitude*, both positively and negatively (shown as -ve). Note that 'Δ' stands for the percentage change from one year to the next.

Δ(Value of New Construction Put in Place - Total) ($r = 0.764$, $p = 0.0001$),
Δ(Labour Force - Total employed),
(-ve) Δ(Producer Price Indexes Capital Equipment),
(-ve) Exchange rates (index of value relative to US $)-Germany,
(-ve) Percent Change in CPI from former year ($r = - 0.469$, $p = 0.032$),

5th Principal Component, PC5: Expenditure factor (private, public, business)

This factor accounts for only 2.7 percent of the variation and loads most highly ($p < 0.04$, $r > 0.46$), all positively, on the following.

Business Expenditure for New Plant and Equipment - All Industries
($r = 0.633$, $p = 0.002$),
Federal Budget Outlays Total ($r = 0.494$, $p = 0.023$),
Average annual Percentage Change in Personal Consumption Expenditure)
($r = 0.462$, $p = 0.035$).

Figures 5.5 and 5.6 on the next page show the final two factors against the sampled firm-years and time.

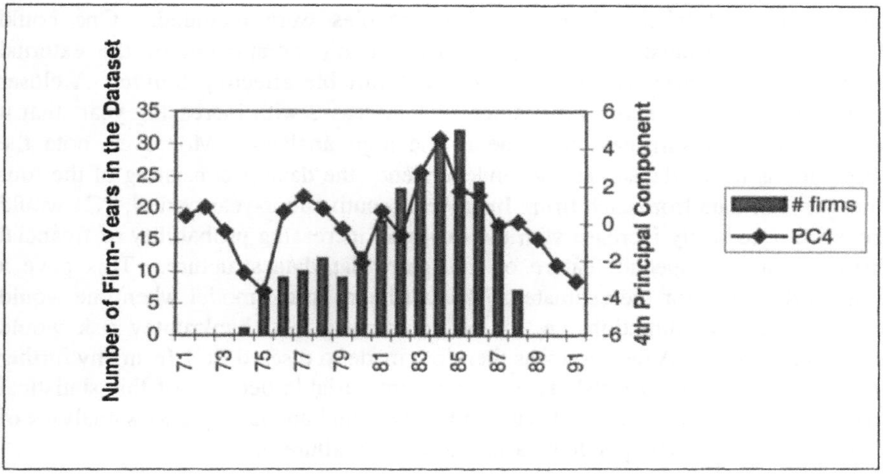

Figure 5.5 Construction Activity Factor and Number of Firm-Years by Year

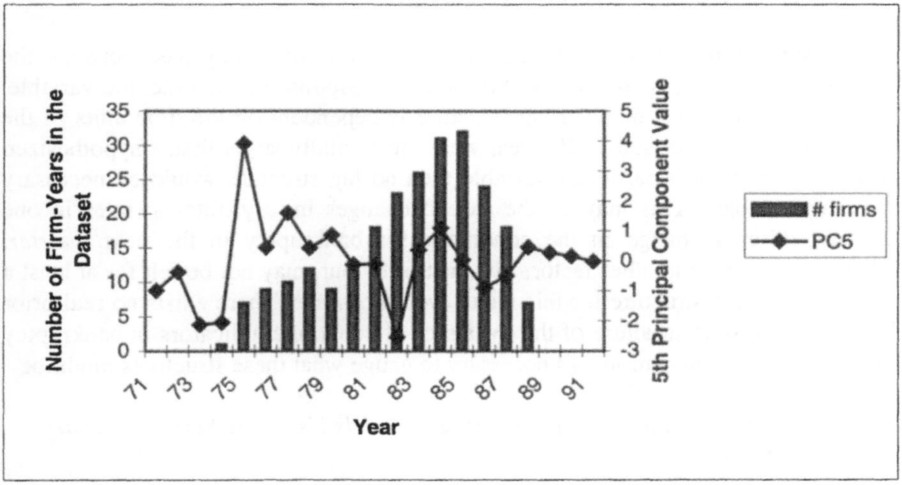

Figure 5.6 Expenditure Factor and Number of Firm-Years by Year

5.2 Statistical Artifact of the 'Economy Growth' Factor

Firstly, note in Figure 5.1, the 'Economy Growth' factor, which shows a strong, approximately linear and virtually unbroken upward temporal trend and, unlike the other PCs, does not exhibit any peaks and troughs. It was the most significant variable in all the logit analyses of failure risk that were subsequently estimated (discussed later) when all the external variables were included. One could

(discussed later) when all the external variables were included. One could therefore well believe that the 'Economy Growth' component of the external economic environment is the most important variable affecting failure. A closer examination, though, reveals that since PC1 increases with increasing year[3] that it was, in effect, a surrogate for time in the logit analysis. Moreover, note the observations in the dataset are not independent: the dataset consisting of the four final years of data from each firm. In any consecutive four-year period, PC1 would therefore necessarily increase with the expected increasing probability of financial distress that is a special feature of this particular data structure. This gave a positive direction for the estimate of its coefficient in the model when one would expect a negative direction, i.e. as the economy grows, bankruptcy risk would diminish, not grow. A decision was therefore made to discard PC1 from any further analysis that used failure risk as the dependent variable because of this statistical artifact. It was not, however, discarded for the simultaneous equations analyses of Chapter 7 using other dependent variables besides failure risk.

5.3 Structuring the Variables Representing the External Environment: Distributed Lag Models on the Principal Components

When constructing models, we recognize that some time may pass between the movement of the independent variables and the response of the outcome variable. The specification of a model's lag structure is dependent on the time units of the data – one year in this study. If a year were substantially larger than a hypothesized reaction period for a particular variable then no lag structure would be necessary for that variable. This may be the case if changes in, say, interest rates in one *quarter* effect a change in the conditions for bankruptcy in the next *quarter*, whereas changes in another factor, say, cost of labour, may not be felt for at least a year and so a lag structure for this factor would be wise. There exists no real prior theory for the time structure of the dynamics of economic indicators in bankruptcy models, so experimentation was necessary to gauge what these structures might be.

5.3.1 Experimentation with Different Lag Models Using the Service Industry Dataset

There are a number of ways in which the impact of economic changes can be distributed over a number of time periods in a *distributed lag model*. If some *a priori* conditions are specified about the form of the lag, the modelling exercise can be simplified, the number of degrees of freedom lost in lengthy lag structures can be reduced, as can multicollinearity between the many lags. Two of the most

---

[3] In Figure 5.1 (series 1) the function increases almost monotonically with time with the exception of 1971, 1974, 1983 and 1987, where slight drops occurred, but nevertheless a very high correlation between PC1 and Year exists.

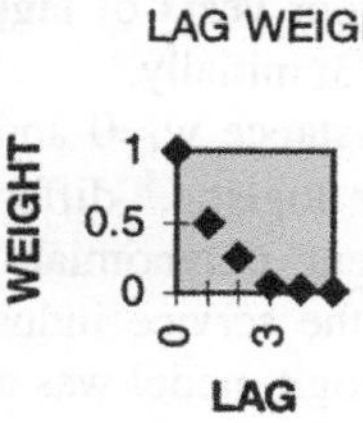

Figure 5.7 Geometric Lag Model

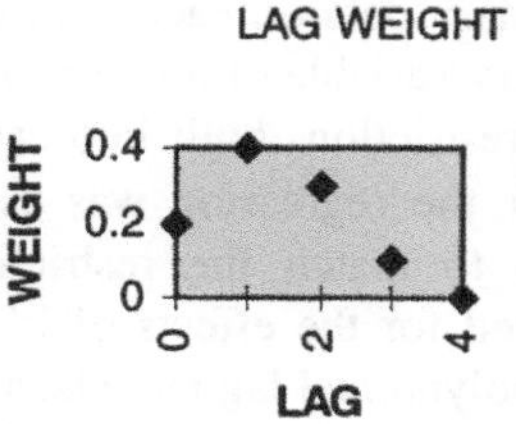

Figure 5.8 Polynomial Lag Model

Figure 5.7 shows a geometric lag structure that assumes that the weights of the lagged explanatory variables are all positive and declining geometrically with time. The model is:

$$Y_t = \alpha + \beta\,(X_t + wX_{t-1} + w^2X_{t-2} + \ldots) + \varepsilon_t$$

$$= \alpha + \beta\,\Sigma\, w^s X_{t-s} + \varepsilon_t \qquad 0<w<1$$

Figure 5.8 shows a more general polynomial lag structure where the weights need not decline with time. For this study, a second-degree polynomial lag structure with a four-period lag was used to explore distributed lags for the second and third principal components, PC2 and PC3 (after the decision was made to drop PC1):

$$Y_t = \alpha + \beta\,(w_0 X_t + w_1 X_{t-1} + w_2X_{t-2} + w_3X_{t-3}) + \varepsilon_t$$

where

$$w_i = c_0 + c_1 i + c_2 i^2 \quad i = 0,1,2,3$$

Any number of lags may be incorporated in the model and different degree polynomials can be used. The significance of adding more terms to the polynomial can be tested statistically if normal errors are assumed.

Either of these specific lag structures may have some theoretical underpinnings when dealing with *one* economic series, say, for a nation's aggregate consumption as a function of aggregate disposable income. In this study, the effects are not so clear and the dataset is more complex. Firstly, we have, within each industry group, N repeated finite series for each explanatory variable to be lagged – i.e. one series for each of the N firms studied; each of which is a subset of the one series for the U.S.A. for that variable, finishing in the year when that firm submitted its final financial statements before being liquidated. Secondly, the outcome of interest is binary and the lags therefore need to be estimated using the method of maximum likelihood with binomial errors in a logistic regression analysis rather than with normal errors in a least squares analysis. A dataset was created which matched each of the four years of binary data on each firm with a stack of four years of lagged data for each explanatory variable of interest - here PC2 and PC3, initially.

of the four years of binary data on each firm with a stack of four years of lagged data for each explanatory variable of interest - here PC2 and PC3, initially.

Depending on the restrictions built into each model, for instance $w_4=0$ and/or $\Sigma w_i = 1$, or whether the regression was assumed linear or logistic,[4] different datasets were created to match the restrictions and different polynomial lag functions were estimated for the effects of PC2 and PC3 on the service industry firms. As well as the polynomial lag models, a no-restrictions logit model was also estimated that showed which of the lagged variables had a significant effect on the outcome.

5.3.2 Conclusions on the Lag Model Weights

All the models gave similar results for the estimated weights for PC2, the Short-Term Cost of Capital Borrowing factor, and PC3, the Labour Market Tightness factor, in that PC2 had little effect on the binary outcome (low weight) in the final year, and approximately equal effects in the previous three years, and PC3 had most effect in the final year and very little effect previous to that.

Because of the similarity across different estimation techniques and the advantages of having orthogonal independent variables, within each lag at least, it was decided to use the raw principal component values and their three-year lags and allow their coefficient estimates from the logistic regression to be their weights, without any geometric or polynomial functional restrictions. In addition, since loss of degrees of freedom is always a problem when too many variables are included in a model, it was decided to include, for analysis in the final model, only those lagged variables from the stack with significant effects on the binary outcome in this preliminary model. This assumes that the economic variables are independent of the financial variables with respect to their effect on failure risk.[5]

5.4 The External Variables Logit Model

The stepwise logit model of failure risk for the service industry using only the four principal components and their lags,[6] gave the following subset for an empirically adequate model of failure risk within the current data set (i.e. no financial variables were included for this analysis):

---

4 The SAS procedure PDLREG for a polynomial distributed lag model uses linear estimation with normal error terms.

5 Since they are not taken account of in this preliminary model, it is assumed that the effects of the economy and the effects of the financial variables on failure risk are additive, within the logit model formulation. There is empirical support for this assumption in this dataset, as discussed in Section 6.1.5.

6 Only the lags that were not linear combinations of other principal components were included in the dataset.

(Variables listed in order of variables entering the stepwise model)

PC3 (no lag) - Labour Market Tightness factor in the final year, ($p = 0.0001$)
PC5 (no lag) - Expenditure factor (private, public, business) in the final year, ($p = 0.0002$)
PC5 (lag 1) - Expenditure factor (private, public, business) in the previous year, ($p = 0.0001$)
PC4 (no lag) - Construction Activity Factor in the final year, ($p = 0.009$)
PC2 (lag 1) - Short-Term Cost of Capital Borrowing factor in the previous year. ($p = 0.0008$)

The model based on this subset has a non-significant lack of fit ($p>0.16$).[7] SAS included these external factors in the stepwise logit model of failure risk for the Service Industry dataset shown below using a significance level of 0.15 for a variable to either enter or be removed from the model at each stage. The overall significance of the final model was $p=0.0001$. See the SAS output in Appendix F for more details.

Model equation (5.1) for the effect of the external variables on failure risk is shown below with variables presented in decreasing order of significance to failure risk. The 3:1 weighting of final to previous years' data was again applied for the same reasons given in the previous chapter – to overcome the otherwise undue weighting of the surviving years in the model.

$$W = \text{logit } P = -0.0351 + 0.8283\,PC3 - 0.6713\,PC5(lag1) - 0.8582\,PC5(no\ lag) + 0.4295\,PC2(lag1) + 0.3334\,PC4(no\ lag) \qquad (5.1)$$

Model (5.1) has an overall classification accuracy for the estimation sample of 72 percent. Surprisingly, this is better than model (4.1) based on the internal ratios (cf. 70.6 percent in (4.1)) but, more importantly, the external variables model has only a 54.2 percent accuracy rate for predicting failing firm-years, which is not much better than chance (c.f. 63.8 percent in (4.1)). The Type II error rate (incorrect classification rate for surviving firm-years) is 22 percent (25.4 percent in (4.1)). Somers' D is only 0.462 (0.52 in model (4.1)).

5.4.1 The Meaning of the External Variables Model

It is always possible that a stepwise regression procedure, which finds the best fitting model from a hypothetical set of independent variables, can produce a fallacious result based on a purely coincidental relationship with the sample data

---

7 Note: In model building, significant variables are added to the model until the lack of fit of the model estimates to the data becomes non-significant. A *minimum adequate* model consisted here of only the first three variables with non-significant lack of fit ($p = 0.077$, in other words, just > 0.05, with 1 fewer degrees of freedom). The addition of extra significant variables at this stage will still add to the fit. When to stop is a matter of judgement.

fallacious result based on a purely coincidental relationship with the sample data set. Just as we had to be careful about statistical artifact in 5.2, when including economic series as explanatory variables in a model for failure risk, it is important to check the meaning of a model that only includes variables external to the firm in its analysis, given its design features. If a particular result were difficult to explain, or even illogical, it may represent a statistical artifact of the data. Unless there are theoretical underpinnings to the results, they have to be viewed with caution.

Table 5.1 Frequency Table of Number of Firms in the Final-Year Prior to Bankruptcy/Liquidation by Year

Year	Frequency
1975	0
1976	0
1977	1
1978	6
1979	2
1980	1
1981	3
1982	3
1983	6
1984	6
1985	8
1986	6
1987	11
1988	7

Here, the estimation dataset consists of 60 small time series of four dependent variables that are all equivalent, with values 0, 0, 0, 1 respectively, and the corresponding economic measures attaching to the four-year window before failure for each firm. Refer to the histogram of final firm-years in Figure 4.1 of the previous chapter, drawn from the table of frequencies for each year (Table 5.1) above, showing the number of firms represented in the dataset each year in their final year prior to failure. These frequencies give the relative weighting that each year and its corresponding economic factors attach to the data for the final year before failure. For each further prior year, the same frequencies occur, respectively, one year earlier. These weightings will be reflected in the model.

Because the data set is not a sample, but a population of failed firms that failed approximately between the years 1978 and 1990[8] in the service industry (or as

[8] Taking into account that the histogram shows us the final years when annual source documents were still produced and we know that it may take up to two years or more before a company actually liquidates or is bankrupted.

frequencies of the '0's and '1's at each year along the timeline is meaningful in terms of how the prevailing economic conditions impacted upon those failed firms during their final four years of trading. In other words, the fact that there are greater or fewer '1's (failures) in certain years is meaningful if we can assume that the total number of service industry firms in existence over the same time period was relatively constant. For instance, the year 1988 (with 1987 as its final year before failure) scored the most failures among service industry firms over the period for which population final-year data were collected. It is not meaningful if we are considering failure rates or other firms in general, and any following comments concerning economic trends and firm failure need to be so qualified.

With the above qualifications in mind, conclusions can be made about the signs of the coefficients in model (5.1) indicating the following economic trends in the final years before failure:

Overall, PC3, the 'labour market tightness' factor, is the most significant variable in relation to failure risk ($p < 0.0001$). Given the positive parameter estimate on PC3 and its high negative loading on the 'total unemployed' (see Appendix G), this is an indication that the model is correctly picking up the impacts of the business cycle on failures. PC5, 'expenditures', both lagged one year and in the final year, are negatively loaded and significant ($p < 0.0001$, $p < 0.0002$ respectively). This, again, is as expected and the two results together indicate support for the failure modelling. Increased spending, either public or private decreases the likelihood of failure. Another external variables significant to failure risk ($p < 0.0008$) is PC2_1, the 'cost of capital borrowing' factor lagged one year (positively). This can be interpreted to represent the time taken for the restriction on credit to take effect. It has the expected sign in that increased cost of capital and borrowing increases the probability of failure. Note that there is nothing in these results that is optimised to maximize goodness of fit specifically for the service industry, increasing the possibility of better results with industry specific variables.

Explaining the positive coefficient on the construction factor, PC4 is problematic, as the model has failure risk *increasing* with increasing percentage change in both the value of new construction and in labour force, and failure risk *decreasing* with both increasing exchange rates with Germany and with increasing percentage change in CPI. The significance of this factor may be spurious or incorrectly interpreted and named. An artifact is supported by a similar pattern in the graph of PC4 over time and the frequency polygon of the firm data evident in Fig. 5.5. These signs are again discussed in more detail in the next chapter when the significant marginal effects of these external factors are considered.

5.5 Conclusions

Zavgren (1983, p. 32) pointed out that 'rising interest rates, a recessionary environment, the availability of credit' might affect a firm's change in financial status. The major aim of this chapter was to find useful variables that represent the

status. The major aim of this chapter was to find useful variables that represent the external environment of the service industry firms in the USA at the time of their demise and for a period of approximately seven years in total before bankruptcy/liquidation (measurements apply to the four observations or firm-years for each firm plus three lag year measurements for each observation). The Principal Components Analysis of the USA economy over the 21 years of the study produced five orthogonal variables accounting for 92 percent of the variation that existed in the economy. The first four, at least, were relatively easy to name on the basis of the economic series upon which they each loaded highly, though it is acknowledged that this is not entirely an objective exercise and others could argue for what they deem to be more appropriate labels for these factors.

While the inclusion of macroeconomic variables as a whole is readily justifiable, there is no rationale, as yet, for incorporating some variables as opposed to others. Conversely, the use of the PCs is justified on the grounds of maximizing the included information while avoiding a large fitting exercise based solely on maximizing goodness of fit and ease of handling data. Thus, while appreciably increasing goodness of fit, PC1 was omitted from the empirical analysis as it gave the wrong sign on its coefficient in any analysis based upon its strong correlative association with YEAR. The reason was the artifactual problem with the temporal nature of the four years of data for each failed firm. Advancing through time toward failure, the periods move closer to failure in a deterministic linear path. This necessarily gives an artificial correlation between the dependent variable and PC1. This artifact serves as an important warning against taking goodness of fit as the main criterion for model building. The omission of PC1 is essentially equivalent to a linear de-trending of the macroeconomic cycle data via the principal component analysis. This operation also helps avoid any spurious correlation between time (YEAR) and failure if, over the time of the sample period, there is a trend towards greater numbers of failures.

A secondary aim of this chapter was to produce a model of individual firm failure based entirely on the external variables, if only for comparison of statistical significance with that of a combined model and for an investigation into the signs of the coefficients. 'Secondary', because it is not usual to model financial distress of the individual firm solely on variables that have nothing to do with the internal workings of the firm or its management, although both Altman (1971) and Rose *et al* (1982) produced models that quantified the relationship at different periods between the *total number* of corporate failures (or business failure *rates* in the latter case) and the corresponding macroeconomic changes as measured by selected economic indicators. Levy (1991) also provides an aggregate econometric analysis of the effects of variations of certain macroeconomic factors on the rate of bankruptcy in the USA, showing that variations in the GNP and the GNP deflator significantly affect the rate of bankruptcy. Notwithstanding these results, one would not expect a model, based solely on variables external to the firm, to perform well at the *individual* firm level as the external variables are conglomerate measures for the USA and apply just as well to *all* firms, failing or surviving, for

These variables representing the external environment can now be used in a combined model of firm failure so that their incremental effect beyond the effect of the financial ratios can be ascertained. Alternatively, these external factors can be controlled for so that a better assessment of the effects of fluctuating financial ratios can be made. The estimation of such a combined model of failure risk is the subject of the next chapter. There is no need to limit the external variables to just the reduced best set from model (5.1) since there are no missing values here to reduce the analysis set as there are for the financial ratios. Consequently, all four principal components and their lags can again be included with the significant financial variables for the combined stepwise analysis of Chapter 6.

Chapter 6

Combining the Impact of the Internal and External Factors on Financial Distress

6.0 Introduction

In this chapter a combined model of failure risk is estimated based on variables both internal and external to the firm, i.e. all the financial ratios that were input into the stepwise regression analysis of Chapter 4 and four[1] of the five principal components and their lags for up to three years[2] from Chapter 5. The same logit functional form that was employed in the previous two chapters will be retained here. Questions to be answered are:

- Do the addition of measures of economic adversity and the consequent improvement in model specification for relevance over time and for model completeness also improve our empirical results?
- Will the structure of the resulting model have vastly different parameter estimates from the corresponding models in previous chapters based on either the internal or the external variables alone?
- Can the results be explained?

6.1 A Combined Financial Distress Model for Bankrupt Service Companies

For this analysis, each firm-year was again treated as independent of every other firm-year (though it is recognized this is not the case but the exercise remains exploratory for the moment); the service industry dataset consisted of the 60 firms by four years each, giving 240 observations. The object of the exercise was to identify best subsets of explanatory variables across the two groups of external and internal variables input into the stepwise analysis, using a branch and bound algorithm of Furnival and Wilson (1974), and to see which variables were most important within these subsets. These best subsets would then provide the reduced

---

1 The first principal component for macro demand/growth was excluded due to statistical artifact (see Chapter 5.2).

2 Only the lags that were not linear combinations of other principal components were included in the dataset.

variable set for model testing when the independence assumption would be dropped. Such a reduced set of predictors would include less redundancy of information among the predictors and hence less multicollinearity, which in the logit analysis leads to smaller standard errors of the model coefficients and hence, more statistical power to their tests of significance. It was also of interest to compare the significance of the variables external and internal to the environment of the firm as to their importance in this regard.

6.1.1 The Significant Financial Variables to Failure Risk

A stepwise[3] failure risk model was estimated on the full set of external and internal variables. With the significant external variables already included, much the same set of financial ratios were still significant ($p < 0.15$) as those in the final model (4.1) of the stepwise analysis of Chapter 4, when the external variables were not included.[4] An exception was the replacement of R6, Return on Assets, in model (4.1) with R15 in this combined model.

(The 1st bracketed p-value is taken from the model equation (4.1) and the 2nd p-value from a combined model including the external as well as the internal variables.)

R2 Working Capital/Total Assets,	($p = 0.0001$, $p = 0.0001$)
R7 Total Liabilities/Total Assets,	($p = 0.002$, $p = 0.0001$)
RC21_1[5] Sales/Net Plant, lowest category,	($p = 0.0001$, $p = 0.0005$)
RC21_4 Sales/Net Plant, highest category,	($p < 0.05$, $p < 0.002$)
RCD18[6] Interest Coverage after Tax, 2nd category,	($p < 0.02$, $p < 0.02$)
R15 Cash Flow from Operations/Total Current Liabilities.	(not included $p < 0.25$, $p < 0.13$)

Here, similar to the situation discussed in Chapter 4, any one of R6, Return on Assets, R5, Retained Earnings/Total Assets, or R14, Cash Flow from Operations/Total Assets, could enter the model individually with $p < 0.15$, once all the other ratios had been included, and result in a slightly lower Type II error at the expense of a rise in the Type I error. Since a reduced Type I error is preferred and in the interest of parsimony, they were all dropped from the final model in favour

---

3 The reasons for using stepwise regression analysis throughout this chapter are explained in Chapter 4.5.

4 Within the internal ratios subset, these ratios contribute most significance irrespective of different weightings placed on each of the four year's of data on each firm and irrespective of the number of lags included in the external subset of variables.

5 R21 categorized as four dummy variables for five categories (See Appendix C): RC21_1=1 if R21 < 5th percentile, the mid-range or base level combines with the intercept term, and RC21_4 =1 if R21 > 95th percentile or +ve divided by zero.

6 R18 categorized as a dummy binary 0-1 variable, either R18< 0, (RCD18=0), or R18 >= 0, (RCD18=1).

of R15. Both R6, Return on Assets and RCD13, Cash Flow from Operations/Sales, were included in the ratios-only model (4.1) but did not add significantly ($p < 0.15$) to this combined model, whereas the opposite was true for R15, Cash Flow from Operations/Total Current Liabilities, which added significantly to this combined model but not to (4.1).

6.1.2 The Significant External Variables to Failure Risk

A stepwise failure risk model was estimated on the full set of external and internal variables. With the significant financial ratios already included, the same set of external variables was still significant ($p < 0.15$) as those in the final model (5.1) of the stepwise analysis of Chapter 5 when the financial ratios were not included.

In the combined model of failure risk the following external variables entered the model with $p < 0.15$:

(The 1st bracketed p-value is taken from the model equation (5.1) and the 2nd p-value from a combined model including the internal as well as the external variables.)

PC3 (no lag) – Labour Market Tightness factor in the final year, (p=0.0001, p=0.0001)

PC5 (lag 1) – Expenditure factor (private, public, business) in the previous year, (p=0.0001, p=0.0001)

PC2 (lag 1) – Short-Term Cost of Capital Borrowing factor in the previous year, (p=0.0008, p=0.0004)

PC5 (no lag) – Expenditure factor (private, public, business) in the final year, (p=0.0002, p=0.002)

PC4 (no lag) – Construction Activity Factor in the final year. (p=0.009, p=0.003)

6.1.3 The Combined Model Equation Assuming Independence Within Firm-Years

As explained in Chapter 4, a weighting of 3:1 for failed: surviving firm-years was used in the analysis to equalise the influence of failed and surviving years in the model estimations. A sensitivity analysis comparing a number of models based on an equal weighting of all the firm-years against a 3:1 weighting was conducted. The model based on a 3:1 weighting always gave better accuracy rates overall and lower Type I errors at the expense of the Type II errors (misclassifying surviving firm-years). This is as expected since the comparative weighting for surviving firm data is reduced in the 3:1 weighted models.

The stepwise regression algorithm included the following ratios and external factors in the final logit model of failure risk for the Service Industry dataset using a significance level of 0.15 for a variable to either enter or be removed from the model at each stage. The overall significance of the final model (6.1), below, was p=0.0001. The combined model is a particular case of the linear predictor (3.4) of the logistic function (3.3) applied to the service industry firms. It is shown below with variables presented in decreasing order of significance to failure risk. It has an overall classification accuracy of 71.9 percent[7] for this estimation sample.[8] This is only slightly better than model (4.1) based on the internal ratios alone (cf. 70.6 percent).

Most importantly, however, the combined model has a 70.7 percent accuracy rate for predicting failing firm-years (cf. 63.8 percent in (4.1)). This means the Type I error rate, or probability of misclassifying failing firm-years, is 29.3 percent compared to the ratios-only model of 36.2 percent – a 7 percent improvement. The Type II error rate (incorrect classification rate for surviving firm-years) is virtually unchanged at 27.7 percent (27.1 percent in (4.1)). Somers' D is 0.685, an improvement over the ratios-only model (0.52 in (4.1)).

Thus, it is in predicting which is to be the singularly important final failing year that the additional explanatory power of the macro-economic factors is most evident, i.e. in reducing the Type I error.[9]

See Appendix H for an extract of the SAS output for this model:

W = logit P = 1.4658 + 0.9115 PC3 – 0.0206 R2 – 0.8011 PC5(lag1) – 0.0166 R7 + 0.4736 PC2(lag1) – 2.2866 RC21_1 + 1.6171 RC21_4 – 0.7695 PC5(no lag) + 0.4133 PC4(no lag) – 0.6916 RCD18 – 0.0821 R15 (6.1)

The five most significant internal variables (including three dummy variables) from model (4.1) that remained highly significant ($p < 0.05$) in the combined model (6.1) were the ratios, 'Working Capital/Total Assets', 'Sales/Net Plant' – highest category and lowest categories, 'Total Liabilities/Total Assets' and 'Interest Coverage after Tax'. When the effects of the internal ratios on failure risk are simultaneously taken into account, all five external variables from model (5.1) remained in the combined model (6.1). This included a representative of each of the four principal components considered – either for the final year or a lagged year: 'Labour Market Tightness' factor – final year, 'Expenditure (Private, Public, Business)' factor – final year, and also in the previous year, 'Short-Term Cost of

7 This is a very crude classification with a cut-off point of 0.5 for failing/surviving firm-years and does not have the same meaning as when it is used in studies involving cross-sectional samples of failed and surviving firms instead of time series panel data of failed firms. One would expect here, for instance, that in the penultimate year (lag 1) the risk of failure would often go over the 0.5 mark and it still survives another year. These figures are presented only for comparisons with the models in Chapters 4 and 5.

8 No holdout sample was used, as prediction is not the focus of this book.

9 Many have argued (Altman *et al*, 1977; White *et al*, 1994) that the Type I error is the one that is most costly. Rose and Giroux (1984) explain the analogous decision framework of the credit decision which confronts bank commercial loan officers every day: - 'A Type I error would be equivalent to granting a bank loan to a firm that eventually went bankrupt and would be associated with the potential for a substantial loan default with the bank recovering nothing. ...A Type II error would be equivalent to rejecting a loan to a solvent and profitable firm' (Rose and Giroux, 1984, p.10).

Capital Borrowing' factor – in the previous year, and 'Construction Activity' factor – final year, though there is some evidence to suggest (as in the previous chapter) that the significance of this factor may be spurious.

6.1.4 The Sign of the Coefficients

(a) The External Variables: The external variables analysis gave the same conclusions for the combined model as for model (5.1):

- As the labour market tightens, i.e. there are fewer unemployed, unions are stronger, and costs of labour are higher, we would expect the risk of failure to increase (+ve sign).
- As the short-term cost of borrowings increases, the costs of production are higher to service borrowings, so one would expect the risk of failure to increase (+ve sign).
- As private, public and business expenditure increases, demand for products is higher so one expects the risk of failure to decrease (–ve sign).

All these expectations are correctly reflected in model (6.1).

The positive coefficient on the construction factor is more complex and, although there may be a statistical artifact acting here (see Chapter 5.4.1), possible explanations for the sign with regard to each of that factor's component parts are as follows:

- With increasing percentage change in the value of new construction, the model has failure risk *increasing*. New construction increases when the economy is healthy and firms are less risk averse and willing to take on more risky projects (even though interest rates are high at this time), so more of them are likely to fail.
- With increasing percentage change in labour force the model has failure risk *increasing*. The labour force increases with increasing construction and the same logic as in the last paragraph then applies.
- With increasing exchange rates with Germany, the model has failure risk *decreasing*. When capital is worth more on the international market it can mean conflicting forces are acting on the firm's financial position. If the firm is an exporter and its products are more expensive as a result of a stronger currency, then this would be expected to increase failure risk, but since this data is from service industry firms this force would be minimal. Rather the sign is reflecting a stronger economy and consequent lower failure risk when the currency is strong.
- With increasing percentage change in CPI, the model has failure risk *decreasing*. Again, this indicates a higher demand for products, which can only help a firm's solvency position.

There are indications in the above that model (6.1) provides evidence that failing firms are more sensitive to cost rather than demand pressures.

(b) The Internal Variables: As in Chapter 4, the sign of the coefficient was not as expected for R7: Total Liabilities/Total Assets, which should be +ve in the same direction as failure risk. Again it is close to zero. This anomaly and others were discussed in more detail in chapter 4.5.4 and will be further investigated in the next chapter when the dependencies within firm-years are recognized and when simultaneous models are used to examine indirect influences on failure risk.

It is interesting that the profitability ratio Return on Assets, R6, of model (4.1) no longer marginally improves the ratio-plus-external-variables model. As footnoted in Chapter 4, Zavgren and Friedman (1988) also found that Return on Invested Capital was not very significant. They note that Ohlson (1980) found that many of his failing firms had profits at least as high as his healthy firms; many even showed a profit during their year of failure (p. 130). These findings led them to conclude that the profitability of failing and healthy firms really do not differ.

The signs on the other ratios and their dummy variables included in the model are as expected and are all explained in Chapter 4.5.4. The additional variable, R15, Cash Flow from Operations/Total Current Liabilities, has a negative coefficient as expected, i.e. it moves in the opposite direction to failure risk, consistent with the findings of other[10] researchers that a lower coverage of current liabilities relates to a higher level of insolvency risk. Recall that Beaver's (1966) best ratio (using a univariate approach) was also 'Cash Flow to Total Debt'.[11]

6.1.5 Independence of the Internal and External Variable Sets on Failure Risk

It is important to note that out of the total set of 23 financial ratios, and 16 external variables, the most important[12] variables within each of the external and internal sets of variables, i.e. those with highest statistical significance in their respective models ($p<0.05$), remained important in determining failure risk *independently* of whether the two subsets were combined or not for the analysis, or whether lagged principal components were used or not, although the order of significance may change. In other words, the effects of the economy and the effects of the financial variables on failure risk are additive, within the logit model formulation. (Note that when the logit is back-transformed, the impacts of the two sets of variables, external and internal, on the risk of failure, are multiplicative or interactive, as

---

10 Viz. Beaver (1966), Blum (1974), Mensah (1983), Norton and Smith (1979), Gilbert *et al* (1990).

11 This statement must be qualified by the fact that Beaver's definition of cash flow, as for many of the early cash flow models, was 'net income plus depreciation, depletion and amortization', which Largay and Stickney (1980) pointed out is not an accurate measure of cash flow but, rather, of working capital.

12 Using a stepwise logit fit with 0.15 as the cut-off significance level for entering and exiting the model.

expected.) This additivity within the linear predictor also points to some stability in the effect of the internal ratios on failure risk since the important financial ratios from the analysis in Chapter 4 remain statistically significant in the respective models with different sets of external variables already included.

6.2 How Important are the Economic Variables Compared to the Financial Variables in Influencing Failure Risk?

Preliminary analyses of the service industry failed firms dataset showed, *in all cases*, that when the principal components and their one, two, and three-year lags are included in stepwise regression models together with the financial ratios, that the most significant variable to enter the model is PC3, the 'Labour Tightness' factor. Also, when best subsets of particular sizes are estimated using the branch and bound algorithm of Furnival and Wilson (1974),[13] both the 'Labour Tightness' factor and the 'Public and Private Expenditure' factor, usually figure first in most best subsets of sizes 1 to 10. Then, depending on the subset size chosen, the 'Short-Term Cost of Capital Borrowing' factor lagged one year or lagged two years, with the 'Public and Private Expenditure' factor lagged one year, figure next in importance to the model along with the internal financial variables listed above. This means that in this dataset, the external economic factors show a stronger relationship with failure risk than do the internal financial ratios. One of the challenges this presents us with is to explain this result (see Chapter 7).

6.3 Comparison of the Average Estimated Probabilities of Failure for Each Lag Year

From a binary input variable that is either '0' or '1', the logit model outputs an estimate of failure risk. It is of interest at this stage to compare these estimates at each period prior to failure. Does this risk increase over time as we would logically expect, and if so, by how much?

From the value of W in the model equation (6.1), the inverse logit of W can be calculated as the logistic function: $P = (1 + \exp\{-W\})^{-1}$, where P is the estimated risk of failure in the next year. In this way a value of failure risk (the output) was estimated from the model for each firm-year and compared with the '1' or '0' that was input, i.e. whether it was, respectively, a failing or surviving year.

The logit model used an independent variable that was only meant to discriminate between the final period (lag 0) before liquidation/bankruptcy – given the value '1' – against the previous three lag years – all given the same value '0'. The following tests were made in order to analyse if the estimated risk of failure

---

13 This algorithm finds a specified number of models with the highest likelihood score (chi-square) statistic for all possible model sizes, from one, two, three variables, and so on, up to the single model containing all of the explanatory variables.

output from the model was able to discern more than a dichotomy and moreover, whether it could quantify an increasing level of risk as the time draws closer to the failure event.

Appendix I displays a table of the estimated failure risks for the 59 firms[14] in the estimation sample for each lag year as well as the scatter plots for each lag year. In general, an inspection shows that there is, indeed, a trend of increasing risk from four years prior (lag 3) to the final year (lag 0) and it is very rare for a firm to have a lower estimate of risk of failure in its final year than in its penultimate years. The results of an Analysis of Variance and associated pairwise z-tests for differences between the estimated risks of failure from the combined model (firm by lag year) are also shown in Appendix I. The mean estimated risks for each lag year are given in the following table. (One to four years prior to failure are denoted LAG0 – LAG3.)

Table 6.1 Estimated Failure Risk at Each Prior Year – Service Firms

Groups	Count	Average Estimated Risk
LAG0	59	0.6704
LAG1	59	0.4304
LAG2	59	0.2644
LAG3	59	0.2562

The F-test for group mean differences in risk is highly significant ($p<0.0001$), meaning that at least one of the means is different from the rest. To test that the risk of failure decreases for each extra lag year, pairwise z-tests for differences in proportions (risks) using one-tail were used. The mean estimated risks do indeed decrease with each lag ($p<0.05$) except for LAG2 and LAG3, for which there is no significant difference in mean estimated failure risk. It can be provisionally concluded from the model that the mean estimated risk of failure increases by a statistically significant amount for the final three years prior to failure. More specifically, it can be seen from Table 6.1 that the estimated risk of failure increases from a little more than one quarter at three and four years prior to failure, to 43 percent at two years prior, to around two thirds at one year prior to failure.

These results are borne out in the histograms of failure risk for each lag year shown in Figure 6.1. The shape of the cumulative frequency ogive gets flatter going from LAG0 to LAG3, as more of the distribution of failure risks is concentrated at the lower risks in the earlier years (larger lags) and further from

---

14 As discussed in a Chapter 4 footnote, Advanced Drilling Systems was excluded as an outlier case on the basis of a number of diagnostic detection tests. This firm gave estimated risk values of 0.00, 0.03, 0.10, and 0.00 respectively for lag0 to lag3.

failure. There is an impressive modal shift from the highest risk category to the lowest in the first lag year, and there it remains for all lags.

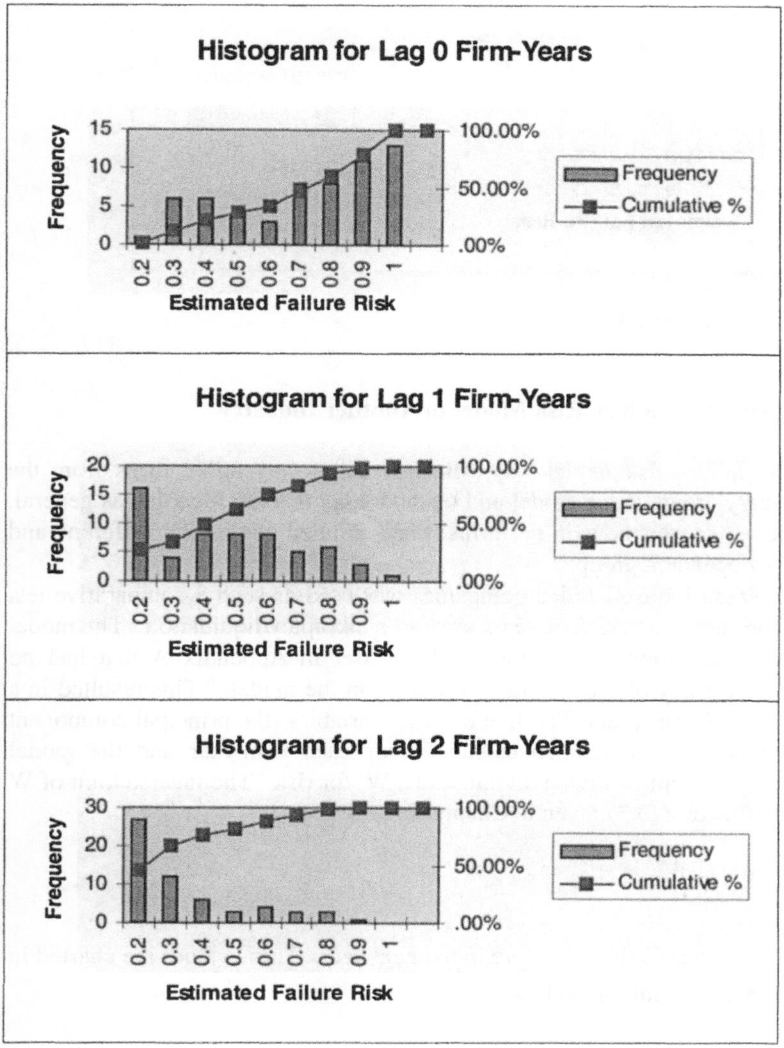

Figure 6.1 Distributions of Estimated Failure Risk for Each Lag Year (Service Industry Firms)

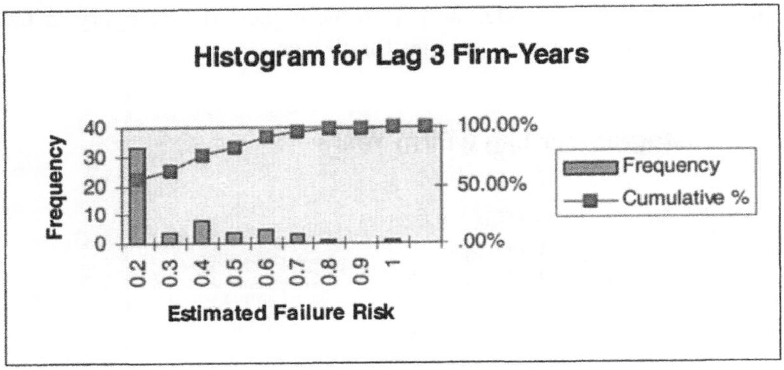

Figure 6.1 (Continued)

6.4 Applying the Failure Risk Model to Another Industry

Although the failure risk model was estimated using only failed firms from the Service Industry group, if the model and methodology is to be regarded as general, it is of interest to see how it performs when applied to a very different and statistically independent group.[15]

A set of Trade Industry failed companies was used as such a comparative test group over the same relative four years prior to bankruptcy/liquidation. The model was applied to all companies in the Trade dataset in Appendix A that had no missing values for any of the five ratio variables in the model.[16] This resulted in a test dataset of 167 firm-years. The five external variables (the principal component values and their lags) were also calculated for each firm-year and the model equation (6.1) was applied giving a logit value, W, for risk. The inverse logit of W is the logistic function (3.3) given in Chapter 3.1[17]

$$P = (1 + \exp\{-W\})^{-1}$$

where P is the estimated risk of failure in the next year. These values are charted in Figure 6.2 as a histogram for each lag year.

---

[15] Research is planned that will apply the model to a group of active Service companies to test its performance in predicting risk, although prediction is not the focus of this book. One would expect that active companies would always have a failure risk of less than 0.5 as long as the companies were sampled at a time period that ensures that they did not subsequently enter bankruptcy for at least a number of years.

[16] The reason for discarding incomplete data is because it would not be appropriate to replace missing values in the Trade dataset with averages from the Service dataset.

[17] As discussed in 3.1.1.

The flattening out of the cumulative density ogive in Figure 6.2 for higher lag years is not as marked as in Figure 6.1 for the Service Industry but is, nevertheless, apparent. The modal value of risk also decreases from Lag0 to Lag3. The average risk of failure for each lag group in the test Trade dataset compared with the estimation Service dataset is tabulated below:

Table 6.2 Comparison of Average Failure Risk at Each Prior Year – Trade and Service Industry Firms

	Trade		Service	
	Count	Risk	Count	Risk
LAG0	43	0.5739	59	0.6704
LAG1	47	0.4602	59	0.4304
LAG2	41	0.3574	59	0.2644
LAG3	36	0.3556	59	0.2562

The fact that reasonable results are obtained when applying the model formulated on the service industry group to the trade industry group is encouraging for tests of external validity in future research.

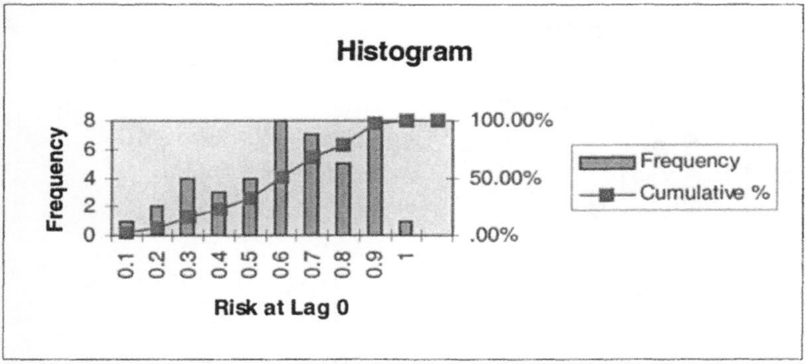

Figure 6.2 Distributions of Estimated Failure Risk for Each Lag Year (Trade Industry Firms)

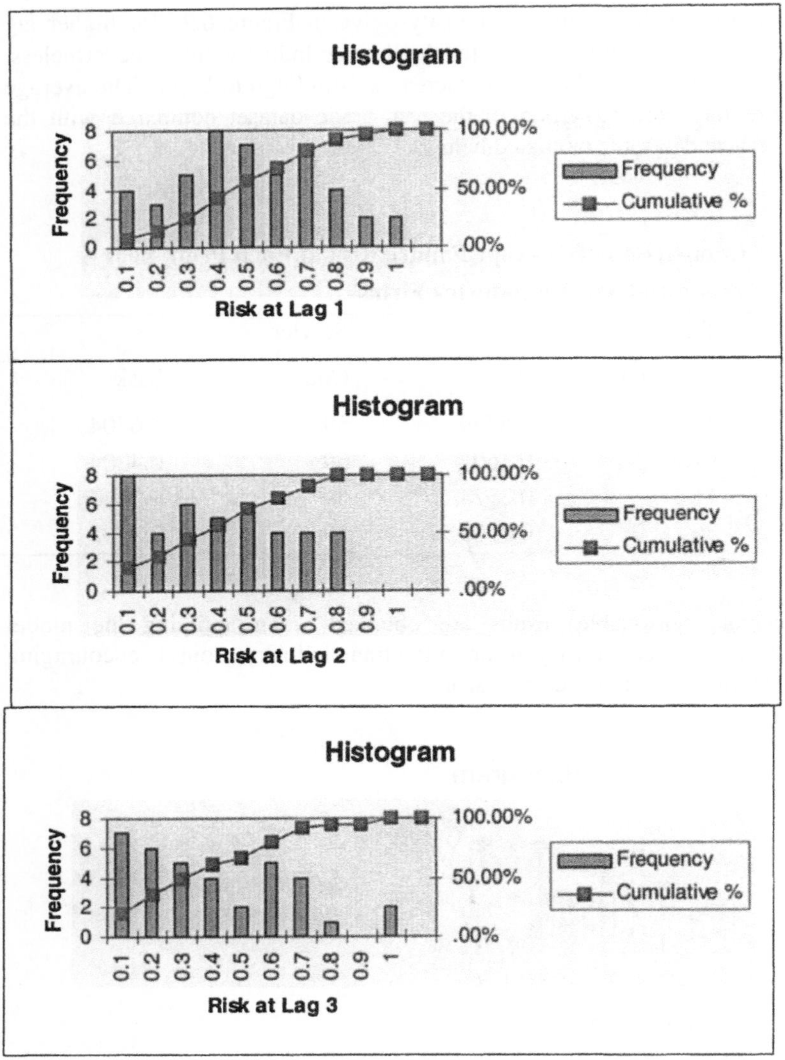

Figure 6.2 (Continued)

6.5 Conclusion

A number of important results are recorded. Firstly, the effects of the economy and the effects of the financial variables on failure risk were found to be mutually non-exclusionary within a logit model (i.e. significant variables remained significant independently of whether separate or combined datasets were used to model risk).

Secondly, although order of entry into a stepwise regression model must always be treated circumspectly, if judged by this criterion, the effects of the important macroeconomic variables are more significant, statistically, than the effects of the important internal financial ratios, to the risk of failure. This suggests that a benign external economic environment will allow a variety of firms of differing capabilities and financial sensitivity to survive and even prosper. This is an important result in the light of the methodological discussion of Chapter 3, lending empirical support to the argument that the static failed/non-failed firms concentrating solely on the internal financial ratios of the firm are flawed for both explanatory and predictive purposes. This is further supported by the use of firms from only one industry (Service) in the modelling design so that inter-industry effects do not confound the results.

With regard to the internal environment of the firms, the liquidity ratio, working capital to total assets vies with the external variables for early entry into the model and is consistent with past studies of financial distress across different research designs and time periods. Since the logit (or log-odds) function of failure risk is monotonic increasing with risk, a positive coefficient in the logit model implies that the risk estimate increases with the ratio and vice-versa if the coefficient is negative. In model (6.1) presented in this chapter, with estimated coefficients shown in Appendix H, working capital to total assets moves in the expected direction, opposite to failure risk. In other words, as this ratio increases and a greater proportion of the firm's assets is liquid, the expected failure risk decreases. On the other hand, cash flow from operations/total current liabilities has a negative coefficient, as expected for this ratio – a new addition to the model set of Chapter 4 when the external environment was excluded. It moves in the opposite direction to failure risk, consistent with other research findings that a lower coverage of current liabilities relates to a higher level of insolvency risk.

Thirdly, the effect of the Labour Market Tightness Factor, an external variable highly weighted (negatively) on the total number unemployed and (positively) on the change in the size of the employed labour force, is the most significant variable to company failure risk. The Expenditure Factor and the Cost of Capital Borrowing Factor, both taken in the previous year are also highly significant to failure risk. Specifically, as the labour market tightens, as the cost of capital borrowings increases, and as private, public and business expenditures decrease, the risk of company failure increases.

Fourthly, and probably most importantly, the logit model based on the variables statistically significant with respect to failure risk and represented by model (6.1) uses only a binary 0–1 input and yet provides a good instrument for measuring failure risk at each period prior to failure. It not only gives a logical result that the risk of failure increases with each period but also that it increases quite markedly in the final three years before failure. The risk is estimated at around one chance in four at three and four years prior, and increases to two chances in three at one year prior to failure – a jump in risk of 41 percent within two years.

In part because no holdout sample exists for the service industry for the same time period, the model formulation (6.1) was applied to a trade industry sample test set. The escalation of risk in the final four years is not as marked but still jumps 21 percent. This is, nevertheless, an encouraging result for the robustness and reliability of the model since one would not expect exactly the same patterns of failure risk across different industry groups.

Chapter 7

A Dynamic Model of Financial Distress: The Path to Failure

7.0 Introduction

In the previous three chapters the models of failure risk have an implicit assumption that the relationship between failure risk and the explanatory variables is independent of the stage reached by the firm on its path to failure. Under this assumption one is able to treat the firm-years as independent cases. This was the situation in the logit model formulation employed in Chapters 4, 5 and 6. Although exploratory in nature, these chapters developed models in their own right and so were informative about the possible comparative effects of the internal ratios and the external economy on failure risk, as well as the means of examining these effects together.

In this chapter the simplifying assumption of independence is dropped and a more explicit attempt made to build dynamic factors into the equations. This follows the philosophy of the book (see especially Chapter 3) in developing more complex models from simpler models situated within a family of related models.

In this chapter the first (exploratory) approach to building a model of failure risk that recognizes the sequential dependence of the firm-years within each firm includes a one-year lagged risk estimate as an explanatory variable (in addition to the internal financial variables and the external macro-economic variables). This is accomplished within a single-equation model of the type discussed in Chapter 3.5. To do this requires an initiating value for the lagged risk and this is taken from the combined model formulation (6.1). Estimates of lagged risk are then improved by successively modelling failure risk on each new lagged estimate in an iterative process. This model takes the form of one equation:

$$\log (P_t / \{1 - P_t\}) = \alpha_0 + \sum_{j=1}^{m} a_j X_{jt} + \beta_1 P_{t-1} \qquad (7.1)$$

where t includes all the years pooled for each firm i.e. t = T, T-1, T-2, T-3, where T is the final year prior to failure, and the X_j are the m explanatory variables, both the financial ratios and the economic factors.

The second approach to modelling failure risk is to incorporate the four years of panel data from each of the 60 firms into a model that recognizes the data from one firm as a single case consisting of a short time series (i.e. four periods that are integral to each other). The model consists of a set of four equations as a system with correlated errors that is viewed as a single model for estimation via generalized least squares. This technique of Seemingly Unrelated Regressions (SUR) was outlined in Chapter 3.4. Here, four separate model equations like formulation (6.1) are estimated and the data are no longer pooled over time for each firm but, rather, each firm contributes one year of its four years of financial and related external data to each of the four models. Each equation expresses the risk of failure for a particular lag period before failure, either one, two, three, or four years prior. These four equations then form a system to be estimated as an entity. By investigating the differences in parameter estimates, as well as their significance with respect to failure risk for each lag period, it is possible, via this method, to investigate the patterns of failure over the final four years of a service industry firm's existence.

The third approach to building a model of failure risk will be to explain some of the unexpected directions of the estimated parameter coefficients in the single-equation model (6.1) by building simultaneity into the set of model equations. Regressors that were treated as independent but which, in reality, are highly correlated, need to be estimated within different equations where they are recognized as dependent upon each other. The methods of two-stage and three-stage least squares[1] will be used to investigate these relationships. The formulation and empirical methodology for a general class of these models was detailed in Chapter 3.4.

7.1 Inclusion of Lagged Risk in a Single-Equation Logit Model of Failure Risk

The data set was modified to include, for each lag year, an estimate of failure risk for the previous year taken from model (6.1). Given there are no fifth year data, no estimate exists for the fifth year prior to failure, so an initial value of zero i.e. the theoretical lower limit of risk, was used as the lagged value for cases four years prior. Subsequently, other initial values were tested for model sensitivity to the initial estimate (in 7.2). Thus the stepwise logit model formulation (6.1) was re-estimated but with the inclusion, for the first time, of a lagged risk variable, PHATLAG1. Note that this estimation conforms to model B in the family of models found in Chapter 3.5.1, and note also that firm-years are still treated as independent observations in these models. See Appendix J for an extract of the SAS output for the stepwise regression procedure results for the final minimum adequate model of this first approach.

---

1 2SLS and 3SLS are often called 'instrumental variable regression' methods, as explained in Chapter 3.5.1.

The minimum adequate model[2] that resulted from the stepwise procedure included the same variables as model (6.1), as well as the variable PHATLAG1, which was found to be very strongly related to failure risk. Given its coefficient is positive, this indicates that failure risk in any year is probably most strongly related to the risk of failure in the previous year. This is a sensible dynamics-related result. In other words, beyond a certain point, movement towards failure can 'feed' forward on itself, making it more difficult to turn the firm's finances around once financial distress has taken hold. This is an important first step in modelling the dynamics as it suggests an 'error propagation' mechanism rather than a dampening mechanism is in operation within failing firms.

Classification comparisons[3] with model (6.1) (without lagged risk) are summarised in Table 7.1 – the Type II error shows some improvement and this is reflected in the overall classification accuracy.

Table 7.1 Classification Comparisons

	Model *with* Lagged Risk	Model *without* Lagged Risk
Overall Classification Accuracy	76.2%	71.9%
Type I Error	29.3%	29.3%
Type II Error	22%	27.7%
Somers' D	0.746	0.685

An Analysis of Variance and associated pairwise z-tests for differences between the estimated risks of failure (firm by lag year) from the model including risks lagged one year show the following:

The F-test for group mean differences in risk is still highly significant ($p<.0001$). Again, the pairwise z-tests for differences in proportions (one-tail) were used to test that the risk of failure decreases for each additional lag year although the risks of failure input into the model were, respectively, 1, 0, 0, 0.[4] The mean estimated risks for each lag year are given in Table 7.2. (One to four years prior to failure are denoted LAG0–LAG3.)

---

2 See Aitken (1974) and Feinberg (1977) for a discussion of adequate models, minimum adequate models, and the principle of parsimony.

3 Note the difference here in the use of classification compared to most bankruptcy studies. Here classification is a diagnostic tool, one among several others, whereas in other studies the classification is an end in itself for predictive purposes.

4 These are the initial values of Y_{ij}: the risk of failure in the next year, as defined in Chapter 4.4.

Table 7.2[5] **Comparisons of Estimated Risk**

Year	Average Risk from Model *with* Lagged Risk	Average Risk from Model *without* Lagged Risk
LAG0	0.6942	0.6704
LAG1	0.4104	0.4304
LAG2	0.2850	0.2644
LAG3	0.1581	0.2562

The mean estimated risks do indeed decrease with each extra lag ($p<.05$), including for LAG2 and LAG3 whereas, in the models tested, there was no significant difference in risk for these two years. Both results can be readily understood. In the new model, the constant estimate of zero input for PHATLAG1 attached to the fourth year prior has an influence on pulling down the value of the estimated average risk in that year. Nevertheless, it can be concluded from the model with estimated risk lagged one year, that the mean estimated risk of failure increases by a statistically significant amount for all four years prior to failure, with the qualification that the risk estimate for the fourth year prior may not be as reliable as the other three. More specifically, it can be seen from the table that the estimated risk of failure increases by more than 12 percent in both the fourth and third years before failure, i.e. a jump from a 16 percent probability at four years prior, to 41 percent at two years prior. The risk then climbs to nearly 70 percent at one year prior; a rise of 28 percent in the penultimate year before failure.

These new results help justify the use of model B in the family of models found in Chapter 3.5.1 in tying together the single-equation model formulations to the more complex multi-equation systems to follow. They also indicate how the uncritical and isolated use of models can provide misleading results. Incorporating a measure of lagged risk into the single-equation model is the simplest way to add the dynamic element into the model specification, yet the improvement in model fit is good and the sequential increase in estimated failure risk from year to year is also more marked than in the model with no dynamic included.

5 Note that given the 3:1:1:1 weighting on the lag years 0 – 3 respectively, and despite the fact that we are estimating single equation models here, these models obey the system-wide constraint that the sum of the average risk estimates should be consistent without enforcing this condition (The prior average risk value of $(\Sigma\Sigma\ w_{ij} \cdot p_{ij})/\Sigma\ \Sigma\ 1 =$ (58.3.1 + 59.1.0 + 59.1.0 + 59.1.0)/235 = 174/235=0.74 should equal the post value which is (58.3.0.6942 + 59.1.0.4104 + 59.1.0.285 + 59.1.0.1581)/235 =171.15/235 = 0.73).

7.1.1 Sensitivity Analysis to Failure Risk Estimated for the Fifth Year Prior to Failure

Two further analyses were conducted using different values of estimated failure risk in the fifth year prior to failure to input into PHATLAG1 in the fourth year prior.

The two values chosen for the constant estimated risk in the fifth year prior were the truncated values output for the fourth year prior (lag 3) in the previous two models discussed; viz. 0.25 for model (6.1) and 0.15 for the new model with lagged risks included. A third analysis used just three years of data and the estimated risk from the fourth year prior in model (6.1) provided the value for the variable PHATLAG1 for the third year prior. Table 7.3, overleaf, summarises the results of the sensitivity analysis.

From Table 7.3 it can be seen that when the failure risk estimate for the fifth year prior is decreased (as a set constant value for each analysis), the significance of PHATLAG1 to the model is increased (as is its coefficient in the model) and the model's accuracy in predicting both failing and non-failing firm-years in the estimate sample is also increased. A reduction in the Type I error results from using only three years of data including the variable risk estimate for the fourth year prior as output from model (6.1), however, the prediction accuracy both overall and for non-failed firm-years is reduced.

Consequently, all four years of data were used for modelling failure risk as an iterative process. In this process PHATLAG1 is updated for the final three years by each new model estimation, and a constant value of zero was used as its estimate input for the observations at four years prior.

7.1.2 Successive Model Iterations of Failure Risk on Lagged Risk

Successive models were estimated using the estimates of failure risk that are output from each previous model, lagging them, and then manually re-inputting them as lagged risks for the next iteration. Iteration was continued until successive models show little difference in the average estimated risks for each lag year, and little or no further improvement in the classification statistics. At each iteration, a stepwise logit model was fitted based on all the variables, internal and external to the firm from model (6.1).

Statistics for the minimum adequate model at each iteration are shown in the tables overleaf. Table 7.4 is an extended version of Table 7.1, and Table 7.5 is an extended version of Table 7.2. Both tables show the results of successive iterations.

Tables 7.4 to 7.6 show that after only three iterations, very close to apparent relative stability is reached. Figure 7.1 illustrates the pattern of the average risks in Table 7.5 for each of the four iterations compared with the initial values from model (6.1) – marked 'iteration0'.

Table 7.3 Classification Table

Constant Value imposed for PHATLAG1 in LAG3 year	Using 0.5 as cut-off failure risk for classification as 'fail' or 'nonfail' **Correct Classification**		**Incorrect Classification**		**Percentages**					
	As Fail	As Nonfail	As Fail	As Nonfail	Overall Correct	Correct Fail	Correct Nonfail	Coefficient PHATLAG1	Model Signif. Level	Somer's D
0.25	39	133	44	19	73.2	67.2	75.1	1.9717	0.0065	0.712
0.15	40	135	42	18	74.5	69.0	76.3	2.579	0.0003	0.726
0	41	138	39	17	76.2	70.7	78.0	3.095	0.0001	0.746
D.N.A.*	42	75	43	16	66.5	72.4	63.6	1.3019	0.085	0.677

* For the model in this row, only three years of data were used for each firm with the estimated PHAT values from the fourth year prior to failure substituting into PHATLAG1 for the third year prior.

Table 7.6 shows the parameter coefficients in the model for each subsequent iteration, i.e. the parameters of the minimum adequate model from a stepwise procedure in each case except for Iteration 4, where the minimum adequate model did not include PC2_1. An extra column has been added to the table for the model including PC2_1 for comparison purposes as some coefficients are altered more than others as a consequence of the dropped variable. Note that when either R6 or R15 were included, similar classification statistics resulted but only the first iteration included R15 before R6 in the final model.[6] Note also the increasing weight on the lagged risk at each successive iteration.

Note: As explained above, the columns in Table 7.6 represent the minimum adequate model for each iteration. Therefore the spaces in the table represent variables that were omitted in that particular model but were included in others.

The stabilized values of Table 7.5 for the 3rd and 4th iterations show increases in the estimated failure risk for the two lag intervals: 100 percent increase for the interval 'three years prior to two years prior to failure' (from around 0.2 to 0.4), and for the interval 'two years prior to one year prior to failure', an 85 percent increase (from around 0.4 to 0.74). The relative magnitude of these increases is more easily visualized in Figure 7.1.

Table 7.4 Classification Statistics for Each Model Iteration

	4th iteration	**3rd iteration**	**2nd iteration**	**1st iteration**	**Model (6.1) without PHATLAG1**
Overall Class'n Accuracy	81.3%	81.7%	77.9%	76.2%	71.9%
Type I Error	25.9%	22.4%	27.6%	29.3%	29.3%
Type II Error	16.4%	16.9%	20.3%	22%	27.7%
Somers' D	0.812	0.814	0.776	0.746	0.685

6 This was also the case for model (6.1).

Table 7.5 Average Estimated Risk for Each Lag Year

Year	4th iteration	3rd iteration	2nd iteration	1st iteration	Model (6.1) without PHATLAG1
LAG0	0.7368	0.7365	0.7054	0.6942	0.6704
LAG1	0.4065	0.3989	0.4374	0.4104	0.4304
LAG2	0.2022	0.2181	0.2347	0.2850	0.2644
LAG3	0.1197	0.1118	0.1483	0.1581	0.2562

Table 7.6 Parameter Estimates for Each Iteration

	Iteration 1	Iteration 2	Iteration 3	Iteration 4	Iteration 4 without PC2_1
INTERCPT	0.4575	0.6889	0.2873	0.335	0.323
PC3	0.7046	0.6972	0.6006	0.5809	0.3486
PC4	0.364	0.3646	0.3613	0.3206	0.2229
PC5	-0.5961	-0.6997	-0.6282	-0.6321	-0.514
PC2_1	0.3529	0.2921	0.2183	0.1946	
PC5_1	-0.7904	-0.7592	-0.731	-0.7608	-0.5843
R2	-0.0196	-0.0211	-0.0214	-0.0206	-0.0206
R7	-0.0167	-0.0173	-0.0175	-0.0163	-0.0161
RCD18	-0.5819	-0.8897	-0.7953	-0.7213	-0.6883
RC21_1	-1.6214	-1.5708	-1.2437	-1.3908	-1.3459
RC21_4	1.6087	1.3646	1.3414	1.5178	1.5096
PHATLAG1	3.0956	4.0181	5.5326	5.5986	5.8372
R15	-0.0779				
R6		0.00719	0.00962	0.00873	0.00948

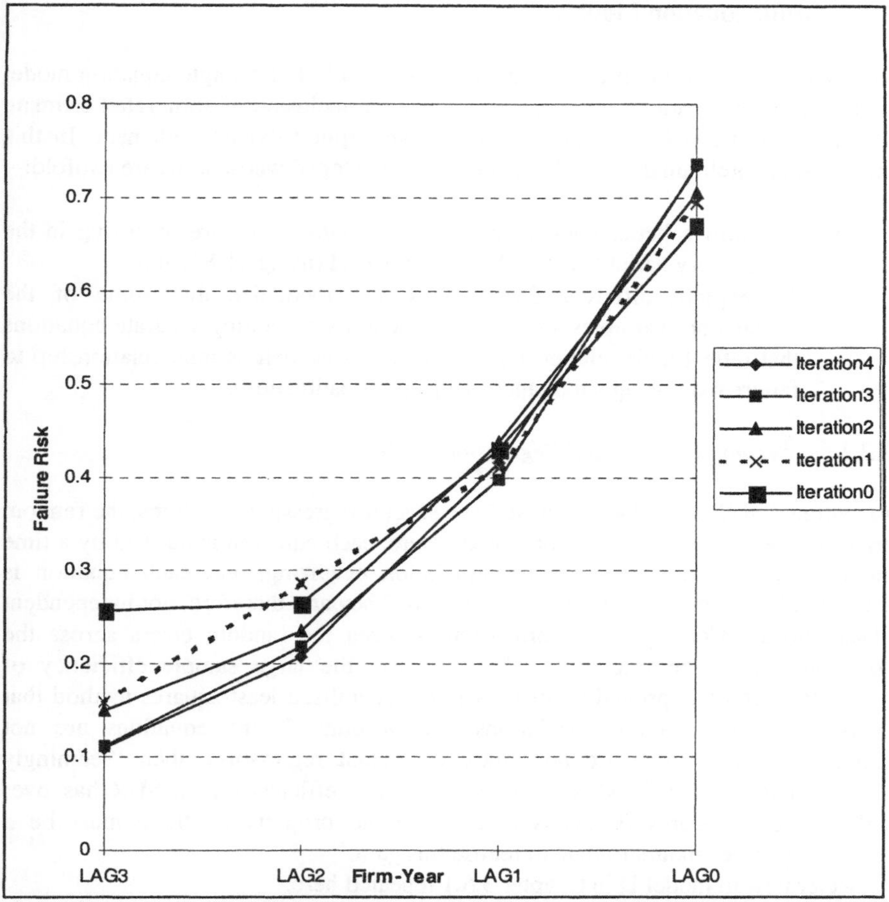

Figure 7.1 Estimated Average Risk of Failure by Lagged Firm-Year for Successive Model Iterations on Lagged Risk

One may conclude that these increases coincide with a very rapid decline in financial stability for these firms as they approach bankruptcy. This rapid decline is borne out by the increasing weight on the lagged risk at each iteration indicating a distress feedback mechanism. To gain more understanding of *how* this occurs, the next step is to investigate the changes that occur at this time in the financial and external indicators. In order to do so, the lag years are analysed via multi-equation estimation.

The reduction in the estimate for the fourth year prior probability of failure, if not entirely due to the input zeros at five years prior, also seems realistic. It forms some justification for the adequacy of a four-year window for this study especially given the consideration that firms are more easily lost to the analysis through censoring (due to missing data) when larger time windows are employed.

7.2 Multi-equation Models

The dual purpose of the previous section was (a) to link the single-equation model specification to the multi-equation systems via the inclusion of an iterated estimate of lagged failure risk and (b) to introduce an explicit dynamic element. In this section some preliminary model structures are developed whose aims are twofold:

- To allow a better understanding of the changes that are occurring in the explanatory variables over the failure period (using SUR), and
- To explore different formulations that recognize that some of the explanatory variables are interdependent, by modelling separate equations that reflect their relationship to each other as well as their relationship to failure risk (using simultaneous equations estimation).

7.2.1 *Seemingly Unrelated Regression Models*

As outlined in Chapter 3.4, when we have several regression equations, the random errors of the equations can be correlated. Here, each equation is defined by a time element relative to bankruptcy or liquidation occurring, and each equation is estimated from a data set of the *same* 60 firms. They are, therefore, not independent observations. Consequently, correlation between the random errors across the equations cannot be ruled out. In this case, the large sample efficiency of estimation can be improved by using a joint generalised least-squares method that takes the cross-equation correlations into account. If the equations are not simultaneous (i.e. there are no jointly dependent regressors), then 'Seemingly Unrelated Regressions' (SUR), can be used. The efficiency gain SUR has over ordinary least squares (OLS) is a large sample property so there must be a reasonably large amount of data to realise this gain.[7]

Refer now to model D in Chapter 3.5.1 repeated here:

$$\text{(i) } \log(P_t / \{1 - P_t\}) = \alpha_t + \sum_{j=1}^{m} a_{t,j} X_{j,t} \qquad (3.18a)$$

$$\text{(ii) } \log(P_{t-1} / \{1 - P_{t-1}\}) = \alpha_{t-1} + \sum_{j=1}^{m} a_{t-1,j} X_{j,t-1} \qquad (3.18b)$$

[7] For a more detailed discussion of SUR, refer to Pindyck and Rubinfeld (1981, pp. 331-3).

$$\text{(iii) } \log(P_{t-2} / \{1 - P_{t-2}\}) = \alpha_{t-2} + \sum_{j=1}^{m} a_{t-2,\, j}\, X_{j,t\,-2} \qquad (3.18c)$$

$$\text{(iv) } \log(P_{t-3} / \{1 - P_{t-3}\}) = \alpha_{t-3} + \sum_{j=1}^{m} a_{t-3,\, j}\, X_{j,.\, t-3} \qquad (3.18d)$$

This equation set was estimated[8] including all the ratios and principal components that were important in the single equation model (6.1) as well as R6 from model (4.1), with 60 replicates for each of the four time periods before failure. The estimates for P_t were taken from a 'full', or rather, a less restricted, single-equation model.[9] This was because if either the binary event outcome values of '0' and '1' or the risk estimates from (6.1) were to be used, the parameter estimates would be either degenerate[10] or biased as a result of a singular system.[11] See Appendix K for an extract of the SAS output for the SUR estimation. For ease of comparison, the parameter estimates for all four equations are shown in Table 7.7, overleaf, along with the approximate significance values of the T ratio for each coefficient parameter and the R-Square value for each equation.

It is important to note that since the dependent variable is only an estimate of risk taken from a less restricted model than the system equations estimated here, the estimation is largely exploratory and experimental rather than being expected to provide definitive parameter estimates. The values in the table are used only for coefficient comparisons between different lag years and are, by no means, absolute values for which generalized conclusions can be made. The following explanation of the system estimates needs to be qualified by this fact.

In particular, evaluation of parameter estimates needs to be tempered by the fact that the SUR is part of an iterated set of estimations. It may, for example, be a consequence of this that the R-Square statistics are all reasonably high. Nevertheless, allowing for this, the results mean that these estimated models explain much more of the variability in the estimated failure risk than a mean model explains. In other words, using model (3.18a) (equation (i)) as an example, the regressors and coefficients shown in Table 7.7 together explain or account for approximately 85 percent of the total variance in the failure risk estimated for the

---

8 Using SUR in SAS/ETS PROC MODEL

9 The 'full' model in this case was a single-equation model like (6.1) only using as many of the regressors (ratios and principal components) that showed significance ($p<0.25$) with failure risk and that did not significantly reduce the number of cases in the analysis set by their inclusion (because of missing values and measurement errors.)

10 The binary outcome disobeys the assumptions of LS regression and, in any case, each equation would have either a set of 1's or 0's as the Y vector, which would give a naive solution equal to a constant value.

11 The SUR estimation would be biased (from singular matrices) if the estimates of p from model (6.1) were used here because the right-hand sides of the equations are exactly the same as in model (6.1). The fit would be almost perfect.

Table 7.7 **The SUR Model**

Coefficient Parameters for SUR Model					Approximate Significance of the t-value for the coefficient			
Variable Name	**Equation (i)**	**Equation (ii)**	**Equation (iii)**	**Equation (iv)**	**Equation (i)**	**Equation (ii)**	**Equation (iii)**	**Equation (iv)**
					Prob>|T|	Prob>|T|	Prob>|T|	Prob>|T|
INTERCEPT	1.5006	1.0887	1.8547	1.1986	0.0001	0.0011	0.0001	0.0016
PC3, LABOUR MARKET TIGHTNESS FACTOR	1.0436	1.4164	0.8864	0.6579	0.0001	0.0001	0.0001	0.0001
R2, WORKING CAPITAL/TOTAL ASSETS	-0.0220	-0.0172	-0.0277	-0.0235	0.0001	0.0001	0.0001	0.0001
PC5(LAG1), EXPENDITURE FACTOR	-0.9058	-1.1573	-0.8328	-0.5154	0.0001	0.0001	0.0001	0.0001
R7, TOTAL LIABILITIES/TOTAL ASSETS	-0.0156	-0.0150	-0.0277	-0.0151	0.0001	0.0001	0.0001	0.0001
RC21_1, SALES/NET PLANT, LOWEST LEVEL	-2.7152	-1.6083	-2.5446	-2.4906	0.0001	0.0024	0.0145	0.0001
RC21_4, SALES/NET PLANT, HIGHEST LEVEL	1.2280	1.4145	2.5893	1.7550	0.0006	0.0165	0.0001	0.0002

Table 7.7 (continued)

PC5, EXPENDITURE FACTOR	-0.8133	-1.1417	-0.7559	-0.3921	0.0005	0.0001	0.0001	0.0021
PC4, CONSTRUCTION ACTIVITY FACTOR	0.5029	0.5951	0.6136	0.3744	0.0001	0.0001	0.0001	0.0001
PC2(LAG1), COST OF CAPITAL BORROWING FACTOR	0.5742	0.8538	0.5376	0.3703	0.0001	0.0001	0.0001	0.0004
RCD18, INTEREST COVERAGE AFTER TAX, HIGHER CATEGORY	-0.6165	-0.5494	-1.1885	-0.8920	0.0058	0.0114	0.0001	0.0001
R15, CASH FLOW FROM OPERATIONS/TOTAL CURRENT LIABS.	-0.1053	0.0464	0.0012	-0.0833	0.003	0.4328	0.9863	0.1395
R6, NET INCOME/TOTAL ASSETS	0.0019	0.0027	0.0003	-0.0002	0.3051	0.0546	0.8694	0.8309
R-SQUARE	**0.85**	**0.74**	**0.88**	**0.88**				

service industry data set[12] in the final year before failure. The best fit occurs three years before failure (lag 2) with a comparative R-Square value of 0.88 and the worst fit at two years prior (lag 1) with an R-Square value of 0.74.

It can be seen from the table that those variables fitted earlier in the stepwise procedure of Chapter 6 (i.e. with the highest joint significance to failure risk in the pooled lag years model) remain highly significant *over all four years* prior to failure and also have consistent signs on the coefficients over the four years. This finding is most important as it lends some weight to the validity of failure model specifications with respect to these variables. As a consequence, these variables can be more confidently used in failure prediction models as their discriminatory powers are reasonably long-term (at least of four years duration before failure). Given this discriminatory robustness over time it may be useful to examine the relative sizes of the coefficients of each of these significant variables over the four lag years. This is in case there are patterns occurring that might help us to understand how a service firm transforms itself from a going concern into a failed firm, at least within the four-year window of this study.

Although some of the parameter estimates change only slightly between the lag years (notably, working capital to total assets, total liabilities to total assets, interest coverage), it is the variables that show larger differences that are of interest here. These are:

PC3, the Labour Market Tightness Factor – This variable has its most pronounced effect in the penultimate year before failure, increasing directly with failure risk, i.e. the more tight the labour market, the higher is the failure risk at this time. The size of the coefficient increases each year from four years prior to two years prior and then drops slightly in the final year. Recall (for all economic factors) that its name does not encompass all that the factor stands for and may not be entirely accurate. If labour is the major factor acting here, then perhaps because key workers cannot easily find work in a tight labour market, they do not leave for other jobs until relatively late, when they realise the firm is really in trouble. The loss of these key workers would then further affect the health of the firm. It is vital to note that PC3 cannot be solely identified with labour market elements. Its use has, however, suggested a new mechanism, i.e. loss of key workers, as an element in firm failure. This is a hypothesis that can be tested in future research.

PC5 and PC5 (LAG1) – The Expenditure Factor, Business, Private and Public measured in the same year and in the previous year: As with PC3, both have their greatest effect in the penultimate year before failure, working against failure risk, i.e. the lower the expenditure in the external economy the higher is the effect on failure risk at this time. The size of both coefficients increases negatively each year from four years prior to two years prior and then they drop slightly in the final year. This indicates that low expenditure levels in the economy have most effect up to two years before failure and after that, perhaps, other factors are more important.

---

12 As measured by the variations in estimated risk from the less restricted model.

This possibility, like the labour market mechanism, is only tentative but testable. It is also very complex. Thus, even small changes in spending may become absolutely crucial when a firm is already very weak but may have little impact when it is sound. The time profile of such impacts is also one worthy of investigation.

Thus, the pattern of effects for these significant external factors is such that the most pronounced effect occurs and increases from four to two years before failure and drops only slightly at one year prior. These results suggest that if the firm is already vulnerable to failure, low expenditure levels in the economy and a tight labour market at this time can have a devastating effect on the ultimate solvency of the firm.

RC21_4, Sales/Net Plant ratio in the highest category – This variable is diminishing in its effect on failure risk in the final three years before failure. When a firm has little or no fixed assets,[13] this ratio is highest and works to increase failure risk. This effect is most pronounced at three years prior to failure and is also statistically most significant at this time ($p=0.0001$). This suggests that (a) whatever fixed assets can be sold are being sold at this time to finance debt (thus reducing the denominator) or (b) many service firms with little or no fixed assets to sell in order to satisfy creditors find their financial position worsening as a result. As a corollary to this logic, RC21_1, Sales/Net Plant ratio in the lowest category, works to reduce failure risk relatively consistently and significantly across all years prior, except for a drop in this effect at two years prior to failure. There is no specific reason for suggesting this variable should have such a pattern of values.

For the variables entering later in the stepwise procedure (i.e. with less significance to failure risk in the pooled-time model (6.1)), the significance levels show, as a rough guide, that at certain lag years these variables have a much more significant effect on failure risk than they do at other lag years. For these variables, the signs on the coefficients can also change between lag years especially when some of these coefficients are not statistically significant at certain lag-years.

It is this very inconsistency of significance (and hence, sign) over time that is the major reason for the lower significance of these variables in the pooled-time single-equation model (6.1). The coefficient effects in the pooled model were averaged out over time and the power of any significance tests applied to them was consequently reduced. In other words, if these are, indeed, important discriminating variables for failure risk but only at certain lag years, then model (6.1), without any dynamic structure, was mis-specified via omitted variables and its isolation from an overall systems model.

Here lies the justification for multi-equation modelling of failure risk using time series as well as cross-sectional data for the analysis. Along with other empirical results stemming from the adoption of a coherent and general modelling

13 Recall from Chapter 4 that service firms often do not own their fixed assets but rather lease them, making the denominator of this ratio small and their financial viability, as a result, more vulnerable.

methodology, this tells us that we must be extremely wary of the strong empirical results that are often purported to flow from the mass of simple, single-equation models that are reported in the literature (see Chapter 2).

Of these variables that enter the model later, the most noticeable difference between the lag years is the significance to failure risk of the cash flow ratio, R15, Cash Flow from Operations/Total Current Liabilities, *in the final year before failure* (p=0.003) – its effect is not significant in the previous two years (p>0.43), and it has only some significance four years prior to failure (p<0.14). In the two years when the parameters are statistically significant, this cash flow ratio moves in the opposite direction to failure risk which is as expected; i.e. the higher the ratio, the lower the failure risk. This ratio measures the ability of the firm to meet its short-term commitments from cash flow. From this empirical evidence, it may just be the most important ratio to trigger failure.

That the cash flow to current liabilities ratio has an immediate association with failure should not be surprising. It is associated with an inability to trade unless financial institutions or other internal and/or external sources of funds are prepared to cover the shortfall. The legal requirements upon operating companies can also play a role in activating this ratio as a trigger. However, if this ratio does represent a short-term inability to trade profitably, then we have seen that longer-term fundamentals in previous years have led the company to this position. Given these sorts of complex mechanisms over time, a dynamic approach has much to recommend it. The simple comparison of failed/non-failed firms must necessarily miss these mechanisms completely and, almost certainly, place too much emphasis on the effect of variables having a major impact only in the failing year.

This allows us to re-assess much of the literature with new insight. Recall that the inclusion of the cash flow from operations/total current liabilities ratio in the single-equation model (6.1) concurred with other research findings[14] that a lower coverage of current liabilities relates to a higher level of insolvency risk and that Beaver's (1966) best ratio (using a univariate approach) was also 'Cash Flow to Total Debt'.[15] This ratio may thus be regarded as a frequent immediate trigger for bankruptcy. If, as is suggested, it is this final trigger, it is not surprising if it is important in the final year but not at other times. Thus the significant result at four years prior to failure (although not strong) is an apparent anomalous empirical result within this work which requires a specific and detailed investigation beyond the scope of this book.

A different pattern of significance was evident for the profitability ratio, R6, Return on Assets. This ratio is significantly related to failure risk (p<0.06) *only* in the second year prior to failure (lag 1), but in no other year (p>0.3). The sign is,

---

14 Viz. Beaver (1966); Blum (1974); Mensah (1983); Norton and Smith (1979); Gilbert *et al* (1990).

15 This statement must be qualified by the fact that Beaver's definition of cash flow, as for many of the early cash flow models, was 'net income plus depreciation, depletion and amortization' which Largay and Stickney (1980) pointed out is not an accurate measure of cash flow but, rather, of working capital.

again, anomalous, moving unexpectedly in the same direction as failure risk as it did in the models of Chapters 4 and 6. As explained in Chapter 4.5.4, this is potentially connected with multicollinearity of the regressors and this problem will be addressed in the next section, when simultaneity is introduced into the equation set. When the set of three equations (3.18a) to (3.18c) also includes an estimate of lagged failure risk on the right-hand side, the parameter estimates hardly change and the coefficient of lagged risk has its highest significance of $p=0.14$ at two years prior to failure (lag 1). (See Appendix L for an extract of the SAS output.) One can conclude that although lagged risk was highly significant to failure risk in the pooled single-equation model (7.1), it is no longer statistically significant at even the 0.1 level within a system of equations where failure risk is estimated separately for each lag year.

7.2.2 Simultaneous Equation Models

If the system of equations is simultaneous, i.e. when a dependent variable in one equation becomes a regressor in another, one can either use 2SLS or combine the 2SLS and SUR methods to take into account both simultaneous equation bias and cross-equation correlation of the errors using 'Three Stage Least-Squares'(3SLS). As outlined in Chapter 3.4.1, to remove the simultaneous equation bias in the linear case, the endogenous variables on the right-hand side of the equations are replaced by the predicted values from a preliminary, first-stage, instrumental variable regression. The instrumental variables are uncorrelated with the random, or observed error term and used as regressors to model the predicted values. In the 2SLS case, the parameter estimates are then obtained by a second regression using the earlier predicted values of the jointly dependent variables as regressors.

In the nonlinear case, nonlinear ordinary least-squares estimation can be performed iteratively to yield a simultaneous equation estimation, as discussed for Model (C) of Chapter 3.5.1.

Because of its importance in this area of research, the simplest form of the logit model, within a simultaneous system, is indicated below. Despite its apparent simplicity, this is an intrinsically nonlinear simultaneous system because of the presence of the logit, dictated by the binary endogenous variable for failure. The formulations for models (3.16) and (3.17a) from Chapter 3.5.1 are repeated here, only extended to n explanatory variables:

$$\text{(i) } \log(P_t / \{1 - P_t\}) = a_0 + a_1 X_{1t} + a_2 X_{2t} + \text{- - - -} \; a_n X_{nt} + b_1 R_{t-1} + b_0 Q_t \qquad (3.16^+)$$

$$\text{(ii) } Q_t = \alpha_0 + \alpha_1 P_t + \sum_{j=1}^{m} a_j X_{jt} \qquad (3.17a)$$

The two equations are defined in terms of variables such that they are each over-identified thus requiring use of a 2SLS or 3SLS estimation. Note, of course, that more than two equations can be included in such a set of simultaneous equations. Exploratory sets of equations of this type were estimated for the service industry failed firms using 2SLS and 3SLS.[16] As in 7.2.1, equation (i) can include the same ratios and principal components that were important in the single-equation models of Chapters 4, 5 and 6, and as this is still a pooled-time equation, it will have exactly the same model formulation as for model (6.1) when both the external and internal variables were included.[17] Consequently, only the effect of the simultaneity with the second equation can change the parameter estimates from those of (6.1).

Owing to the large significant correlations between three of the ratios included in equation (i),[18] i.e. variables R2, R7 and R6, as discussed in Chapter 4.5.4, the addition of equation (ii) and further simultaneous equations to the equation system can provide an avenue for deeper exploration into these relationships. For instance, some of the anomalies surrounding the signs of some of the ratio coefficients (specifically that of R7 and R6) can, perhaps, be explained in part by the theoretical construction and estimation of such a system. Other relationships of interest that can be explored here might be, in particular, the interactions of the internal and the external variables to the firm.[19] One such relationship of interest, among others, might be between the Cost of Capital Borrowing (PC2) and Interest Coverage after Tax (RCD18).

Examples of these theoretical constructions are given in the following sections.

7.2.3 *Working Capital/Total Assets as a Dependent Variable*

A number of these relationships were explored initially using stepwise linear regressions, isolating the empirically important (i.e. statistically significant, $p < 0.15$) from the full set of variables in the data set. Note that the first principal component, the 'Economy Growth' factor, which was omitted from regressions estimating failure risk due to a statistical artifact,[20] can be, and was reintroduced for these stepwise procedures.

The linear stepwise regression method with the most significant ratio to failure risk, Working Capital/Total Assets, R2, employed as the dependent variable gave the following model:

---

16 Using SAS/ETS PROC MODEL

17 Note: The lagged endogenous variable R_{t-1} (eg. P_{t-1}) is not included in model (6.1) and so was left out of particular formulations of (3.16^{+}) at this stage though it was included in particular formulations of (3.17a) for the stepwise procedure estimates of various examples of Q_t in this chapter. As we will see, P_{t-1} turned out to be not significant in all cases of these system model examples. Later, when P_{t-1} is included in the model of equation (7.4) and (7.5), it is also not significant to that system of equations.

18 Specifically in models (4.1), (6.1) and (7.1).

19 No interactions can occur between the external variables as they are principal components which, by definition, are orthogonal, and any linear dependencies between lagged principal components has been eliminated by stepwise regressions in the models of Chapters 5, 6 and 7.

20 Detailed in Chapter 5.2.

(All variables have p<=0.0001 and are shown in order of stepwise entry into the model. See Appendix M for an extract of the SAS output.)

$$R2 = 90.2114 - 0.7692\, R7 - 68.9445\, P_t(\text{est.}) + 4.589\, PC3 + 2.5700\, PC1 + 0.1423\, R6 \qquad (7.2)$$

where R7 = Total Liabilities/Total Assets,

P_t(est.) = Estimate of failure risk, P_t, from a less restricted model (See 7.2.1)

PC3 = Labour Market Tightness Factor

PC1 = Economy Growth Factor

R6 = Return on Assets

Note that this model is allowed to be determined by a stepwise procedure. This is for two reasons; first, we are not testing a well-defined theoretical model for R2, which would precisely determine the variables and their form to be entered, and second, we require a well-defined empirical equation for the simultaneous system.

The expected strong negative correlation between Working Capital/Total Assets and Total Liabilities/Total Assets is borne out by the negative sign on R7 in the model equation. As Total Liabilities becomes a larger multiple of Total Assets, then Working Capital becomes a smaller multiple (or a negative one) of Total Assets. The strong positive correlation between Working Capital/Total Assets and Return on Assets (Net Income/Total Assets) gives a positive sign on the coefficient of R6. This reflects the movement of Net Income with Working Capital. The positive sign on PC1, the Economy Growth Factor, shows that Working Capital/Total Assets moves with general growth in the economy. Similarly, the positive sign on PC3, the Labour Market Tightness Factor, indicates that in periods of high employment (tight labour market), Working Capital is a larger multiple of Total Assets. The large negative coefficient on the estimate of failure risk in the same period means that a firm for which the model predicts a high risk of failure (financially distressed) has a smaller or negative working capital ratio (low liquidity).[21]

Including equation (7.2) in a simultaneous equations system together with an equation with the formulation of model (6.1) gave the estimated parameters for the system model shown in Table 7.8, above. At this stage it is absolutely vital to note that this is a purely illustrative system of equations. It is intended to show the modelling methodology in operation rather than being a test of a specific theory of bankruptcy. Generally such a test will be explicit in such models.

---

21 Note: The estimate of failure risk lagged one period was not included in the final model under the stepwise procedure (p > 0.85) once P_t had already been included.

Table 7.8 Parameter Estimates for the First System Model

Equation For Failure Risk Variables Included	System model		Comparison with Model (6.1)	
	Estimate	Prob>|T|	Estimate	Approx. Prob>|T|
INTERCEPT	-0.0078	0.9542	1.4658	0.0002
PC3, LABOUR MARKET TIGHTNESS FACTOR	0.8283	0.0001	0.9115	0.0001
R2, WORKING CAPITAL/TOTAL ASSETS	0.0010	0.0534	-0.0206	0.0001
PC5_1, EXPENDITURE FACTOR LAGGED 1 YEAR	-0.7500	0.0001	-0.8011	0.0001
RC21_1,SALES/NET PLANT LOWEST VALUES	-2.3854	0.0001	-2.2866	0.0005
RC21_4,SALES/NET PLANT HIGH VALUES	1.4931	0.0001	1.6171	0.0018
PC5, EXPENDITURE FACTOR	-0.7227	0.0001	-0.7695	0.0021
PC4, CONSTRUCTION ACTIVITY FACTOR	0.4005	0.0001	0.4133	0.0032
PC2_1, COST OF CAPITAL BORROWING FACTOR LAG1	0.4526	0.0001	0.4736	0.0004
RCD18,INTEREST COVERAGE AFTER TAX ≥0 (DUMMY)	-0.6827	0.0001	-0.6916	0.0192
R15,CASH FLOW FROM OPERATIONS/TOTAL CURRENT. LIAB	-0.1106	0.0011	-0.0821	0.1239
R7, TOTAL LIABILITIES/TOTAL ASSETS	excluded		-0.0166	0.0001

Table 7.8 (continued)

Equation For Working Capital/Total Assets	**System Model**		**Compare With Model (7.2)**	
	Estimate	Prob>|T|	Estimate	Prob>|F|
INTERCEPT	71.0104	0.0001	90.2114	0.0001
R7, TOTAL LIABILITIES/TOTAL ASSETS	-0.7731	0.0001	-0.7692	0.0001
R6, NET INCOME/TOTAL ASSETS	0.1160	0.0001	0.1423	0.0001
P_t,ESTIMATED RISK OF FAILURE (FROM FULL MODEL)	-20.0970	0.0001	-68.9445	0.0001
PC3, LABOUR MARKET TIGHTNESS FACTOR	1.8227	0.0001	4.5891	0.0001
PC1,ECONOMY GROWTH FACTOR	1.2375	0.0001	2.5670	0.0001

Coefficient values are tabulated in Table 7.8, together with significance values for the T and F ratios shown as well as comparisons with the corresponding non-system estimates of models (6.1) and (7.2). See Appendix N for an extract of the more detailed SAS output.

The method used was 3SLS instrumental regression as explained in Chapter 3.4.1.[22] An extra consideration in estimating system models is that there needs to be at least as many instruments as the maximum number of parameters (including the intercept term) in any equation for unbiased parameter estimates, i.e. the identification problem. Note that the eleven-variable model (6.1) is reduced here to ten, excluding R7, Total Liabilities/Total Assets. R7 was removed from equation (i) because (a) its relationship to failure risk became statistically not significant in that equation (p=0.59), and (b) the relationship of R7 with failure risk appears, therefore, to be indirect, through its highly significant (p=0.0001) relationship with R2 in equation (ii).

These results occurred because R7 is highly correlated with the endogenous variable, R2, Working Capital/Total Assets and so is an instrumental variable in equation (ii) for estimating R2. Recall that the direction of the coefficient of R7 was unexpectedly negative in the single-equation risk models of Chapters 4, 6 and 7. (See discussion of indirect factors in Chapter 4.5.4.)

The additional equation for R2 has caused that ratio's coefficient in equation (i) to be reduced in magnitude and to change direction from its value in model (6.1). Similarly, the weighting on the estimated risk of failure in the same period is much

[22] Note that few econometric textbooks discuss the selection of instruments for nonlinear models. Refer to Bowden and Turkington (1984), p. 180-182.

reduced in the system model from its value in the non-system model (–20 cf. –69 respectively) but it is still highly significant ($p<0.0001$).

Note also that when the formulation of model (6.1) was replaced by that of model (7.1) in equation (i), i.e. including an estimate of lagged risk, there was very little difference in the parameter estimates and this was due to the statistically insignificant contribution of P_{t-1} ($p=0.38$) within this system of equations. All other parameters were still statistically significant ($p<0.15$). For illustration only, the parameter estimates from the 2SLS analysis including the non-significant P_{t-1} are shown for this system of two equations:

$$\text{(i) } W = \text{logit } P = 0.1717 + 0.8303\ PC3 + 0.0015\ R2 - 0.7680\ PC5(lag1) + 0.4598\ PC2(lag1) - 1.9877\ RC21\_1 + 1.3461\ RC21\_4 - 0.7136\ PC5(\text{no lag}) + 0.3290\ PC4(\text{no lag}) - 0.8970\ RCD18 - 0.0501\ R15 + 0.3453 P_{t-1}(\text{est.}) \quad (7.4)$$

$$\text{(ii) } R2 = 73.3484 - 0.7752\ R7 + 0.1217\ R6 + 2.5953\ PC3 - 29.752\ P_t(\text{est.}) + 1.6567\ PC1 \quad (7.5)$$

The contribution of P_{t-1} in equation (i) is, nevertheless, still positive and working to increase failure risk at each subsequent period.

These results and differences clearly indicate that a properly-specified system estimation can have more than a marginal impact on parameter estimates and their statistical significance. Consequently it cannot be ignored any longer in bankruptcy research.

7.2.4 *Interest Coverage after Tax as a Dependent Variable*

Another of the relationships explored, using stepwise linear regressions to isolate the important (i.e. statistically significant, $p < 0.15$) variables from the full set of variables in the data set, was that between the external factor, PC2, Cost of Capital Borrowing, and the leverage ratio, R18, Interest Coverage after Tax. R18 is calculated as Net Income before Extraordinary Items plus Interest Expense/Interest Expense. In eighteen cases within the data this ratio had a zero denominator, so the earlier analyses used a dummy 0/1 variable, RCD18, where a '1' denoted that either the interest was covered or, if there was no interest expense, then the numerator was positive. Here, a continuous variable measure was preferred for a stepwise linear regression with R18 as dependent variable, so the positive and negative infinite values were replaced by, respectively, the 95th and 5th percentile values from the full data set.

The linear stepwise regression method with R18 as dependent variable gave the following model:

(All variables have $p<=0.14$ and are shown in order of stepwise entry into the model. See Appendix O for an extract of the SAS output.)

$$R18 = -5.4391 + 0.1300\ R6 + 2.1023\ R15 - 21.7212\ RC21\_2 + 3.4304\ R4$$

$$+ 0.1841\,R7 + 0.0407\,R5 - 21.0339\,P_t(est.) - 23.3336\,RC21\_1 + 12.8033\,RC20\_3 + 1.1806\,PC2 \qquad (7.3)$$

where: R18=Interest Coverage after Tax
R6 = Net Income/Total Assets
R15=Cash Flow from Operations/Total Current Liabilities
RC21_2=Sales/Net Plant 5-25% values
R4=Quick ratio or Acid Test ratio
R7=Total Liabilities/Total Assets
R5=Retained Earnings/Total Assets
P_t(est.)=Estimate of Failure Risk from full model
RC21_1=Sales/Net Plant lowest values
RC20_3=Sales/Inventory 75th-95th percentile
PC2=Cost of Capital Borrowing Factor

The Cost of Capital Borrowing Factor, PC2, does indeed have a significant relationship with the dependent variable but in an unexpected direction. Taken literally the results indicate that at times when interest rates are high, the firm is more likely to be able to cover its interest expense. On the face of it this result is nonsensical and no specific explanation for the result can be offered.

Similarly, the ratio, Total Liabilities/Total Assets has an unexpected negative correlation with the Interest Coverage ratio. If the firm relies increasingly on debt finance and it suffers a trading downturn then it is more likely to be unable to meet its debt repayment commitments. For this reason, one would expect that the Interest Coverage ratio would be inversely related to the leverage ratio, Total Liabilities/Total Assets, but the data does not support this.

The first variable to enter the model was Net Income/Total Assets (R6). Its relationship with the Interest Coverage ratio is positive along with the other profitability ratio: Retained Earnings/Total Assets (R5), a liquidity ratio: the Quick or Acid Test ratio (R4), and the cash flow ratio: Cash Flow from Operations/Total Current Liabilities (R15). One would expect that high values for these four ratios would be reflected in the ability of a firm to meet it's interest payments and the positive sign on each ratio confirms this.

The coefficients of the turnover ratio dummies for Sales/Inventory(RC20) and Sales/Net Plant(RC21) also support the expectations one would have about their values and the ability to repay the firm's loans. Reasonably high values for Sales/Inventory (RC20_3, between the 75th and 95th percentile) are reflected in a higher ability to cover the firm's interest expense and for the lowest values of Sales/Net Plant (RC21_1 and RC21_2, less than the 25th percentile), a large negative sign on both these dummy variables supports a lower ability to repay loans.

Importantly, the coefficient on the estimate of failure risk in the same period is negative. The data shows that as this risk increases, the ability of the firm to cover its interest expense is much reduced.

Table 7.9 Parameter Estimates for the Second System Model

Equation (i) For Failure Risk -Variables	System Model		Compare with Model (6.1)	
	Estimate	Prob>|T|	Estimate	Prob>|T|
INTERCEPT	0.0985	0.4711	1.4658	0.0002
PC3, LABOUR MARKET TIGHTNESS FACTOR	0.7336	0.0001	0.9115	0.0001
R2, WORKING CAPITAL/TOTAL ASSETS	0.0010	0.0806	-0.0206	0.0001
PC5_1, EXPENDITURE FACTOR LAGGED 1 YEAR	-0.6518	0.0001	-0.8011	0.0001
RC21_1,SALES/NET PLANT LOWEST VALUES	-2.1632	0.0001	-2.2866	0.0005
RC21_4,SALES/NET PLANT HIGH VALUES	1.3532	0.0001	1.6171	0.0018
PC5, EXPENDITURE FACTOR	-0.5970	0.0005	-0.7695	0.0021
PC4, CONSTRUCTION ACTIVITY FACTOR	0.3209	0.0006	0.4133	0.0032
PC2_1, COST OF CAPITAL BORROWING FACTOR LAG1	0.3820	0.0001	0.4736	0.0004
RCD18,INTEREST COVERAGE AFTER TAX ≥0(DUMMY)	-0.7360	0.0001	-0.6916	0.0192
R15,CASH FLOW FROM OPER'NS/TOTAL CUR.LIAB	-0.0808	0.0038	-0.0821	0.1239
R7, TOTAL LIABILITIES/TOTAL ASSETS	excluded		-0.0166	0.0001

Equation (ii) for Working Capital/Total Assets	System Model		Compare with Model (7.2)	Prob>|F|
INTERCEPT	65.4656	0.0001	90.2114	0.0001
R7, TOTAL LIABILITIES/TOTAL ASSETS	-0.7636	0.0001	-0.7692	0.0001
R6, NET INCOME/TOTAL ASSETS	0.1493	0.0001	0.1423	0.0001
P_t,ESTIMATED RISK OF FAILURE (FROM FULL MODEL)	-8.2660	0.3922	-68.9445	0.0001
PC3, LABOUR MARKET TIGHTNESS FACTOR	1.1542	0.1638	4.5891	0.0001
PC1, ECONOMIC GROWTH FACTOR	1.2609	0.0197	2.5670	0.0001

Table 7.9 (continued)

Equation (iii) for Interest Coverage after Tax	System Model		Compare With Model (7.3)	
	Estimate	Prob>|T|	Estimate	Prob>|F|
INTERCEPT	-6.7355	0.3097	-5.4391	0.4588
R6, NET INCOME/TOTAL ASSETS	0.1646	0.0001	0.1300	0.0033
R15, CASH FLOW FROM OPER'NS/TOTAL CURR.LIABS	2.3898	0.0223	2.1023	0.0688
RC21_2, SALES/NET PLANT 5TH-25TH PERCENTILE	-17.3345	0.0040	-21.7212	0.0025
R4, QUICK RATIO-ACID TEST	3.3786	0.0013	3.4304	0.0031
R7, TOTAL LIABILITIES/TOTAL ASSETS	0.1999	0.0002	0.1841	0.0020
R5, RETAINED EARNINGS/TOTAL ASSETS	0.0430	0.0026	0.0407	0.0107
P_t,ESTIMATE OF FAILURE RISK FROM FULL MODEL	-23.7126	0.0254	-21.0339	0.0317
RC21_1, SALES/NET PLANT LOWEST VALUES	-23.6290	0.0076	-23.3336	0.0321
RC20_3, SALES/INVENTORY 75TH-95TH PERCENTILE	12.4160	0.0572	12.8033	0.0983
PC2, COST OF CAPITAL BORROWING FACTOR	1.3140	0.0396	1.1802	0.1342

Including equation (7.3) for Interest Coverage after Tax in a simultaneous equations system together with model formulation (6.1), and model formulation (7.2) for Working Capital/Total Assets gave the estimated parameters for the system model tabulated in Table 7.9 above, with significance values of the T and F ratios shown and comparisons with the corresponding non-system estimates. See Appendix P for an extract of the more detailed SAS output.

The inclusion of the additional equation (7.3) to the system changes the coefficients and the significance values only slightly. The only exception is in model equation (ii) for Working Capital/Total Assets, where the effect of the estimated failure risk in the same period, P_t, is reduced to the point where it is no longer significant ($p>0.3$) to that model.

7.3 Model Dynamics

Of tremendous importance in any family of dynamic models are the stability properties. In principle and in practice, any useful methodology that is quantitative *and* lays claim to being dynamic must be capable of allowing the stability properties of conceptually valid estimated models to be examined – usually by calculation of eigenvalues from parameter estimates. In the case of failing to failed firms we would expect to be able to put theoretical limits on the possible range of dynamic behaviour and characteristics of these firms.

In principle we can solve for reduced forms for all linear and some non-linear systems of equations, then, given either qualitative (+/– etc.) or quantitative parameter information, we can discover the stability properties of the system of equations. The importance of this is that it can tell us if, once on the path to bankruptcy, the process dynamics become self-propagating, i.e. part of the way sliding down the path, too much momentum is gathered for the company to be able to stop.

Thus, of major interest is whether P_t converges to $P_t = 1.0$ or some other high value. If $P_t = 1.0$ this would clearly end the process as the firm fails at that point. No further movement can occur, and the system ceases to exist. In most cases, however, we would expect the firm would cease to exist long *before* values of the variables in the equations would yield 1.0. What may be of interest is what we would expect to happen to the value of financial ratios as P_t approaches the final value. We can then examine these behaviours as a whole to see (a) whether they make theoretical sense, and (b) if they do, what other insights they may yield.

However, discovering the stability properties of nonlinear systems like the ones considered in this chapter is a much more difficult task than for linear systems. Establishing general properties for such systems is not possible as the generality and simplicity that are features of linear systems no longer apply. Non-linear systems must be dealt with on a case by case basis, and analytical methods for solution may not always be available as in the case of linear systems.

For the single equation case of model (7.1) with lagged risk of failure, the method is intuitively clear and straightforward. The coefficient of the lagged risk in Table 7.6 is always positive (it is also greater than 1) for each iteration, so the logit of the risk probability, P_t, would inflate quite quickly over time. This corresponds with P_t approaching 1, as logit P_t approaches infinity, i.e.

$$\lim_{P_t \to 1} \log (P_t / \{1 - P_t\}) = +\infty$$

Of course, as stated above, we would expect firms to cease existence long before this point is reached. In the purely illustrative two equation system of (7.4) and (7.5), the coefficient of the lagged risk is, again, positive; its contribution thus acting to increase failure risk over time.[23]

In general, when systems of equations are being considered it becomes necessary to examine the eigenvalues of the coefficient matrix of the reduced form equations that relate P_t and P_{t-1} in a first-order difference equation system. In order to examine the possibility that the particular systems of equations estimated in this chapter lend themselves, even with modifications, to a dynamic analysis, it is instructive to consider the general linear case.

Consider an m equation model that is linear in the parameters and variables. Each equation of this model will usually relate, or be associated with, a given variable of interest to theory. In other words, these 'basic' equations explain the behaviour and interrelations of the endogenous variables and are termed 'structural' equations. The 'basic endogenous variables' typically appear on the left-hand side of the equation and their coefficients are, implicitly, unity. Some of the basic endogenous variables may also appear on the right-hand side of the structural equations.

If the structural equations are solved for the endogenous variables in terms of just the disturbance terms and the predetermined variables i.e. the exogenous variables and the lagged endogenous variables but *not* any other endogenous variables, the resulting equations are the reduced-form equations.
Refer back to Chapter 3 for the structural model (3.9):

$$X_t = A_0X_t + A_1X_{t-1} + A_2X_{t-2} + \text{---------} + A_kX_{t-k} + B\,Z_t + e_t \qquad (3.9)$$

and its reduced forms:–

$$X_t = (I-A_0)^{-1} A_1X_{t-1} + \text{----------} + (I-A_0)^{-1} BZ_t + (I-A_0)^{-1} e_t \qquad (3.10)$$

or

$$X_t = A^*_1X_{t-1} + A^*_2X_{t-2} + \text{----------} + B^*Z_t + \epsilon_t \qquad (3.11)$$

where $A^*_i = (I-A_0)^{-1} A_i$, $B^* = (I-A_0)^{-1} B$, and $\epsilon_t = (I-A_0)^{-1} e_t$.

Equation (3.11) can be treated as an augmented first-order difference system and then solved for the eigenvalues.[24]

Note that in the non-linear examples examined in this chapter, the internal variables X_t in model (3.9) include the outcome variable Y which is a 0/1 variable or, rather, its replacement by the estimate of the probability of failure in the next year, which in turn was replaced by the logit transformation of this probability, as well as two other postulated endogenous variables to the system; R2, the working capital to total assets ratio and R18, the interest coverage ratio. Only in the example system represented by equations (7.4) and (7.5) is there an $\mathbf{X}_{t-1}$ included. P_{t-1}, the lagged probability of failure, proved to be non significant in all the system

[23] Though the effect of the lagged risk was not statistically significant within the system model (p=0.38).

[24] See Forster (1980), pp.62-73

equation estimations of this chapter and was, therefore, omitted from the models represented in Table 7.8 and Table 7.9. The Z_t vector contains all the other predetermined variables that here consist of the financial ratios, except R2, and the macroeconomic variables.

An extra complication is the binary dummy form of the endogenous variable R18 that was used on the right-hand side of the equation for logit P_t, for reasons that it was more appropriate in explaining failure (as evidenced by its statistical significance). The final model is a set of simultaneous equations which are linear in the parameters but, in the examples in this chapter, the vector X_t contains non-linear functions of the endogenous variable P_t, the logit function, $\log (P_t / (1-P_t))$.

The procedure under 2SLS, if the system were linear in all the endogenous variables, would be, first, to regress each endogenous variable separately on *all* the predetermined variables in the two-equation model example of (7.4) and (7.5).[25] But P_t appears, untransformed, only on the right-hand side of the equation and, anyway, we are unable to validly derive a least squares regression for an untransformed probability value. Kelejian and Oates (1989, p.314), terms this an 'additional endogenous variable' as distinct from a 'basic endogenous variable' though this term usually applies to functions of basic endogenous variables on the right-hand side of the equation, and gives rules (p.319) for obtaining consistent parameter estimates in such cases. Thus, in this example, it is still possible to estimate these equations, using 2SLS, if they are properly identified[26] but it may *not* be possible to derive the reduced form equations i.e. with all the endogenous variables only on the left-hand side of the matrix equation as in (3.11) above.

Therefore, in our non-linear example it is not possible to calculate a linear augmented matrix from the reduced model and, hence, neither can we examine the stability of this particular model by investigating the nature of its eigenvalues. Given the basic methodology, future work can better specify more enlightening model formulations with regards to the dynamics of non-linear systems of equations. This could occur, for instance, by changing the right-hand side representation of the probability of failure to the logit transform of P_t and testing other forms of the interest coverage ratio that are appropriate as both regressor and outcome variable in the same measure. With these modifications, and the treatment of the logit transform of P_t as one entity, it may be possible to treat all endogenous variables as basic endogenous and then estimate the coefficient matrix of the

---

[25] Note: If some of the predetermined variables in the theory are unavailable, it may still be possible to estimate a subset of the equations that do have all the necessary predetermined variables in that equation available. This is the identification problem; a problem of specification.

[26] Under the counting rule (Kelejian and Oates, 1989, p.314-315) that, for each equation to be estimated, the number of basic endogenous variables appearing on the right-hand side of the equation needs to be less than or equal to the number of predetermined variables and additional endogenous variables appearing in the model but not appearing in that equation.

reduced form equations, which can then be more readily examined for its stability properties.

7.4 Conclusions

The empirical work presented in this chapter is given as instances of the family of models put forward and applied to the service industry failed group. These few examples of the many formulations that are possible out of the general forms given in Chapter 3 have produced a number of complex results; some that follow our theoretical expectations and/or previous empirical results about firms in distress and some that do not; that is the potential nature and outcome of empirical research. The challenge of results that do not fit into a current paradigm is either to improve or extend the specification of the underlying model in line with new theoretical hypotheses or to abandon the paradigm. Nevertheless, the results need to be summarized and integrated into the overall book argument before further research can be contemplated.

The three significant ratios to failure risk in models (4.1), (6.1), and (7.1) that exhibited high multi-collinearity in the data are the liquidity ratio: Working Capital over Total Assets, the leverage ratio: Total Liabilities over Total Assets, and the profitability ratio: Net Income over Total Assets. Including a second linear equation in a simultaneous equation set with Working Capital over Total Assets as a jointly dependent variable overcame the problem of an incorrect sign on the coefficient of Total Liabilities over Total Assets experienced in the single-equation logit models. The incorrect sign was due to the multi-collinearity of supposedly 'independent' predictors.

Most important, however, are the moves in this chapter towards:

- simultaneous equation modelling of bankruptcy (with mixed empirical results),
- the introduction of dynamics into the modelling and, associated with both of the above,
- the explicit modelling of a time path to failure.

All of these have been accomplished within the methodological framework constructed within this book.

PART III
DISCUSSION AND CONCLUSIONS

Chapter 8 summarizes and integrates the book. The major purposes of this chapter are:

- to summarize the research conducted and its results,
- to show how this book breaks new ground in the modelling of financial distress,
- to outline the limitations of the research,
- to draw out the implications of the findings and
- to indicate further profitable avenues for research in this domain.

Chapter 8

Conclusion

8.0 Introduction: Towards Methodological Cohesion

This book has presented a methodology for examining the *process* of failure of firms. In doing this it represents a break from the past in that it moves away from models that attempt to *discriminate* between failed and non-failed firms. For this departure it has employed the methodology to examine a set composed purely of firms which all fail. Nevertheless, it is a property of the methodology that it can accommodate discrimination models within the family of models that it includes. In this context these models can be seen as partial or special case models so that their failings and/or special assumptions are made more explicit and apparent. This is not only shown to be the situation at the methodological level through the construction of a family of models, but the more general models tested within the methodological framework are empirically more successful than the partial, special case models. At the critical level alone this makes a contribution: it clearly indicates that the great mass of results in the literature are potentially all biased and damaged by their partialness/special case limitations.

While this is not the first work to attempt to move away from the discrimination framework and the testing of such partial models, it appears to be the first to attempt to do so within a coherent and methodological framework.

8.1 Departures from the Past

As part of constructing a new framework, the following departures from past work in the area of financial distress prediction are key features of this book:

- This work attempts to produce a failed firm model that examines financial distress before eventual failure and tests financial distress as a process. Since not all distressed firms become bankrupt, a critical examination of those that do may provide additional insights into the failure process. In this context, the use of only failed firms can be likened to survival studies in biostatistics, whereas the traditional method using cross-sectional data on failed and non-failed firms can be likened to case-control studies. Again it is important to note that the methodology can accommodate both approaches.

- One objective toward which the work in this book attempts to move is a model that either (a) can be utilized to discriminate between 'at risk' firms that survive and 'at risk' firms that fail or (b) gives an indication of which factors are involved when a firm that was surviving becomes one that is failing. This is a fine distinction and the design represents a far more difficult predictive environment than previous studies where the two groups of failed and nonfailed observations were usually already well separated in multidimensional space. Therefore, it is contended that in such an environment, 'explanation' rather than 'prediction' is the target to which researchers can realistically aim, so the focus of the work here is on the former. This aim leaves the testing of specific theories (hypotheses) of bankruptcy and then construction of predictive models as next steps, after reporting, description and general process-oriented explanations have been satisfactorily accomplished.
- The interest here in process over state contains two implications for modelling. The first is that the firm's own internal dynamics of financial distress are more open to analysis. Very few studies have analysed the failure process (Partington *et al*, 1991; Theodossiou, 1993; Hill *et al*, 1996; Cybinski, 2000). In our view, the aim of path-to-failure studies is to understand the dynamics of the process and ultimately how the condition of the firm in one period helps determine the financial health of the firm in subsequent periods. In addition, a move away from static comparisons of failed and non-failed firms avoids a largely unrecognized methodological problem common to all such studies.
- This problem is that empirical studies using final year data are necessarily heavily biased towards viewing business failure in terms of insolvency related (financial) variables. Any such final year analysis is compounded in this error by the use of failed/non-failed comparisons, as the non-failed firms are necessarily solvent. This explains why such empirical modelling can demonstrate high statistical explanatory measures yet still be of little use for failure prediction purposes when applied to other non-failed firms. This has highly negative implications for both the academic and commercial use of such models. Finally, path to failure modelling, as represented by probability of failure estimates for each of the final four years of life in the model presented here, has the potential to distinguish different types of paths to failure and to examine their determinants. Thus those firms that are characterized by sudden, catastrophic paths to failure can be distinguished from those that experience more gradual declines over several years.
- As well as facilitating the goal of creating an explicitly dynamic, testable model of business failure, it is argued there are several reasons for wishing to study the failure process, including the use of only firms that ultimately fail in the empirical analysis. In the current analysis, the impacts of changing macroeconomic conditions upon the same firm can be accounted for, as well as its position in the business cycle during the failure process. This flows from the

argument that the combined financial history of the firm and its environment is as important as conditions in the current year in determining the probability of a firm's failure. This allows a move away from failure models that are essentially financial-health models, but which ignore economic conditions.

- So in addition to incorporating a dynamic element in the equations to be estimated, by using failed firms and examining the same firms over time prior to failure, an *absolute* time element has been added in the form of macro-economic variables. The internal financial histories of failed firms traditionally used for estimating such models have been augmented by the data that describes the external economic environment in which these firms operated. The results indicate not only that such incorporation was sensible and theoretically relevant, but also that parametric estimation can be crucially affected.

- Rather than use single-equation modelling exclusively, multi-equation model sets are used including non-linear formulations. While these multi-equation models are relatively primitive and are used mainly to demonstrate the application of the methodology, they allow the researcher:
  (i) To better understand the changes that are occurring in the explanatory variables over the failure period, and
  (ii) To explore different formulations that recognise that some of the explanatory variables are interdependent, by modelling separate equations that reflect their relationship to each other as well as their relationship to failure risk.

8.2 Empirical Results

It is argued that this book is concerned with explanation and understanding of the process of firm failure rather than upon prediction and forecasting. It may seem contradictory then, that in the empirical work undertaken, no specific theory is tested that provides specific and exclusive explanation. This arises because the methodology constructed is being 'tested' but in a different sense than is usual in parametric estimation. Nevertheless, some of the empirical results do have interesting implications and others confirm the conclusions made in earlier studies that particular symptoms are precursors to failure.

It is demonstrated that even when embedded in simple and deliberately non-optimised model structures, the alternative methods for analysing firm failure presented in this book are capable of producing good empirical results. In practical terms this was accomplished using readily available data sources exhibiting cyclical variability. The approach employed is both methodologically empirically valid and, especially when compared to failed/non-failed studies, capable of considerable development and refinement. The vast majority of studies to the present have emphasized predictive ability at the expense of explanation and understanding, yet these studies have had little success in prediction.

In these terms, the focus of this book is critical and methodological, backing up those arguments with a demonstration of a way forward in the empirical analysis of business failure.

Results from the most simple single-equation model within the family of models tested on the service industry data are summarised below:

- The effects of the economy and the effects of the financial variables on failure risk were found to be mutually reinforcing.

- The effects of the important macroeconomic variables are more significant, statistically, than the effects of the important internal financial ratios to the risk of failure; at least as judged by their order of entry into a forward stepwise selection logit model.

- The liquidity ratio, working capital to total assets, is statistically the most significant ratio to failure risk.[1] This is consistent with past studies of financial distress across different research designs and time periods in that, as this ratio increases, failure risk decreases. Another ratio consistently displaying predictive ability across several major research studies is cash flow from operations/total current liabilities. Encouragingly, it also shows some significance to the combined model of failure risk of Chapter 6. The lower significance of the cash flow ratio belies its importance to the model, since in further research on this data set it proved to be the ratio that changed the most in the final four years before failure, and where it shows the most significance to failure risk is in the final of the four years. This is when the inability to cover short-term commitments with cash flow can be argued to have become most crucial. It is this changing significance over time that is the major reason for the lower statistical significance of this variable in the pooled-time single-equation model. Because the coefficient effect in the pooled model was averaged out over time, the power of any significance test applied to it is correspondingly reduced.

- The effect of the 'labour market tightness' factor, a complex external variable derived as a principal component, highly weighted (negatively) on the total number unemployed and (positively) on the change in the size of the employed labour force, is the most significant variable, overall, to failure risk. The interpretation of this result is very much tentative for definitional reasons and its unexpectedness.

---

1 In addition, when combined with the external variables, it vies with the external variables for early entry into the stepwise model.

- The logit model based on the variables statistically significant to failure risk used only a binary 0/1 input variable for the events 'fails in the next year'/ 'survives the next year' and yet provided a good instrument for measuring failure risk at each period prior to failure. It not only has given a logical result that the risk of failure increases with each period but also that it increases quite markedly in the final three years before failure. The risk is estimated at around one chance in four at three and four years prior, and increases to two chances in three at one year prior to failure – an absolute jump in risk of 41 percent within two years. This is a strong indication that a reorientation to process dynamics is very much overdue.

- Incorporating a measure of lagged risk into the single-equation model is the simplest way to add the dynamic element into the model specification, yet the improvement in model fit is good and the sequential increase in estimated failure risk from year to year is also more marked than in the model with no dynamic included.

- One may conclude that these increases coincide with a very rapid decline in financial stability for these firms as they approach bankruptcy. This rapid decline is borne out by the increasing weight on the lagged risk when its value was consecutively iterated until stability was reached – indicating a distress feedback mechanism.

Results from the multiple equation models within the family of models tested on the service industry data are summarized below:

- The finding that at certain lag years some variables have a much more significant effect on failure risk than they do at other lag years (or they may not be statistically significant in some years) offers considerable justification for the multi-equation modelling of failure risk using time series as well as cross-sectional data for the analysis set. In these situations, the coefficient effects in the single-equation model are averaged out over time and the power of any significance tests applied to them is consequently reduced. The result is that these effects are usually deemed statistically insignificant under a single-equation failure model specification.

- One such variable is 'cash flow from operations to total liabilities' which appears to be an immediate trigger for bankruptcy in the final year before failure. As such it is important in the final year but not at other times. Consequently this variable is not useful as an early pointer since a drop in its value is predictive of failure only at too short an advance period.

- This may also be the reason for the controversy over cash flow variables in general as to whether they contain information value beyond that of accrual variables in bankruptcy prediction analyses (discussed in Chapter 2.3). Thus, studies may reach very different conclusions with respect to this variable depending on the time of the measurement of variables as opposed to the point of time of failure. That the cash flow to current liabilities ratio was found to have an immediate association with failure should not be surprising. It is associated with an inability to trade unless financial institutions or other internal and/or external sources of funds are prepared to cover the shortfall. One would expect financial institutions to be less prepared to do this in business downturns. In addition, the legal requirements upon operating companies can also play a role in activating this ratio as the immediate trigger to failure. However, if this ratio does represent a short-term inability to trade profitably, then the failure-process methodology shows that longer-term fundamentals in previous years have led the company to this position. Given these sorts of complex mechanisms over time, a dynamic approach has much to recommend it.

- By investigating the differences in parameter estimates and their significance to failure risk for each prior year before failure by the method of seemingly unrelated regressions, some insights into the patterns of failure over the final four years of a service industry firm's existence have been gained here. Firstly, an important result is that some variables not only remain highly significant *over all four years* prior to failure but also have consistent signs on the coefficients over those four years. This finding lends some weight to the validity of some single-equation failure model specifications with respect to these variables. As a consequence, these variables can be confidently used in these simple failure prediction models, as their discriminatory powers are reasonably long term (at least of four years duration before failure).

- Because of this discriminatory robustness over time it was useful to examine the relative sizes of the coefficients of each of these significant variables over the four lag years. The variables that showed little difference in size from year to year were working capital to total assets, total liabilities to total assets, and interest coverage. Again, despite the comments in the point above, no stress is laid here on the strength of individual variables.

- The variables that show larger differences from year to year are of even greater interest. The 'labour market tightness' factor and the 'expenditure (business, private and public)' factor – the latter measured both in the same year as the firm's final financial statements were submitted as well as in the previous year – all increased in their effects on failure risk as failure approached, having the most pronounced effect in the penultimate year before failure and this effect dropped only slightly in the final year prior. These results suggest that if the firm is already vulnerable to failure, low expenditure levels in the economy and a tight labour market at this time can have a devastating effect on the ultimate solvency of the firm.

- Of the financial ratios, sales to net plant showed a considerably larger positive effect on failure risk at three years prior to failure. Particularly if this ratio was large, it was associated with an increased failure risk at this time. One possible reason for this effect is that the value of fixed assets was eroded at this time by selling off assets, rather than by sales increasing.

- The three significant ratios to failure risk that exhibit high multi-collinearity in the data are the liquidity ratio: working capital to total assets, the leverage ratio: total liabilities to total assets, and the profitability ratio: net income to total assets. Including a second linear equation in a simultaneous equation set with working capital to total assets as a jointly dependent variable overcame the problem of an unexpected negative sign on the coefficient of total liabilities to total assets in the single-equation logit models of earlier chapters. The incorrect sign was concluded to be due to the multi-collinearity of supposedly 'independent' predictors.

8.3 Limitations

It is proper to indicate at this stage those applications for which this work is *not* useful. Because the empirical work presented in this book is given as instances of the family of models put forward and applied to the service industry failed group, it is of limited use, for reasons of external validity, for groups concerned with the assessment of a particular firm's insolvency risk other than in that industry and for other than failed firms. It *is* useful, nevertheless, for future research into insolvency risk and the further study of the causes of failure, which can be based on this new methodology.

This research was limited to a four-year data window for each failed firm. It would be advantageous for this research to repeat this work with a larger time period before failure and hence, a larger event history to analyse. A disadvantage of increasing the time window is always that many firms with incomplete data over the full period of time would have to be censored from the analysis.

Firms examined in this project were firms deleted from the Compustat database, which does not include small firms. The bias in this project, as with most studies in bankruptcy research, is an important one since small firms are especially prone to bankruptcy. New firms, which also have a high propensity for bankruptcy, are likely to be excluded because of the requirement for inclusion of four years of data.

The most immediate progression in this research would be to redress some of the important limitations mentioned above, though these limitations do not preclude the application of this study's findings in a practical way. Although exploratory in nature, the single-equation formulations for failure risk constituted models in their own right and so were informative concerning the possible comparative effects of the internal ratios and the external economy on failure risk and the means of examining these effects together. The fact that reasonable results were obtained when the single-equation combined model for the service industry was applied to the trade industry group is an encouraging result for testing external validity in future research.

8.4 Implications of the Research and Possible New Directions

This book does not complete a research program: rather it attempts to propose and initiate one. Consequently, its most important contribution probably lies in its implications for future research into insolvency risk. This brief section makes some specific suggestions for future research.

Since many of the challenges facing researchers of financial distress could only be addressed by a totally new research design and modelling methodology, the work in this book concentrated on extending the *potential* for bankruptcy analysis from single-equation modelling to multi-equation analysis; providing the tools for understanding the different forces that are simultaneously acting from within and without the firm and that impact on failure risk. It also offers some specific directions for research to go in testing the new methodology by suggesting a number of specific equation sets to be tested. But the number of other possible sets, even with limited data, is large. This opens up whole new areas for testing hypotheses about the various internal and external processes acting on the firm in order to explain the bankruptcy process. The results emphasize that not just further research, but new research directions are needed to understand and explain the characteristics of bankrupt and financially distressed firms.

An ongoing challenge to researchers of corporate bankruptcy has been to produce a model that distinguishes distressed firms filing bankruptcy from others, also at risk, but avoiding it. In other words the real question of interest to this book that will continue to be for future research is: 'How do firms transform from surviving or even successful ones into failed ones.'

One way to investigate this question is to continue further in the direction of researchers using the statistical techniques drawn from survival analysis, knowing that the potential to fail always exists *ex ante*. Other promising avenues for further research are: the failing firm model of Flagg *et al* (1991) that include postulated events signalling that a firm is experiencing financial distress; the sequential dynamic failure prediction model of Theodossiou (1991) using multivariate time-series which can detect the critical point at which a firm's financial variables shift from a 'good performance' distribution to a 'bad performance' distribution; and the application of non-linear dynamics to the problem of bankruptcy prediction with the chaos-derived models of Lindsay and Campbell (1996). The new approach described in this book consists of a family of models, described in Chapter 3, that allow for a comparison of each firm with itself over time – from when the firm was surviving, or avoiding bankruptcy, to when it failed.

A number of tentative reasons for the key findings of the empirical work in Chapter 7 are hypothesized. These are often complex but testable in further work. For instance, indications in the data are that low expenditure levels in the economy have most effect up to two years before failure and after that, perhaps, other factors come to the fore. Thus, at this time even small changes in spending may become absolutely crucial when a firm is already very weak, but which may have little impact when it is sound. The time profile of such impacts is one worthy of investigation.

There are also indications that if the labour market is tight, the failure risk is higher at this time. If labour is the major factor acting here, i.e. the principal component involved is appropriately named, then it is postulated that because key workers can't easily find work in a poor labour market, they don't leave for new employment until it is obvious that the firm is in real financial difficulty. The loss of these key workers could then further negatively affect the health of the firm. It's use has, however, suggested a new mechanism, i.e. a 'flight from failure', implying a loss of key workers as an element in firm failure which may be more rigorously tested.

A peculiarity of service industry firms is that they often don't own their fixed assets but lease them, making the denominator of the ratio, sales to net plant, small, and their financial viability, as a result, more vulnerable. The data show that at three years prior to failure, this ratio has its greatest effect, acting to increase failure risk at this time particularly for firms whose values fall into the highest category. The hypothesis put forward for further testing is that whatever fixed assets can be sold are being sold at this time to finance debt or that many service firms with little or no fixed assets to sell, find their financial position worsening as a result.

8.5 Concluding Comments

Studies of bankruptcy have largely reached a standstill. The literature review in this book indicates that the major contributions had largely stopped by the late 1970s/early 1980s. Since then improvements have been at the margins and within the existing paradigm, i.e. including many repetitions using different data sets or comparing prediction accuracies between MDA and logit formulations, and lately, between these formulations and those arising from emerging technologies.

Without consciously adopting an iconoclastic view it is suggested that all the signs are there for a paradigm shift in the Kuhnian sense (Kuhn, 1962). These include not only the mainstream works but also the attempts to break away using new methods (e.g. neural networks), which do not alter the basic foundations, and those that may be genuine precursors (e.g. based on dynamics).

This work may best be seen as such a precursor but, rather than taking a specific dynamic model and testing that, it has attempted to create a more general methodological framework. Within this methodological framework it has not only been possible to develop new models and to test them, but by using the concept of a 'family' of models, those models which are now current can be more readily seen as special cases and all the drawbacks this entails.

What will be most interesting is to see how rapidly these changes will take to occur.

PART IV
APPENDICES

Appendix A

Data Collection: The Internal Financial Variables

Creating Company Sets In PC Plus and Retrieving Data From the COMPUSTAT Firms Database

Internal financial data were collected from Standard and Poor's COMPUSTAT PC Plus, which is a data screening and access system for financial analysis.[1] The system is a CD-ROM database interfaced to a PC. The database includes financial and market data for different reporting categories, or classifications, used to organize data by entity types, such as active company, research company, Canadian company, aggregate, index, business or geographic segment, issue, or country. The software allows the user to select, access, and present data from the database through a menu-driven software program. The main goal of a PC Plus session is to take data from the database and store it for further manipulation. For this study, only the set of research companies were of interest. Research companies contain only historical information. Data is no longer collected for these companies due to a merger, acquisition, bankruptcy, liquidation, etc.

Creating Company Sets in PC Plus

In order to create a number of company sets from the large population of all companies[2] in the database, a screening method was used. Screening allows the researcher to refine a large population of companies into a smaller, more useful one, using common attributes of the companies that are to be included in the company set. The screening process involves two steps. The first step is to define the screening criteria by creating a set of rules, called a screening worksheet. Common screening variables are State, Stock Exchange, Standard Industry Code

---

1 I am indebted to the Faculty of Commerce and Business Administration at the University of British Columbia in Vancouver, Canada, for allowing me to access their licensed COMPUSTAT database whilst on study leave at that institution in 1991.

2 Companies are the fundamental units of the database. A company is a publicly held corporation that trades common stock or a wholly owned subsidiary that trades preferred stock and/or debt. At the time of collection, there were approximately 7000 active companies and 6100 Research companies in COMPUSTAT PC Plus. Most companies are industrial.

[SIC],[3] Current Period [CPD],[4] and Reason for Deletion [Research file]. The second step is to run the screening worksheet to isolate the subset of companies that meet the criteria. The resulting subset is then saved as a company set. The companies are identified by their ticker symbols, which are eight-character code that identifies a security for trading purposes. For this study *eight data sets* were created – one for each of the *last four years* before a company's Date of Deletion[5] and from *two different Industry Codes.* Only bankrupt and liquidated firms were acceptable as Reasons for Deletion. The sets comprised:

All 63 Trade companies [SIC 5000-5999]
All 60 Service companies [SIC 7000-8999]

Retrieving Data from COMPUSTAT

Next, a report is run on the company set to retrieve the data that the researcher needs on each company for further analysis. The PC PLUS software has a library of predefined reports of commonly used financial statements or the researcher is able to create customized reports with a report builder that can be linked to a spreadsheet application such as EXCEL. For this study an individual template was defined for storing a limited number of financial items from the total set in a columnar or table report, which is a spreadsheet that lists data items by columns and company names by rows. In this way, the necessary financial data from the financial statements of U.S. bankrupt and liquidated public companies were downloaded from the COMPUSTAT Research file.

The above sets of bankrupt and liquidated firms were selected from the COMPUSTAT Research file because they filed chapter X [not chapter XI] bankruptcy proceedings in the period 1971-91, and had at least three years of financial statements submitted prior to the final year's submission.

---

3 A four-digit Standard Industry Classification code that identifies the principal products manufactured or major services provided by each company.

4 For each firm, the current period is the most recent time frame for which data is available for that firm, so the current period for one company may differ from that of another, depending on the most current data available for each. For this study, data were collected for each company in the dataset for periods CPD, CPD-1, CPD-2, and CPD-3.

5 This is the month and year that the company was moved from the Active Companies set to the Research Companies set. For instance, the average time period between current period, CPD, and Date of Deletion, is about two years for companies in the Service industry group. The author does not know the trigger for file deletion. One would need access to the Capital Changes Reporter to gauge when, either in the intervening period or later, the firm was actually liquidated. At collection in October-November 1991, the COMPUSTAT file was current for deletion dates to July 1991.

Appendix B

The Internal Variables Employed – The Financial Ratios

The following list are the ratio labels, [bracketed by type] that were included in the initial models of bankruptcy risk with their definitions and explanation notes [and the formula using COMPUSTAT names] as well as the authors who were among the first to advocate their inclusion in such models.

R1. [SIZE] LOG[TOTAL ASSETS/CPI (price level index)]. [Log [AT/CPI]] - take logs since it is not normally distributed but right skewed. Ohlson

R2. [LIQUIDITY] WORKING CAPITAL/TOTAL ASSETS [%] where WORKING CAPITAL = [CURRENT ASSETS-CURRENT LIABILITIES]. [[ACT-LCT]/AT x100] Altman, Ohlson

R23. [LIQUIDITY] CASH AND MARKETABLE SECURITIES/TOTAL ASSETS. Calculated [Cash and Equivalents minus Total Receivables] as numerator, i.e. calculated as [CHE/AT] Zavgren
This is like the acid test ratio, R4, only with AT in the denominator instead of LCT, and RECT is not included in the numerator.
Note: All the liquidity ratios, R2, R23, R3, R4 would be expected to move in the opposite direction to the probability of failure, i.e. firms with a higher proportion of current assets, especially quick assets, relative to total assets or current liabilities are more likely to survive.

R3. [LIQUIDITY] CURRENT RATIO =TOTAL CURRENT ASSETS/TOTAL CURRENT LIABILITIES [ACT/LCT] equivalent to COMPUSTAT ratio CR.
Zavgren replaced the CR with the acid test ratio or quick ratio, R4, as inclusion of inventories reduces its meaning as a measure of liquidity. Ohlson used its inverse.

R4. [LIQUIDITY] QUICK RATIO OR ACID TEST RATIO =[CURRENT ASSETS-INVENTORY] /LCT calculated as:
[CASH+CASH EQUIVALENTS+TOTAL RECEIVABLES]/LCT Zavgren

R5. [PROFITABILITY] RETAINED EARNINGS/TOTAL ASSETS [%]. [RE/AT x 100] Altman, Zavgren
The numerator is the accumulation of net income minus dividends every year.
Note: Some authors interpret RE/AT as a surrogate for the operating age of the business. There is a higher probability that the longer a company has been operating the larger the ratio will become if it is trading profitably. In Altman's

[1968] original Z score model, Altman *et al*'s [1977] Zeta model, Lincoln's [1984] manufacturing and retail model, and McNamara *et al*'s [1988] private company model this ratio was a good predictor of survival. This ratio may also indicate the 'reserve' available to a company to withstand a period of poor profit performance. [McNamara *et al*, 1988]

R6. [PROFITABILITY] NET INCOME/TOTAL ASSETS [%] = ROA, RETURN ON ASSETS. [IB/AT x 100] Ohlson, Zavgren
This return on total funds shows the return on a firm's total investment.
We rather use IB [Income before Extraordinary items] than EBIT [Earnings before interest and tax, calculated as net operating profit before tax minus capital profits plus interest paid less miscellaneous] that was used by Altman, since high interest is damning and should be taken into account.

R7. [LEVERAGE] TOTAL LIABILITIES/TOTAL ASSETS [%] or the debt ratio [LT/AT x 100] Ohlson
This ratio is interpreted as a measure of the firm's capital structure [Weston and Brigham, 1975]. The higher the debt ratio, the greater the chance of predicting failure. [Izan, 1984, Lincoln, 1984, McNamara *et al*, 1988]

R8. [LEVERAGE] TOTAL DEBT/TOTAL ASSETS [%] = [Long Term Debt+Debt in Current Liabilities]/Total Assets [[DLTT+DLC]/AT x 100] COMPUSTAT ratio, DAT

The following are COMPUSTAT profitability ratios with sales [SALE] in the denominator [often zero for the Service industry group]:

R10. [PROFITABILITY] NET PROFIT MARGIN [%] = NI before extraordinary items/ Net Sales [%] [IB/SALE[1] x100]

R11. [PROFITABILITY] OPERATING MARGIN BEFORE DEPRECIATION [%] = Operating income plus depreciation expense/Sales [%]
[OIADP+ DP] / SALE[1] x 100

R12. [PROFITABILITY] PRETAX PROFIT MARGIN [%] = NI before taxes and Extraordinary items / Net Sales [%] [PI / SALE[1] x100]

The following are cash-flow ratios using Cash Flow defined as "Funds from Operations + Working Capital Changes" = [FOPT+WCAPCH] – both items are

---

[1] The denominator of the ratio is often zero so there is a need to categorize this ratio.

found in the Working Capital Statement from a Statement of Changes/ Statement of Cash Flows.[2]

R13. [CASH FLOW] CASH FLOW FROM OPERATIONS/SALES [FOPT +WCAPCH] /SALE[3]

R14. [CASH FLOW] CASH FLOW FROM OPERATIONS/TOTAL ASSETS [FOPT +WCAPCH]/AT

R15. [CASH FLOW] CASH FLOW FROM OPERATIONS/TOTAL CURRENT LIABITIES [FOPT+WCAPCH]/LCT

R16. [LEVERAGE or PROPRIETY or GEARING RATIO] LONG TERM DEBT/SHAREHOLDERS' EQUITY [%] [DLTT/CEQx100] COMPUSTAT ratio, DSE.

R18. [LEVERAGE] INTEREST COVERAGE AFTER TAX = [Net income before extraordinary items+interest expense]/Interest expense [IB+XINT]/XINT[3] COMPUSTAT ratio, IC.

The following group of TURNOVER or ACTIVITY RATIOS [sales or part of sales e.g. receivables, or what would be sales, i.e. inventories, or income from sales, is in the numerator] mean less in service industries where sales is often zero.

R9. [TURNOVER] SALES/TOTAL ASSETS [SALE/AT] Altman

R17. [TURNOVER] RECEIVABLES TURNOVER =NET SALES/AVERAGE TOTAL RECEIVABLES [SALE/RECT] COMPUSTAT ratio, RECX.

R19. [TURNOVER] INVENTORY TURNOVER = COST OF GOODS SOLD/AVERAGE INVENTORY calculated as [COGS/INVT[3]] COMPUSTAT ratio, INVX.

R20. [TURNOVER] SALES/INVENTORY [SALE/INVT[3]] Zavgren

---

2 If either quantity is not available, Cash Flow is defined as it is in the Compustat ratios as Net Income before Extraordinary Items plus Depreciation. [IB+DP].

3 The denominator of the ratio is often zero so there is a need to categorize this ratio.

Appendix C

SAS Code for Categorizing Variables

```
libname service 'c:\mysasdir';
data service.servcat; set service.servmean;
/*categorize if many n or p or outliers */
/*always 5 levels with boundaries:<5% or n, 1st and 3rd quartiles, >95% or p*/
if r5<-675 or r5=.n then rc5=1;
if -675<=r5<=-108.6 or r5=.n then rc5=2;
if -108.6<r5<12.7 then rc5=3;
if 12.7<=r5<=57.3 then rc5=4;
if r5>57.3 or r5=.p then rc5=5;

if r7<10.5 then rc7=1;
if 10.5<=r7<=40.4 then rc7=2;
if 40.4<r7<95.2 then rc7=3;
if 95.2<=r7<=238.5 then rc7=4;
if r7>238.5 or r7=.p then rc7=5;

if r10<-342.9 or r10=.n then rc10=1;
if -342.9<=r10<=-22.1 then rc10=2;
if -22.1<r10<4.5 then rc10=3;
if 4.5<=r10<=24.5 then rc10=4;
if r10>24.5 or r10=.p then rc10=5;

if r11<-280.1 or r11=.n then rc11=1;
if -280.1<=r11<=-11.6 then rc11=2;
if -11.6<r11<13.6 then rc11=3;
if 13.6<=r11<=55.2 then rc11=4;
if r11>55.2 or r11=.p then rc11=5;

if r12<-342.8 or r12=.n then rc12=1;
if -342.8<=r12<=-23.9 then rc12=2;
if -23.9<r12<8 then rc12=3;
if 8<=r12<=35.6 then rc12=4;
if r12>35.6 or r12=.p then rc12=5;

if r13<-3.31 or r13=.n then rc13=1;
if -3.31<=r13<=-0.26 then rc13=2;
if -0.26<r13<0.24 then rc13=3;
if 0.24<=r13<=0.89 then rc13=4;
if r13>0.89 or r13=.p then rc13=5;
```

```
if r16<-172.5 or r16=.n then rc16=1;
if -172.5<=r16<=0 then rc16=2;
if 0<r16<71 then rc16=3;
if 71<=r16<=657.4 then rc16=4;
if r16>657.4 or r16=.p then rc16=5;

if r17<0.1 then rc17=1;
if 0.1<=r17<=3.1 then rc17=2;
if 3.1<r17<9.2 then rc17=3;
if 9.2<=r17<=59.8 then rc17=4;
if r17>59.8 or r17=.p then rc17=5;

if r18<-39.5 or r18=.n then rc18=1;
if -39.5<=r18<=-5.6 then rc18=2;
if -5.6<r18<0 then rc18=3;
if 0<=r18<2.4 then rc18=4;
if 2.4<=r18<=24.3 then rc18=5;
if r18>24.3 or r18=.p then rc18=6;
if r19<0.97 then rc19=1;
if 0.97<=r19<=4.3 then rc19=2;
if 4.3<r19<28.3 then rc19=3;
if 28.3<=r19<=185.8 then rc19=4;
if r19>185.8 or r19=.p then rc19=5;

if r20<1.4 then rc20=1;
if 1.4<=r20<=6.7 then rc20=2;
if 6.7<r20<48.6 then rc20=3;
if 48.6<=r20<=328.9 then rc20=4;
if r20>328.9 or r20=.p then rc20=5;

if r21<0.17  then rc21=1;
if 0.17<=r21<=1.18 then rc21=2;
if 1.18<r21<9.26 then rc21=3;
if 9.26<=r21<=42.28 then rc21=4;
if r21>42.28 or r21=.p then rc21=5;

if r22<0.11 then rc22=1;
if 0.11<=r22<=0.26 then rc22=2;
if 0.26<r22<0.57 then rc22=3;
if 0.57<=r22<=0.91 then rc22=4;
if r22>0.91 or r22=.p then rc22=5;
/*use categories [declare as nominal] in SAS Insight to get significant [<0.05]
ratios -then create dummy variables */
/* for  stepwise PROC LOGISTIC [logit analysis]  where declaration of nominal
variables not an option*/
```

```
Title "Creating [ #levels-1] dummy variables for the important categorized
variables from SAS INSIGHT analysis";
data service.dummy; set service.servcat;
SELECT[RC7];
WHEN [1] DO; RC7_1=1; RC7_2=0; RC7_3=0;RC7_4=0;END;
WHEN [2] DO; RC7_1=0; RC7_2=1; RC7_3=0;RC7_4=0; END;
WHEN [3] DO; RC7_1=0; RC7_2=0; RC7_3=0;RC7_4=0;END;/*middle group is
base value*/
WHEN [4] DO; RC7_1=0; RC7_2=0; RC7_3=1;RC7_4=0;END;
WHEN [5] DO; RC7_1=0; RC7_2=0; RC7_3=0;RC7_4=1;END;
END;

SELECT[RC5];
WHEN [1] DO; RC5_1=1; RC5_2=0; RC5_3=0;RC5_4=0; END;
WHEN [2] DO; RC5_1=0; RC5_2=1; RC5_3=0;RC5_4=0; END;
WHEN [3] DO; RC5_1=0; RC5_2=0; RC5_3=0;RC5_4=0;END;
WHEN [4] DO; RC5_1=0; RC5_2=0; RC5_3=1;RC5_4=0;END;
WHEN [5] DO; RC5_1=0; RC5_2=0; RC5_3=0;RC5_4=1;END;
END;

SELECT[RC13];
WHEN [1] DO; RC13_1=1; RC13_2=0; RC13_3=0;RC13_4=0; END;
WHEN [2] DO; RC13_1=0; RC13_2=1; RC13_3=0;RC13_4=0; END;
WHEN [3] DO; RC13_1=0; RC13_2=0; RC13_3=0;RC13_4=0;END;
WHEN [4] DO; RC13_1=0; RC13_2=0; RC13_3=1;RC13_4=0;END;
WHEN [5] DO; RC13_1=0; RC13_2=0; RC13_3=0;RC13_4=1;END;
END;
if rc18<=3 then rcd18=0;
ELSE RCD18=1;

SELECT[RC19];
WHEN [1] DO; RC19_1=1; RC19_2=0; RC19_3=0;RC19_4=0; END;
WHEN [2] DO; RC19_1=0; RC19_2=1; RC19_3=0;RC19_4=0; END;
WHEN [3] DO; RC19_1=0; RC19_2=0; RC19_3=0;RC19_4=0;END;
WHEN [4] DO; RC19_1=0; RC19_2=0; RC19_3=1;RC19_4=0;END;
WHEN [5] DO; RC19_1=0; RC19_2=0; RC19_3=0;RC19_4=1;END;
END;

SELECT[RC20];
WHEN [1] DO; RC20_1=1; RC20_2=0; RC20_3=0;RC20_4=0; END;
WHEN [2] DO; RC20_1=0; RC20_2=1; RC20_3=0;RC20_4=0; END;
WHEN [3] DO; RC20_1=0; RC20_2=0; RC20_3=0;RC20_4=0;END;
WHEN [4] DO; RC20_1=0; RC20_2=0; RC20_3=1;RC20_4=0;END;
WHEN [5] DO; RC20_1=0; RC20_2=0; RC20_3=0;RC20_4=1;END;
```

```
END;

SELECT[RC21];
WHEN [1] DO; RC21_1=1; RC21_2=0; RC21_3=0;RC21_4=0; END;
WHEN [2] DO; RC21_1=0; RC21_2=1; RC21_3=0;RC21_4=0; END;
WHEN [3] DO; RC21_1=0; RC21_2=0; RC21_3=0;RC21_4=0;END;
WHEN [4] DO; RC21_1=0; RC21_2=0; RC21_3=1;RC21_4=0;END;
WHEN [5] DO; RC21_1=0; RC21_2=0; RC21_3=0;RC21_4=1;END;
END;
run;

/* binary dummies were later created for R7 and R13*/
/*if rc7_3=1 or rc7_4=1 then rcd7=1; else rcd7=0;*/
/*if rc13_1=1 or rc13_2=1 then rcd13=1; else rcd13=0; run;*/
```

Appendix D

Summary Statistics of the Twenty-Three Internal Ratios

SAS output from PROC SUMMARY, using CLASS LAG:

N1-N23 Number of Cases excluding cases with missing values [and one outlier-see Chapter 4.0]

MISS!-MISS23 Number of missing values for each ratio - all types[refer to Chapter 4.3]

MEAN!-MEAN23 Mean value for each ratio calculated excluding all missing values and one outlier firm.

[refer to ratio label at end of this appendix along with each variable's min and max value]

LAG	N1	N2	N3	N4	N5	N6	N7	N8	N9	N10	N11	N12	N13	N14	N15
all years	205	188	188	204	200	203	204	204	203	194	194	193	194	202	196
0	59	50	50	57	55	58	58	58	58	53	53	52	53	57	53
1	55	51	51	53	55	54	55	55	54	52	52	52	52	54	52
2	47	44	44	47	46	47	47	47	47	45	45	45	45	47	47
3	44	43	43	47	44	44	44	44	44	44	44	44	44	44	44

LAG	N16	N17	N18	N19	N20	N21	N22	N23	MISS1	MISS2	MISS3	MISS4	MISS5	MISS6	MISS7	MISS8
	201	177	176	138	130	190	121	188	31	48	48	32	36	33	32	32
0	56	44	50	37	33	50	30	50	0	9	9	2	4	1	1	1
1	55	48	46	36	35	51	33	51	4	8	8	6	4	5	4	4
2	47	42	39	32	31	45	28	44	12	15	15	12	13	12	12	12
3	43	43	41	33	31	44	30	43	15	16	16	12	15	15	15	15

LAG	MISS9	MISS10	MISS11	MISS12	MISS13	MISS14	MISS15	MISS16	MISS17	MISS18	MISS19
.	33	42	42	43	42	34	40	35	59	60	98
0	1	6	6	7	6	2	6	3	15	9	22
1	5	7	7	7	7	5	7	4	11	13	23
2	12	14	14	14	14	12	12	12	17	20	27
3	15	15	15	15	15	15	15	16	16	18	26

LAG	MISS20	MISS21	MISS22	MISS23	MEAN1	MEAN2	MEAN3	MEAN4	MEAN5	MEAN6
·	106	46	115	48	4.82049	-9.9998	2.04351	1.68005	-124.939	-17.3941
0	26	9	29	9	4.69254	-46.6242	1.83200	1.47754	-228.493	-20.1776
1	24	8	26	8	4.81182	-12.6141	2.13549	2.26226	-148.179	-25.3204
2	28	14	31	15	4.91617	8.4536	1.93091	1.64340	-69.310	-11.2277
3	28	15	29	16	4.90068	16.8047	2.29558	1.30574	-24.601	-10.5841

LAG	MEAN7	MEAN8	MEAN9	MEAN10	MEAN11	MEAN12	MEAN13	MEAN14	MEAN15
.	92.175	47.5416	1.17483	-57.521	-33.4932	-28.0927	-0.08052	-0.23960	0.05520
0	121.759	58.3140	1.05155	-74.065	-20.9664	-23.9500	-0.30396	-0.45175	-0.62736
1	96.405	49.0115	1.21704	-114.464	-98.8648	-59.5002	0.11115	-0.35167	-0.02288
2	76.257	42.5351	1.20000	-16.764	-3.2651	-14.5718	-0.14000	-0.06787	0.48745
3	64.897	36.8520	1.25864	-11.982	-2.2402	-9.6989	0.02295	-0.01068	0.50795

LAG	MEAN16	MEAN17	MEAN18	MEAN19	MEAN20	MEAN21	MEAN22	MEAN23
.	-19.964	22.5102	-3.73455	43.5955	98.044	7.6947	9.0769	0.43021
0	152.661	51.0364	-8.63100	51.7962	196.349	6.4838	9.2363	0.41980
1	98.836	14.9000	-4.87217	35.8717	65.283	7.1261	10.4524	0.42196
2	74.793	14.2814	2.81513	44.4125	57.686	7.3164	7.9629	0.44386
3	-500.304	9.8530	-2.71707	42.0345	70.743	10.1166	8.4440	0.43814

Variable	Minimum	Maximum	Label
R1	0	7.230000	LOG[TOTAL ASSETS/CPI]
R2	-1323.260000	85.710000	WORKING CAPITAL/TOTAL ASSETS
R3	0.010000	19.840000	TOTAL CURRENT ASSETS/TOTAL CURRENT LIAB
R4	0	19.040000	[CURRENT ASSETS-INVENTORY] /LCT
R5	-6356.590000	93.340000	RETAINED EARNINGS/TOTAL ASSETS
R6	-417.900000	548.800000	NET INCOME/TOTAL ASSETS
R7	6.210000	1712.400000	TOTAL LIABILITIES/TOTAL ASSETS
R8	0	380.620000	TOTAL DEBT/TOTAL ASSETS [%]
R9	0	5.640000	SALES/TOTAL ASSETS
R10	-3433.330000	76.240000	NET PROFIT MARGIN[%]
R11	-3346.670000	262.160000	OPERATING MARGIN BEFORE DEPREC[%]
R12	-3433.330000	1379.300000	PRETAX PROFIT MARGIN[%]
R13	-8.570000	34.000000	CASH FLOW FROM OPERATIONS/SALES
R14	-7.500000	1.310000	CASH FLOW FROM OPERATIONS/TOTAL ASSETS
R15	-22.490000	6.840000	CASH FLOW FROM OPERATIONS/TOTAL CURRENT
R16	-24339	2363.530000	LONG TERM DEBT/SHAREHOLDERS' EQUITY[%]
R17	0	1628.570000	NET SALES/AVERAGE TOTAL RECEIVABLES
R18	-248.000000	330.000000	INTEREST COVERAGE AFTER TAX
R19	0.330000	645.850000	COST OF GOODS SOLD/AVERAGE INVENTORY
R20	0.520000	4492.200000	SALES/INVENTORY
R21	0	119.060000	SALES/NET PLANT
R22	0	99.000000	RECEIVABLES/INVENTORY
R23	0.020000	1.000000	CASH & MARKETABLE SECURITIES/T. ASSET

Appendix E

Results of Stepwise Logit Model of Risk Based on the Internal Ratios Alone

[SAS Extract]

Model Fitting Information and Testing Global Null Hypothesis BETA=0

Criterion	Intercept Only	Intercept and Covariates	Chi-Square for Covariates
AIC	488.564	421.061	.
SC	492.023	448.737	.
-2 LOG L	486.564	405.061	81.503 with 7 DF (p=0.0001)
Score	.	.	69.750 with 7 DF (p=0.0001)

Analysis of Maximum Likelihood Estimates

Variable	DF	Parameter Estimate	Standard Error	Wald Chi-Square	Pr > Chi-Square	Standardized Estimate	Odds Ratio
INTERCPT	1	1.0507	0.3358	9.7895	0.0018	.	.
R2	1	-0.0150	0.00369	16.4543	0.0001	-1.431575	0.985
R6	1	0.00478	0.00307	2.4132	0.1203	0.235442	1.005
R7	1	-0.00981	0.00314	9.7336	0.0018	-1.131461	0.990
RCD13	1	0.6972	0.3311	4.4344	0.0352	0.213128	2.008
RCD18	1	-0.7032	0.2946	5.6969	0.0170	-0.237418	0.495
RC21_1	1	-2.5360	0.6309	16.1551	0.0001	-0.525845	0.079
RC21_4	1	0.9033	0.4552	3.9388	0.0472	0.185051	2.468

Association of Predicted Probabilities and Observed Responses

Concordant = 75.9%	Somers' D = 0.520
Discordant = 23.9%	Gamma = 0.521
Tied = 0.2%	Tau-a = 0.194
(10266 pairs)	c = 0.760

Residual Chi-Square = 5.8766 with 3 DF (p=0.1178)

Analysis of Variables Not in the Model

Variable	Score Chi-Square	Pr > Chi-Square
R5	0.4957	0.4814
R14	1.0847	0.2977
R15	1.3532	0.2447

NOTE: No (additional) variables met the 0.15 significance level for entry into the model.

Classification Table

	Correct		Incorrect		Percentages				
Prob Level	Event	Non-Event	Event	Non-Event	Correct	Sensi-tivity	Speci-ficity	False POS	False NEG
0.500	37	129	48	21	70.6	63.8	72.9	56.5	14.0

Appendix F

Results of Stepwise Logit Model of Risk Based on the External Variables Alone

[SAS Extract]

```
                                  The LOGISTIC Procedure
      Data Set: WORK.DATA1
      Response Variable: BANK      OUTCOME Y VARIABLE BINARY 0/1
      Response Levels: 2
      Number of Observations: 236
      Weight Variable: W
      Sum of Weights: 354
      Link Function: Logit
                              Response Profile

                     Ordered                               Total
                       Value     BANK      Count          Weight

                           1        1         59       177.00000
                           2        0        177       177.00000

     Model Fitting Information and Testing Global Null Hypothesis BETA=0

                                     Intercept
                       Intercept        and
     Criterion           Only       Covariates    Chi-Square for Covariates

     AIC               492.748        430.356             .
     SC                496.212        451.139             .
     -2 LOG L          490.748        418.356        72.392 with 5 DF [p=0.0001]
     Score                .              .           60.710 with 5 DF [p=0.0001]


                       Analysis of Maximum Likelihood Estimates

                   Parameter   Standard      Wald        Pr >     Standardized      Odds
 Variable    DF     Estimate      Error   Chi-Square  Chi-Square     Estimate       Ratio

 INTERCPT     1      -0.0351     0.1940       0.0327      0.8565            .           .
 PC5          1      -0.8582     0.2273      14.2561      0.0002    -0.646354       0.424
```

PC3	1	0.8283	0.1740	22.6682	0.0001	1.699634	2.289
PC4	1	0.3334	0.1277	6.8193	0.0090	0.405986	1.396
PC2_1	1	0.4295	0.1282	11.2247	0.0008	1.037593	1.537
PC5_1	1	-0.6713	0.1678	16.0023	0.0001	-0.584800	0.511

Association of Predicted Probabilities and Observed Responses

Concordant	= 69.3%	Somers' D	= 0.462
Discordant	= 23.2%	Gamma	= 0.499
Tied	= 7.5%	Tau-a	= 0.174
[10443 pairs]		c	= 0.731

Classification Table

	Correct		Incorrect		Percentages				
Prob Level	Event	Non-Event	Event	Non-Event	Correct	Sensi-tivity	Speci-ficity	False POS	False NEG
0.500	32	138	39	27	72.0	54.2	78.0	54.9	16.4

Appendix G

Principal Components Analysis of the USA Economy 1970-1991

Using tables from *Abstracts of the USA* [1992] and matching the table names with earlier years' publications going back to 1970. EXCEL spreadsheet column labels A-BX are the variable labels used in the Principal Components Analysis. Amounts are in Current dollars.

X=not included in Principal Components Analysis due to many missing values. In other series, single missing values are interpolated or extrapolated.

Each row represents the variable label, along with its Table Number[6] and the name of the variable.

A DNA years covered 1970-1991 - not used in PCA
B 449 All Governments - Debt outstanding [bil.$]
C 491 Federal Budget Surplus or Deficit[-] [mill $]
D Gross Federal Debt as percent of GNP
E 494 Federal Budget Outlays Total [mill $]
F Net Interest Payments [mill $]
G 501 Total Funds Loaned in U.S. Credit Markets[bill $]
H 525 National Defense Outlays [bil $]
I 608 Labour Force - Total employed ['000]
J - Toal Unemployed['000]
K*X 623 Weekly Hours [*missing 1971-74, 1975-78]
L*X 624 Total Self-employed Workers['000] [*missing 1971-4,1976-9,1981-2]
M 673 GDP -all in current $ [bil $] - GNP only available for early [7] years
N Personal Consumption Expenditures[bil $]
O Gross private Domestic Investment [bil $]
P =ΔM 675 Average annual Percentage Change in GDP from former year
Q =ΔN Average annual Percentage Change in Personal Consumption Expenditure
R* 683 Gross Savings [bil $]
S* Gross Investment [bil $] [*missing 1971]
T 738 Consumer Price Indexes [base ave 1982-84]

[6] This number applies to the 1992 publication of *Abstracts of the USA*.

U =ΔT	739	Percentage Change in CPI from former year	
V	746	Producer Price Indexes	Crude Materials [base 1982]
W			Intermediate Materials
X			Finished Goods
Y			Capital Equipment
Z*X	778	Insured Commercial Banks -	Provisions for Loan Losses [bil $]
AA*X		Percentage of Banks Losing Money [*missing 1970-79]	
AB*	789	Mortgage Debt Outstanding - Commercial [bil $] [*missing 1981,1991]	
AC	802	Money Stock and Liquid Assets	M1 Total
AD		[bil $]	M2 Total
AE*			M3 Total [*missing 1971-72]
AF*	806	Money Market Interest Rates	Commercial paper 3 mth
AG*			Prime Rate charged by banks
AH*			US Govt Securities 1yr Treasury bill
AI*X	808	Security Prices - Bond Prices -Dow Jones	Yearly High
AJ*X		[*missing 1971-74,1976-77,1982]	Yearly Low
BB		replace above bond prices with Standard and Poor's Municipal	
AK*	809	Bond and Stock Yields [%]-US Treasury constant maturities	3 -year
AL*		[*missing 1971-72] Replaced 72 with S&P's preferred 10 stocks	5 -year
AM*			10-year
AN	862	Business Expenditure for New Plant and Equipment-All Industries[bil $]	
AO*	864	Composite Indexes of Economic Cyclical Indicators-	Leading Indicat's
AP*		[1982=100]	Coincident Indicators
AQ*		[*missing 1991]	Lagging Indicators
AR*	866	Manufacturing and Trade	Sales
AS*		[*missing 1971]	Inventories [NA 1990-91]
AT*	925	Fossil Fuel prices - Crude Oil [cents per million Btu] [*missing 1971,1991]	
AU	1204	Value of New Construction Put in Place - Total [mill $]	
AV	1250	Manufacturers'	Shipments
AW		[bil $]	Inventories
AX			New Orders
AY	1315	US International Transactions -	Balance on Current Account [bil $]*
AZ	1407	Exchange rates [index of value relative to US $]	Germany
BA		[1982=100]	Japan

The following series were added. They are the rates of change [denoted Δ] of many of the above series.

BC = ΔE 494 Federal Budget Outlays Total
BD = ΔF Net Interest Payments
BE = ΔI 608 Labour Force - Total employed
BF = ΔR 683 Gross Savings
BG = ΔS Gross Investment
BH = ΔY 746 Producer Price Indexes Capital Equipment
BI = ΔAC 802 Money Stock and Liquid Assets M1 Total
BJ = ΔAD M2 Total
BK = ΔAE M3 Total
BL = ΔAF 806 Money Market Interest Rates Commercial paper 3 mth
BM = ΔAG Prime Rate charged by banks
BN = ΔAH US Govt Securities 1yr Treasury bill
BO = ΔAK 809 Bond and Stock Yields [%]-US Treasury constant maturities 3 - year
BP = ΔAL 5 -year
BQ = ΔAM 10-year
BR = ΔAN 862 Business Expenditure for New Plant and Equipment - All Industries
BS = ΔAR 866 Manufacturing and Trade Sales
BT = ΔAS Inventories
BU = ΔAU 1204 Value of New Construction Put in Place - Total
BV = ΔAV 1250 Manufacturers' Shipments
BW = ΔAW Inventories
BX = ΔAX New Orders

PRINCIPAL COMPONENTS ANALYSIS

1st PRINCIPAL COMPONENT:
Economy Growth (Level Of Activity/Demand)

This factor is a surrogate for YEAR as it is highly correlated with YEAR [an increasing function -almost monotonic.]

PC1 [54% of variation explained] loads highest [**p<=0.0002**] on:
[in *descending order* of correlation magnitude]
[all **+ve** unless stated as **-ve**]

E 494 Federal Budget Outlays Total [mill$]
T 738 Consumer Price Indexes
AS 866 Manufacturing and Trade Inventories

AE 802 Money Stock and Liquid Assets M3 Total
AD 802 Money Stock and Liquid Assets M2 Total
M 673 GDP -all in current $ [bil $] - GNP only available for early [7] years
N 673 Personal Consumption Expenditures [bil $]
AR 866 Manufacturing and Trade Sales
AN 862 Business Expenditure for New Plant and Equipment All Industries
Y 746 Producer Price Indexes Capital Equipment
AV 1250 Manufacturers' Shipments
AX 1250 Manufacturers' New Orders
AW 1250 Manufacturers' Inventories
X 746 Producer Price Indexes Finished Goods
AU 1204 Value of New Construction Put in Place - Total [mill $]
M 673 Gross private Domestic Investment [bil $]
S 683 Gross Investment [bil $]
R 683 Gross Savings [bil $]
W 746 Producer Price Indexes Intermediate Materials
C -ve 491 Federal Budget Surplus or Deficit[-] [mill $]
Composite Indexes of Economic Cyclical Indicators
AO 864 -Leading Indicators
AP 864 -Coincident Indicators
AY –ve 1315 US International Transactions - Balance on Current Account [bil $]

2nd PRINCIPAL COMPONENT
Cost Of Capital Borrowing Factor

PC2 [17.6% of variation accounted for] loads highest [**p<=.0005**] on :
[in *descending order* of correlation magnitude]

AF 806 Money Market Interest Rates Commercial paper 3 mth
BP[ΔAL]809 Δ[Bond and Stock Yields [%]US Treasury constant maturities 5-yr]
AH 806 Money Market Interest Rates US Govt Securities 1yr Treasury bill
BO[ΔAK]809 Δ[Bond and Stock Yields [%]US Treasury constant maturities 3-yr]
BD[ΔF] 494 Δ[Net Interest Payments]
BQ[ΔAM]809 Δ[Bond and Stock Yields [%]US Treasury constant maturities10yr]
AG 806 Money Market Interest Rates Prime Rate charged by banks
BM[ΔAG]806 Δ[Money Market Interest Rates Prime Rate charged by banks]
AK 809 Bond and Stock Yields [%]-US Treasury constant maturities 3 -yr
BN[ΔAH]806 Δ[Money Market Interest Rates US Govt Securities 1yr Treas. bill]
AL 809 Bond and Stock Yields [%]-US Treasury constant maturities 5-yr
U[ΔT] 739 Average Annual percentage change,Δ[CPI], from former year
BL[ΔAF]806 Δ[Money Market Interest Rates Commercial paper 3 mth]
AM 809 Bond and Stock Yields [%]-US Treasury constant maturities 10-yr

3rd PRINCIPAL COMPONENT
Labour Market Tightness Factor

PC3 [12.4% of variation accounted for] loads highest [**p<=0.02**] on :-
[in *descending order* of correlation magnitude]

J **[-ve]** 608 Labour Force - Total Unemployed ['000]
BB 808 Security Prices -Standard and Poor's Municipal
BE[ΔI] 608 Δ[Labour Force - Total employed]
AM**[-ve]**809 Bond and Stock Yields [%]-US Treasury constant maturities 10-yr
AL**[-ve]** 809Bond and Stock Yields [%]-US Treasury constant maturities 5-yr
BL[ΔAF]806 Δ[Money Market Interest Rates Commercial paper 3 mth]
AK**[-ve]** 809 Bond and Stock Yields [%]-US Treasury constant maturities 3-yr
BG[ΔS] 683 Δ [Gross Investment]
BM[ΔAG]806 Δ[Money Market Interest Rates Prime Rate charged by banks]
BN[ΔAH]806 Δ[Money Market Interest Rates US Govt Securities 1yr Treas. bill]
BX[ΔAX]1250 Δ[Manufacturers' New Orders]
AT**[-ve]** 925 Fossil Fuel prices - Crude Oil [cents per million Btu]
BF[ΔR] 683 Δ[Gross Savings]
BJ[ΔAD] **[-ve]**802 Δ[Money Stock and Liquid Assets-M2 Total]
BV[ΔAV]1250 Δ[Manufacturers' Shipments]
BS[ΔAR]866 Δ[Manufacturing and Trade Sales]

4th PRINCIPAL COMPONENT
Construction Activity Factor

PC4 [accounting for 5.6% of the variation] loads highest [**p<0.03**] on:

BU[ΔAU]1204 Δ[Value of New Construction Put in Place - Total]
BE[ΔI] 608 Δ[Labour Force - Total employed]
BH[ΔY]**[-ve]** 746 Δ[Producer Price Indexes Capital Equipment]
AZ**[-ve]** 1407 Exchange rates [index of value relative to US $] Germany
U[ΔT]**[-ve]** 739 Percent Change, Δ [CPI], from former year

5th PRINCIPAL COMPONENT
Expenditure Factor [Private, Public, Business]

PC5 [accounting for 2.7% of the variation] loads highest [**p<0.04**] on:

BR ΔAN 862 Busines Expenditure for New Plant and Equipment - All Industries
BC ΔE494 Federal Budget Outlays Total
Q=ΔN 675 Average annual Percentage Change ,Δ[Personal Consumption Exp.]

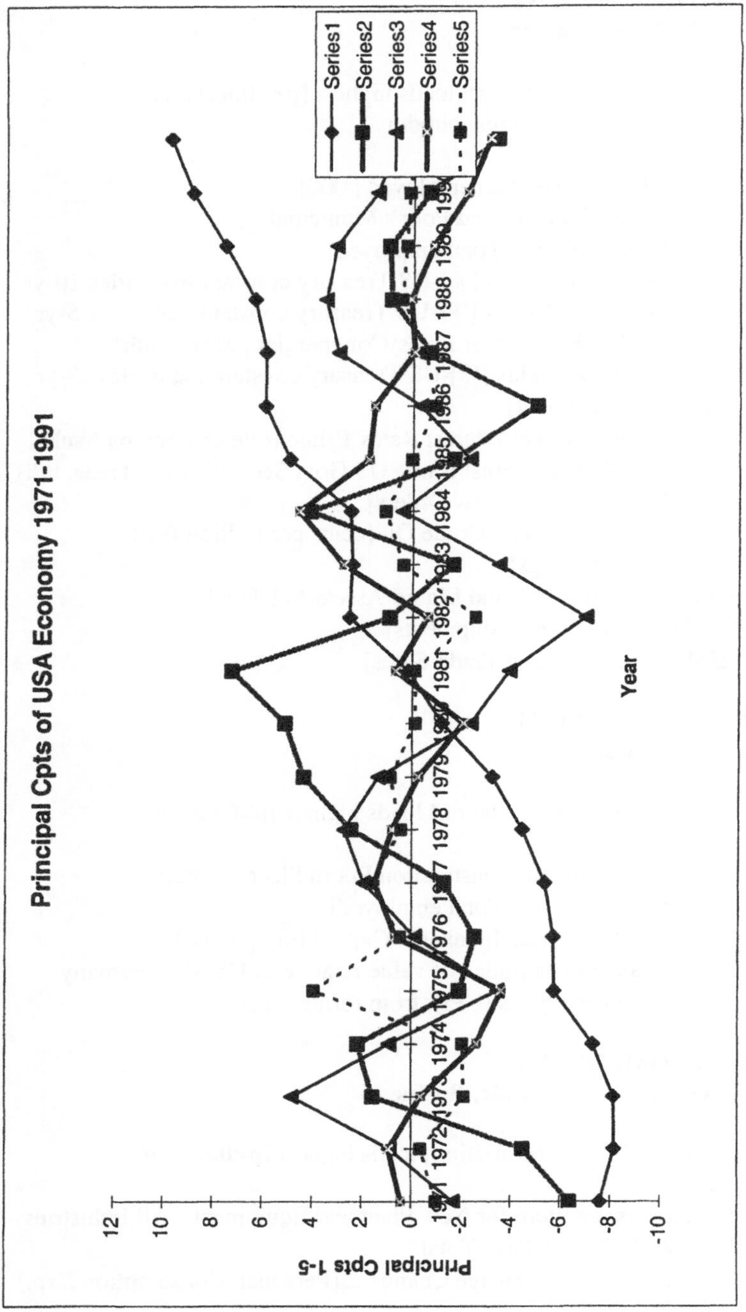
Principal Cpts of USA Economy 1971-1991
Principal Cpts 1-5
Year
Series1
Series2
Series3
Series4
Series5
12
10
8
6
4
2
0
-2
-4
-6
-8
-10
1971
1972
1973
1974
1975
1976
1977
1978
1979
1980
1981
1982
1983
1984
1985
1986
1987
1988
1989
1990
1991

Principal Component Values For Each Year 1971-1991

Year	PC1	PC2	PC3	PC4	PC5
1971	-7.60082	-6.3848	-1.6758	0.42372	-0.99014
1972	-8.1711	-4.5077	0.86538	0.91028	-0.37112
1973	-8.1421	1.54885	4.80185	-0.37125	-2.1183
1974	-7.31004	2.14973	0.9094	-2.64179	-2.0528
1975	-5.74793	-1.93763	-3.47421	-3.63041	3.91908
1976	-5.71699	-2.54768	-0.12456	0.65381	0.45551
1977	-5.365	-1.30231	1.924	1.47728	1.59671
1978	-4.45419	2.44495	2.71621	0.79998	0.4368
1979	-3.2585	4.35636	1.34594	-0.25933	0.86666
1980	-1.19871	5.10705	-2.37138	-2.07398	-0.11592
1981	0.16006	7.24294	-3.92377	0.67408	-0.09657
1982	2.52881	0.92366	-6.97712	-0.60285	-2.54115
1983	2.42333	-1.62607	-3.49235	2.77404	0.37209
1984	2.49448	4.13505	0.4227	4.57363	1.09929
1985	4.94474	-1.65367	-2.30862	1.77265	0.04334
1986	5.93131	-5.01364	-0.29983	1.54374	-0.89717
1987	5.91623	-0.69367	3.00586	-0.0423	-0.49738
1988	6.37102	0.87707	3.51841	0.10776	0.46596
1989	7.55218	0.95228	3.09072	-0.81168	0.27598
1990	8.88222	-0.66597	1.46578	-2.18756	0.16509
1991	9.76102	-3.40479	0.5814	-3.08981	-0.01597

Eigenvalues of the Correlation Matrix

[SAS Extract]

	Eigenvalue	Difference	Proportion	Cumulative
PC1	37.7808	25.4705	0.539725	0.539725
PC2	12.3102	3.6419	0.175861	0.715586
PC3	8.6683	4.7241	0.123833	0.839419
PC4	3.9442	2.0403	0.056346	0.895765
PC5	1.9040	.	0.027200	0.922965

Appendix H

The Preliminary Logit Model Based on the Internal and the External Variables

[SAS Extract]

NOTES AND SAS OUTPUT FOR THE RESULTS OF THE FINAL STEPWISE ANALYSIS - PROC LOGISTIC

The LOGISTIC Procedure

Model Fitting Information and Testing Global Null Hypothesis BETA=0

Criterion	Intercept Only	Intercept and Covariates	Chi-Square for Covariates
AIC	488.564	359.146	.
SC	492.023	400.661	.
-2 LOG L	486.564	335.146	151.418 with 11 DF [p=0.0001]
Score	.	.	120.776 with 11 DF [p=0.0001]

Analysis of Maximum Likelihood Estimates

Variable	DF	Parameter Estimate	Standard Error	Wald Chi-Square	Pr > Chi-Square	Standardized Estimate	Odds Ratio
INTERCPT	1	1.4658	0.3972	13.6212	0.0002	.	.
PC3	1	0.9115	0.1818	25.1319	0.0001	1.840710	2.488
PC4	1	0.4133	0.1404	8.6650	0.0032	0.502279	1.512
PC5	1	-0.7695	0.2497	9.4930	0.0021	-0.567249	0.463
PC2_1	1	0.4736	0.1327	12.7349	0.0004	1.129773	1.606
PC5_1	1	-0.8011	0.1790	20.0306	0.0001	-0.699404	0.449
R2	1	-0.0206	0.00441	21.8895	0.0001	-1.975457	0.980
R7	1	-0.0166	0.00383	18.8065	0.0001	-1.916435	0.984
R15	1	-0.0821	0.0533	2.3675	0.1239	-0.149701	0.921
RCD18	1	-0.6916	0.2952	5.4874	0.0192	-0.233494	0.501
RC21_1	1	-2.2866	0.6560	12.1513	0.0005	-0.474131	0.102
RC21_4	1	1.6171	0.5183	9.7339	0.0018	0.331274	5.038

Residual Chi-Square = 8.8668 with 4 DF [p=0.0645]

Note:the residual chi-square value is just not significant at 0.05 level -i.e. lack-of-fit is not significant. This is a minimum adequate model.

Association of Predicted Probabilities and Observed Responses

Concordant	= 84.2%	Somers' D	= 0.685
Discordant	= 15.7%	Gamma	= 0.685
Tied	= 0.1%	Tau-a	= 0.256
[10266 pairs]		c	= 0.842

Analysis of Variables Not in the Model

Variable	Score Chi-Square	Pr > Chi-Square
R5	2.3894	0.1222
R6	2.5783	0.1083
R14	1.7911	0.1808
RCD13	0.4420	0.5062

Note: Classification accuracy is no better with R6 and/or R5 included'[p<0.15] and probability[type I error] is worse. The other variables have already been eliminated in earlier stepwise analyses-analysed in stages to reduce the number of missing cases in the final analysis.]

Classification Table

	Correct		Incorrect		Percentages				
Prob Level	Event	Non-Event	Event	Non-Event	Correct	Sensi-tivity	Speci-ficity	False POS	False NEG
0.500	41	128	49	17	71.9	70.7	72.3	54.4	11.7

Note:
Probability[Type I Error] = 17/58 = 29.3% misclassifying failing firm-years
Probability[Type II Error]= 49/177= 27.7% misclassifying surviving firm-years

Appendix I

Analysis of Estimated Failure Risk by Lag Year for Each Failed Service Industry Firm

	Estimated risk of failure at each lag-year (Each row denotes one failed firm) LAG			
Firm	**0**	**1**	**2**	**3**
1	.	0.84	0.15	0.88
2	0.97	0.32	0.60	0.10
3	0.76	0.04	0.02	0.34
4	0.58	0.28	0.01	0.01
5	0.37	0.48	0.27	0.11
6	0.91	0.87	0.84	0.55
7	0.82	0.19	0.54	0.35
8	0.96	0.66	0.00	0.00
9	0.85	0.48	0.04	0.01
10	0.25	0.69	0.73	0.06
11	0.68	0.71	0.32	0.01
12	0.77	0.53	0.10	0.01
13	0.68	0.30	0.22	0.32
14	0.71	0.19	0.17	0.52
15	0.34	0.16	0.15	0.49
16	0.64	0.77	0.27	0.18
17	0.81	0.21	0.38	0.52
18	0.87	0.65	0.56	0.66
19	0.27	0.77	0.39	0.70
20	0.86	0.17	0.39	0.36
21	0.76	0.36	0.24	0.35
22	0.90	0.38	0.03	0.13
23	0.96	0.90	0.62	0.59
24	0.84	0.41	0.72	0.26
25	0.93	0.69	0.36	0.28
26	0.81	0.41	0.23	0.34
27	0.93	0.85	0.44	0.61
28	0.43	0.24	0.10	0.64

Estimated risk of failure at each lag-year (Each row denotes one failed firm) LAG				
Firm	0	1	2	3
29	0.63	0.16	0.22	0.12
30	0.84	0.43	0.21	0.31
31	0.60	0.59	0.58	0.26
32	0.96	0.13	0.03	0.13
33	0.55	0.12	0.02	0.05
34	0.92	0.45	0.30	0.45
35	0.85	0.55	0.02	0.02
36	0.30	0.14	0.21	0.10
37	0.26	0.10	0.70	0.42
38	0.28	0.01	0.00	0.97
39	0.98	0.84	0.73	0.07
40	0.93	0.78	0.06	0.07
41	0.62	0.72	0.06	0.03
42	0.80	0.36	0.03	0.13
43	0.92	0.32	0.28	0.46
44	0.33	0.41	0.01	0.01
45	0.76	0.51	0.18	0.19
46	0.45	0.10	0.66	0.51
47	0.79	0.61	0.03	0.13
48	0.67	0.35	0.07	0.11
49	0.82	0.43	0.22	0.37
50	0.82	0.52	0.47	0.01
51	0.99	0.24	0.01	0.00
52	0.26	0.12	0.02	0.05
53	0.31	0.32	0.15	0.18
54	0.64	0.52	0.07	0.11
55	0.39	0.56	0.49	0.03
56	0.32	0.19	0.16	0.09
57	0.47	0.51	0.36	0.14
58	0.79	0.7	0.27	0.24
59	0.43	0.04	0.02	0.02

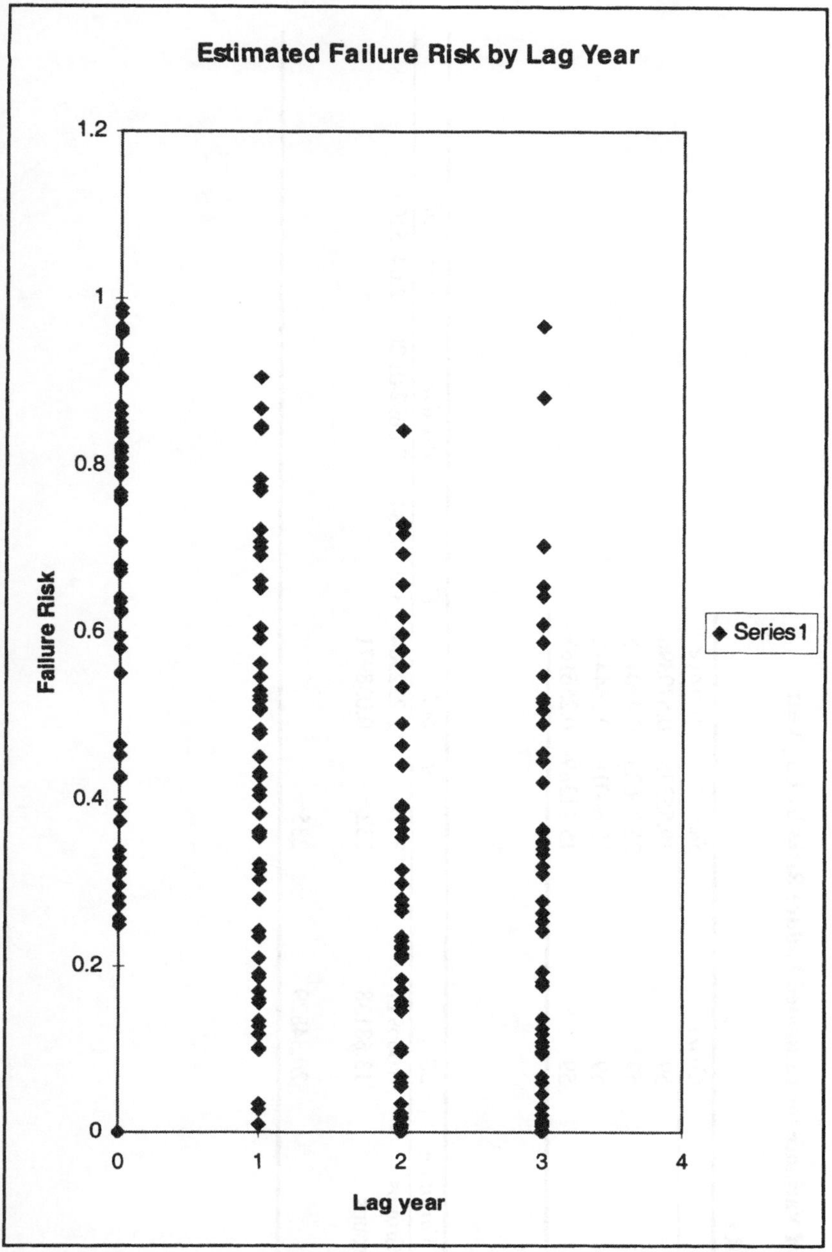
Estimated Failure Risk by Lag Year
1.2
1
0.8
0.6
0.4
0.2
0
Failure Risk
0
1
2
3
4
Lag year
Series1

Analysis of Variance for Estimated Failure Risks by Lag Year

SUMMARY

Groups	*Count*	*Sum*	*Average*
LAG0	59	39.55335	0.670396
LAG1	59	25.39625	0.430445
LAG2	59	15.60018	0.264410
LAG3	59	15.11389	0.256168

ANOVA

Source of Variation	*SS*	*df*	*MS*	*F*	*P-value*	*F critical*
Between Groups	6.666911	3	2.222304	37.684384	7.06924E-20	2.6435103
Within Groups	13.68138	232	0.058971			
Total	20.34829	235				

Pairwise z-tests for proportions — **Test for differences between average estimated failure risk for each lag year** — **H_0: $p_i > p_j$ one-tail or H_0: $p_i = p_j$ two-tail**

	<u>LAG3</u>	<u>LAG2</u>		<u>LAG1</u>	<u>LAG2</u>	
Mean	0.256168	0.26441		0.430445	0.26441	
s.e. $_{[pi - pj]}$	0.0808			0.086		
	Z= 0.103	NOT SIG.	accept H_0	Z=1.925	SIGNIF	reject H_0
		$p_2=p_3$	[two-tail]	$p_1>p_2$	[one-tail]	[p<0.03]
	<u>LAG0</u>	<u>LAG1</u>		<u>LAG0</u>	<u>LAG2</u>	
Mean	0.670396	0.430445		0.670396	0.26441	
s.e. $_{[pi - pj]}$	0.0883			0.0837		
	Z=2.717	SIGNIF	reject H_0	Z=4.846	SIGNIF	reject H_0
	$p_0>p_1$	[one-tail]	[p=0.0033]	$p_0>p_2$	[one-tail]	[p<<0.0001]

Note: Using the Normal variate $z = [p_i - p_j] / s.e._{[pi - pj]}$
where: $s.e._{[pi - pj]} = \sqrt{[p_i q_i / n_i + p_j q_j / n_j]}$ where $q_i = 1 - p_i$
to test H_0: $p_i > p_j$ [one-tail] or H_0: $p_i = p_j$ [two-tail]

Appendix J

A Logit Model Based on the Internal and External Variables Plus Estimated Risk Lagged One Year

[SAS extract]

First iteration: Analysis of Maximum Likelihood Estimates [SAS extract]

Variable	DF	Parameter Estimate	Standard Error	Wald Chi-Square	Pr > Chi-Square	Standardized Estimate	Odds Ratio
INTERCPT	1	0.4575	0.4527	1.0213	0.3122	.	.
PC3	1	0.7046	0.1798	15.3509	0.0001	1.422858	2.023
PC4	1	0.3640	0.1296	7.8865	0.0050	0.442357	1.439
PC5	1	-0.5961	0.2284	6.8114	0.0091	-0.439434	0.551
PC2_1	1	0.3529	0.1344	6.8983	0.0086	0.841871	1.423
PC5_1	1	-0.7904	0.1861	18.0304	0.0001	-0.690058	0.454
R2	1	-0.0196	0.00456	18.5229	0.0001	-1.877778	0.981
R7	1	-0.0167	0.00393	18.0844	0.0001	-1.930321	0.983
R15	1	-0.0779	0.0517	2.2730	0.1316	-0.142081	0.925
RCD18	1	-0.5819	0.3118	3.4831	0.0620	-0.196463	0.559
RC21_1	1	-1.6214	0.6744	5.7799	0.0162	-0.336209	0.198
RC21_4	1	1.6087	0.5138	9.8031	0.0017	0.329553	4.996
PHATLAG1	1	3.0956	0.6714	21.2550	0.0001	0.556652	22.100

The LOGISTIC Procedure

Association of Predicted Probabilities and Observed Responses

Concordant	= 87.2%	Somers' D	= 0.746
Discordant	= 12.6%	Gamma	= 0.747
Tied	= 0.1%	Tau-a	= 0.279
[10266 pairs]		c	= 0.873

Classification Table

	Correct		Incorrect		Percentages				
Prob Level	Event	Non-Event	Event	Non-Event	Correct	Sensi-tivity	Speci-ficity	False POS	False NEG
0.500	41	138	39	17	76.2	70.7	78.0	48.8	11.0

PROBABILITY[TYPE I ERROR] = 17/58 = 29.3% -MISCLASSIFYING FAILING FIRM-YEARS
PROBABILITY[TYPE II ERROR]= 39/177= 22% -MISCLASSIFYING SURVIVING FIRM-YEARS
Note: Similar model classification statistics result from R6 replacing R15 except for a larger Type II error of 31%. Lack of Fit is not significant **** Residual Chi-Square = 7.7044 with 4 DF [p=0.1030]

Appendix K

Seemingly Unrelated Regressions Model

[SAS Extract]

```
LIBNAME  SERVICE "C:\MYSASDIR";
DATA  A;SET SERVICE.SERV60F;
MISSING N P;RUN;
PROC MODEL ;
phatF = 1/[1 + EXP[-A1 - B1*PC3 -C1*R2 -D1*PC5_1 - E1*R7 - F1*RC21_1
- G1*RC21_4 - H1*PC5 - I1*PC4 - J1*PC2_1 -K1*RCD18 - L1*R15 -
M1*R6]];
phatFl1 = 1/[1 + EXP[-A2 - B2*PC3L1 -C2*R2L1 -D2*PC5_1L1 - E2*R7L1 -
F2*RC21_1L1 - G2*RC21_4L1 -H2*PC5L1 - I2*PC4L1 - J2*PC2_1L1 -
K2*RCD18L1 - L2*R15L1 - M2*R6]];
phatFL2 = 1/[1 + EXP[-A3 - B3*PC3L2 -C3*R2L2 -D3*PC5_1L2 - E3*R7L2 -
F3*RC21_1L2 - G3*RC21_4L2 -H3*PC5L2 - I3*PC4L2 - J3*PC2_1L2 -
K3*RCD18L2 - L3*R15L2 - M3*R6]];
phatFL3 = 1/[1 + EXP[-A4 - B4*PC3L3 -C4*R2L3 -D4*PC5_1L3 - E4*R7L3 -
F4*RC21_1L3 - G4*RC21_4L3 -H4*PC5L3 - I4*PC4L3 - J4*PC2_1L3 -
K4*RCD18L3 - L4*R15L3 - M4*R6]];
FIT phatF phatFL1 phatFL2 phatFL3 / SUR ;
RUN;
```

```
                                          MODEL Procedure
                                          SUR Estimation

                                      SUR Estimation Summary
                                   Parameters Estimated        52

                                       Minimization Summary
                                   Method                   GAUSS
                                   Iterations                   7

                                   Final  Convergence  Criteria
                                   R                   0.00078464
                                   PPC[M4]               0.016509
                                   RPC[M4]               0.023497
                                   Object              4.40871E-7
                                   Trace[S]            0.04691776
                                   Objective Value     3.05572373
                                      Observations Processed
                                   Read                        59
                                   Solved                      59
                                   Used                        58
                                   Missing
```

Nonlinear SUR Summary of Residual Errors

Equation	Model	DF Error	DF SSE	MSE	Root MSE	R-Square	Adj R-Sq
PHATF	13	45	0.55689	0.01238	0.11124	0.8455	0.8043
PHATFL1	13	45	0.83712	0.01860	0.13639	0.7417	0.67
PHATFL2	13	45	0.36091	0.00802	0.08956	0.8814	0.8498
PHATFL3	13	45	0.35638	0.00791	0.08899	0.8801	0.8482

Nonlinear SUR Parameter Estimates

Parameter	Estimate	Approx. Std Err	'T' Ratio	Approx. Prob>|T|
A1	1.500561	0.30809	4.87	0.0001
B1	1.043628	0.16731	6.24	0.0001
C1	-0.021964	0.0030834	-7.12	0.0001
D1	-0.905753	0.15791	-5.74	0.0001
E1	-0.015606	0.0028006	-5.57	0.0001
F1	-2.715166	0.64303	-4.22	0.0001
G1	1.227973	0.33412	3.68	0.0006
H1	-0.813269	0.21613	-3.76	0.0005
I1	0.502940	0.12028	4.18	0.0001
J1	0.574168	0.11993	4.79	0.0001
K1	-0.616536	0.21266	-2.90	0.0058
L1	-0.105347	0.03359	-3.14	0.0030
M1	0.00186500	0.0017979	1.04	0.3051
A2	1.088727	0.31186	3.49	0.0011
B2	1.416383	0.23284	6.08	0.0001
C2	-0.017233	0.0038274	-4.50	0.0001
D2	-1.157268	0.20977	-5.52	0.0001
E2	-0.014992	0.0032760	-4.58	0.0001
F2	-1.608250	0.49957	-3.22	0.0024
G2	1.414450	0.56761	2.49	0.0165
H2	-1.141736	0.22068	-5.17	0.0001
I2	0.595104	0.12925	4.60	0.0001
J2	0.853849	0.16194	5.27	0.0001
K2	-0.549377	0.20818	-2.64	0.0114
L2	0.046352	0.05856	0.79	0.4328
M2	0.00267101	0.0013532	1.97	0.0546
A3	1.854691	0.31707	5.85	0.0001
B3	0.886436	0.12200	7.27	0.0001
C3	-0.027669	0.0049277	-5.61	0.0001
D3	-0.832786	0.10462	-7.96	0.0001
E3	-0.027730	0.0039777	-6.97	0.0001
F3	-2.544577	1.00102	-2.54	0.0145
G3	2.589319	0.50015	5.18	0.0001
H3	-0.755920	0.16810	-4.50	0.0001
I3	0.613621	0.11307	5.43	0.0001
J3	0.537624	0.09129	5.89	0.0001
K3	-1.188459	0.22725	-5.23	0.0001
L3	0.00118013	0.06819	0.02	0.9863
M3	0.00029389	0.0017779	0.17	0.8694
A4	1.198648	0.35610	3.37	0.0016
B4	0.657936	0.10124	6.50	0.0001
C4	-0.023484	0.0047377	-4.96	0.0001
D4	-0.515410	0.10002	-5.15	0.0001
E4	-0.015130	0.0036240	-4.17	0.0001
F4	-2.490608	0.35094	-7.10	0.0001
G4	1.754953	0.43140	4.07	0.0002
H4	-0.392134	0.12017	-3.26	0.0021
I4	0.374358	0.08078	4.63	0.0001
J4	0.370259	0.09591	3.86	0.0004
K4	-0.891998	0.18759	-4.76	0.0001
L4	-0.083333	0.05540	-1.50	0.1395
M4	-0.00017163	0.0007990	-0.21	0.8309

Number of Observations		Statistics for System	
Used	58	Objective	3.0557
Missing	1	Objective*N	177.2320

Appendix L

Seemingly Unrelated Regressions Model with Lagged Risk

[SAS Extract]

```
LIBNAME SERVICE "C:\MYSASDIR";
DATA  A;SET SERVICE.SERV60F;
PROC MODEL DETAILS;
phatF = 1/[1 + EXP[-A1 - B1*PC3 -C1*R2 -D1*PC5_1 - E1*R7 - F1*RC21_1- G1*RC21_4
- H1*PC5 - I1*PC4 - J1*PC2_1 -K1*RCD18 - L1*R15 - M1*R6 - N1*PHTF_1]];
phatFL1 = 1/[1 + EXP[-A2 - B2*PC3L1 -C2*R2L1 -D2*PC5_1L1 - E2*R7L1 - F2*RC21_1L1
- G2*RC21_4L1-H2*PC5L1 - I2*PC4L1 - J2*PC2_1L1 - K2*RCD18L1 - L2*R15L1 - M2*R6
- N2*PHTF_1L1]];
phatFL2 = 1/[1 + EXP[-A3 - B3*PC3L2 -C3*R2L2 -D3*PC5_1L2 - E3*R7L2 - F3*RC21_1L2
 - G3*RC21_4L2-H3*PC5L2 - I3*PC4L2 - J3*PC2_1L2 - K3*RCD18L2 - L3*R15L2 - M3*R6
 - N3*PHTF_1L2]];
phatFL3 = 1/[1 + EXP[-A4 - B4*PC3L3 -C4*R2L3 -D4*PC5_1L3 - E4*R7L3 - F4*RC21_1L3
 - G4*RC21_4L3-H4*PC5L3 - I4*PC4L3 - J4*PC2_1L3 - K4*RCD18L3 -L4*R15L3 -M4*R6]];

FIT phatF phatFL1 phatFL2 phatFL3 / SUR BLOCK out=predsur1 outpredict;
RUN;
```

```
        Minimization Summary
Method                        GAUSS
Iterations                        9
Final  Convergence  Criteria
R                        0.00076237
PPC[M4]                    0.019052
RPC[M4]                    0.026148
Object                  3.47914E-7
Trace[S]                 0.04731961
Objective Value          2.98764506

      Observations Processed
Read                             59
Solved                           59
Used                             58
Missing                           1
```

MODEL Procedure
SUR Estimation
Nonlinear SUR Summary of Residual Errors

Equation	DF Model	DF Error	SSE	MSE	Root MSE	R-Square	Adj R-Sq
PHATF	14	44	0.55345	0.01258	0.11215	0.8465	0.8011
PHATFL1	14	44	0.82283	0.01870	0.13675	0.7461	0.6711
PHATFL2	14	44	0.35633	0.0080983	0.08999	0.8829	0.8483
PHATFL3	13	45	0.35740	0.0079423	0.08912	0.8798	0.8477

Nonlinear SUR Parameter Estimates

Parameter	Estimate	Approx. Std Err	'T' Ratio	Approx. Prob>|T|
A1	1.453598	0.37360	3.89	0.0003
B1	1.039543	0.18211	5.71	0.0001
C1	-0.021984	0.0032753	-6.71	0.0001
D1	-0.918872	0.16373	-5.61	0.0001
E1	-0.015750	0.0029635	-5.31	0.0001
F1	-2.665742	0.66595	-4.00	0.0002
G1	1.192788	0.33631	3.55	0.0009
H1	-0.792059	0.22670	-3.49	0.0011
I1	0.495248	0.12488	3.97	0.0003
J1	0.569947	0.12918	4.41	0.0001
K1	-0.591270	0.21755	-2.72	0.0094
L1	-0.106714	0.03376	-3.16	0.0028
M1	0.00181450	0.0017835	1.02	0.3145
N1	0.190169	0.48920	0.39	0.6993
A2	1.276786	0.33620	3.80	0.0004
B2	1.569915	0.25948	6.05	0.0001
C2	-0.019095	0.0040397	-4.73	0.0001
D2	-1.275120	0.22553	-5.65	0.0001
E2	-0.016614	0.0034523	-4.81	0.0001
F2	-1.680827	0.49957	-3.36	0.0016
G2	1.681892	0.59629	2.82	0.0072
H2	-1.282341	0.24337	-5.27	0.0001
I2	0.689249	0.14700	4.69	0.0001
J2	0.944469	0.17528	5.39	0.0001
K2	-0.486855	0.20919	-2.33	0.0246
L2	0.048959	0.05829	0.84	0.4055
M2	0.00278039	0.0013743	2.02	0.0492
N2	-0.709351	0.47364	-1.50	0.1414
A3	1.810556	0.31193	5.80	0.0001
B3	0.927636	0.13070	7.10	0.0001
C3	-0.025767	0.0048676	-5.29	0.0001
D3	-0.809096	0.10275	-7.87	0.0001
E3	-0.025957	0.0039543	-6.56	0.0001
F3	-2.703064	0.98832	-2.73	0.0090
G3	2.434493	0.49579	4.91	0.0001
H3	-0.845011	0.18665	-4.53	0.0001
I3	0.666120	0.12164	5.48	0.0001
J3	0.556866	0.09325	5.97	0.0001
K3	-1.152379	0.22250	-5.18	0.0001
L3	0.010858	0.06760	0.16	0.8731
M3	0.000050351	0.0017552	0.03	0.9772
N3	-0.605318	0.42981	-1.41	0.1661
A4	1.137348	0.35593	3.20	0.0026
B4	0.653037	0.10074	6.48	0.0001
C4	-0.022888	0.0047120	-4.86	0.0001
D4	-0.518936	0.09922	-5.23	0.0001
E4	-0.014873	0.0036091	-4.12	0.0002
F4	-2.463170	0.34930	-7.05	0.0001
G4	1.766778	0.42977	4.11	0.0002
H4	-0.389889	0.11953	-3.26	0.0021
I4	0.376049	0.08097	4.64	0.0001
J4	0.369759	0.09562	3.87	0.0004
K4	-0.865371	0.18615	-4.65	0.0001
L4	-0.083528	0.05485	-1.52	0.1348
M4	-0.00014196	0.0007938	-0.18	0.8589

Number of Observations		Statistics for System	
Used	58	Objective	2.9876
Missing	1	Objective*N	173.2834

Appendix M

Stepwise Regression Analysis for Working Capital/Total Assets, R2

[SAS Extract]

```
LIBNAME SERVICE "C:\MYSASDIR";
DATA;SET SERVICE.PREDF;
MISSING N P;
option ps=60;
/*AFTER REMOVING UNCORRELATED VARIABLES WITH R2[P>0.15] USING INSIGHT*/
proc reg;
model R2=R7 R6 PHATFULL PHATFLG1 PC1-PC5 PC2_1-PC2_3 PC4_1-PC4_3 PC5_1
  /selection=stepwise
  slentry=0.15
  slstay=0.15
  details;
  run;
```

EXTRACT OF SAS OUTPUT

	DF	Sum of Squares	Mean Square	F	Prob>F
Regression	5	2727915.1975303	545583.03950607	644.58	0.0001
Error	170	143891.85772807	846.42269252		
Total	175	2871807.0552584			

Variable	Parameter Estimate	Standard Error	Type II Sum of Squares	F	Prob>F
INTERCEP	90.21144316	4.67182662	315600.09537168	372.86	0.0001
R7	-0.76921206	0.01599853	1956677.6524370	2311.70	0.0001
R6	0.14233757	0.03629395	13018.40700631	15.38	0.0001
PHATFULL	-68.94453856	8.36616575	57482.29618363	67.91	0.0001
PC1	2.56697994	0.61559616	14717.71693286	17.39	0.0001
PC3	4.58910628	0.88217673	22905.10760183	27.06	0.0001

All variables left in the model are significant at the 0.1500 level.
No other variable met the 0.15 significance level for entry into the model.

Summary of Stepwise Procedure for Dependent Variable R2

Step	Variable Entered Removed	Number In	Partial R**2	Model R**2	C[p]	F	Prob>F	Label
1	R7	1	0.9266	0.9266	73.7355	2197.5113	0.0001	TOTAL LIABILITIES/TOTAL ASSETS
2	PHATFULL	2	0.0103	0.9369	41.2825	28.2104	0.0001	ESTIMATED FAILURE RISK FULL MODEL
3	PC3	3	0.0051	0.9420	26.1609	15.1675	0.0001	LABOUR MARKET TIGHTNESS FACTOR
4	PC1	4	0.0033	0.9454	16.9953	10.4337	0.0015	LEVEL OF ACTIVITY/DEMAND FACTOR
5	R6	5	0.0045	0.9499	3.8127	15.3805	0.0001	NET INCOME/TOTAL ASSETS

Appendix N

3SLS Analysis for Simultaneous Equations Estimation: Failure Risk and Working Capital/Total Assets

[SAS Extract]

```
DATA;SET SERVICE.PREDF;
MISSING N P; RUN;
OPTION PS=60;
OPTION LINESIZE=80;
PROC MODEL BLOCK ; /*CHECK NO. OF INSTRUMENTS MUST BE >=NO. OF
PARAMETERS ESTIMATED IN ANY EQUATION*/
EXOGENOUS R7 R6 RC21_1 RC21_4 RCD18 R15 PC1 PC3 PC5 PC4 PC2_1 PC5_1 ;
ENDOGENOUS PHATFULL;
/* EQN 1:CHAPTER 6 MODEL MINUS R7*/
/*AND INCLUDING R7 IN EQN 2 FOR R2 SINCE HIGH PAIRWISE CORR*/

PHATFULL = 1/[1 + EXP[-INT1 - B1*PC3 -C1*R2 -D1*PC5_1 - F1*RC21_1
- G1*RC21_4- H1*PC5 - I1*PC4 - J1*PC2_1 -K1*RCD18 - L1*R15]];/*11
PARAMETERS*/

/* EQN 2: */

R2=INT + A*R7 + B*R6 + C*PHATFULL + D*PC3 + E*PC1;/*6 PARAMETERS*/

FIT PHATFULL R2 /3SLS DETAILS OUT=PREDFSIM OUTACTUAL OUTPREDICT;
INSTRUMENTS _EXOG_;/*12 INSTRUMENTS*/

LABEL BANK="OUTCOME Y VARIABLE BINARY 0/1"
 R2="WORKING CAPITAL/TOTAL ASSETS"
 R6="NET INCOME/TOTAL ASSETS"
 R7="TOTAL LIABILITIES/TOTAL ASSETS"
 R15="CASH FLOW FROM OPERATIONS/TOTAL CUR.LIAB"
 RCD18="INTEREST COVERAGE AFTER TAX"
 RC21_1="SALES/NET PLANT LOWEST VALUES"
 RC21_4="SALES/NET PLANT HIGH VALUES"
 PC1="LEVEL OF ACTIVITY/DEMAND FACTOR"
 PC2_1="COST OF CAPITAL BORROWING FACTOR LAG1"
 PC3="LABOUR MARKET TIGHTNESS FACTOR"
 PC5="EXPENDITURE FACTOR"
 PC5_1="EXPENDITURE FACTOR LAGGED 1 YEAR"
 PC4="CONSTRUCTION ACTIVITY FACTOR"
 PHATFULL="ESTIMATE RISK OF FAILURE FULL MODEL"; RUN;
                                              Model Summary

                                    Model Variables          14
                                      Endogenous              1
                                      Exogenous              12
                                    Parameters               17
                                    Equations                 2

                                    Number of Statements      2

 Model Variables: R7 R6 RC21_1 RC21_4 RCD18 R15 PC1 PC3 PC5 PC4 PC2_1
                  PC5_1 PHATFULL R2
 Parameters: INT1 B1 C1 D1 F1 G1 H1 I1 J1 K1 L1 INT A B C D E
```

```
Equations: PHATFULL R2

                         Model Structure Analysis
            [Based on Assignments to Endogenous Model Variables]
Exogenous Variables: R7 R6 RC21_1 RC21_4 RCD18 R15 PC1 PC3 PC5 PC4
PC2_1 PC5_1
Endogenous Variables: PHATFULL R2
        NOTE: The System Consists of a Single Block.
        The 2 Equations to Estimate are:
PHATFULL = F[ INT1, B1, C1, D1, F1, G1, H1, I1, J1, K1, L1 ]
R2       = F[ INT[1], A[R7], B[R6], C[PHATFULL], D[PC3], E[PC1] ]
Instruments: 1 R7 R6 RC21_1 RC21_4 RCD18 R15 PC1 PC3 PC5
                        PC4 PC2_1 PC5_1

                          2SLS Estimation Summary:
                         Parameters Estimated       17
                         Unique Instruments         13
                            Minimization Summary
                         Method                  GAUSS
                         Iterations                  4

                  Nonlinear 2SLS Summary of Residual Errors
              DF    DF
Equation    Model Error SSE       MSE       Root MSE  R-Square  Adj R-Sq

 PHATFULL    11    459  16.65116  0.03628   0.19047    0.6580    0.6505
 R2           6    464  205742    443.41007 21.05730   0.9638    0.9634

                   Nonlinear 2SLS Parameter Estimates
                                        Approx.        'T'    Approx.
                Parameter    Estimate   Std Err       Ratio  Prob>|T|

                INT1         0.039124   0.13290        0.29    0.7686
                B1           0.817136   0.13696        5.97    0.0001
                C1         0.00099732  0.0005226       1.91    0.0569
                D1          -0.742256   0.12480       -5.95    0.0001
                F1          -2.349398   0.40533       -5.80    0.0001
                G1           1.465821   0.21694        6.76    0.0001
                H1          -0.707842   0.17346       -4.08    0.0001
                I1           0.381464   0.09704        3.93    0.0001
                J1           0.445019   0.09566        4.65    0.0001
                K1          -0.719052   0.12455       -5.77    0.0001
                L1          -0.100954   0.03248       -3.11    0.0020
                INT         70.947726   2.43615       29.12    0.0001
                A           -0.775419  0.0080725     -96.06    0.0001
                B            0.105960   0.01762        6.01    0.0001
                C          -19.875642   5.10661       -3.89    0.0001
                D            1.806947   0.42606        4.24    0.0001
                E            1.203404   0.28593        4.21    0.0001
                 Number of Observations         Statistics for System
                 Used                 470       Objective       6.5008
                 Missing                2       Objective*N       3055

                          3SLS Estimation Summary
                             Minimization Summary
                         Method                  GAUSS
                         Iterations                  3

             Nonlinear 3SLS Summary of Residual Errors

              DF    DF
Equation    Model Error    SSE       MSE       Root MSE  R-Square  Adj R-Sq

PHATFULL     11    459    16.67495  0.03633    0.19060    0.6575    0.6500
R2            6    464    205746    443.41906  21.05752   0.9638    0.9634
```

Nonlinear 3SLS Parameter Estimates

Parameter	Estimate	Approx. Std Err	'T' Ratio	Approx. Prob>|T|
INT1	-0.00775494	0.13497	-0.06	0.9542
B1	0.828312	0.13980	5.93	0.0001
C1	0.00100591	0.0005194	1.94	0.0534
D1	-0.750044	0.12644	-5.93	0.0001
F1	-2.385388	0.41466	-5.75	0.0001
G1	1.493077	0.21800	6.85	0.0001
H1	-0.722726	0.17858	-4.05	0.0001
I1	0.400528	0.10009	4.00	0.0001
J1	0.452572	0.09725	4.65	0.0001
K1	-0.682742	0.12338	-5.53	0.0001
L1	-0.110606	0.03378	-3.27	0.0011
INT	71.010383	2.43304	29.19	0.0001
A	-0.773057	0.0080333	-96.23	0.0001
B	0.115974	0.01730	6.70	0.0001
C	-20.096945	5.09914	-3.94	0.0001
D	1.822686	0.42588	4.28	0.0001
E	1.237485	0.28539	4.34	0.0001

Number of Observations		Statistics for System	
Used	470	Objective	0.0372
Missing	2	Objective*N	17.5063

Appendix O

Stepwise Regression Analysis for Interest Coverage after Tax, R18

[SAS Extract]

```
DATA=SERVICE.PREDF;RUN;
LIBNAME SERVICE "C:\MYSASDIR";
DATA;SET SERVICE.predF;
MISSING N P;
if r18=.p then r18=27.15; /*REPLACE UNDEFINED +VE R18[ZERO DENOMS]WITH 95TH PERCENTILE*/
if r18=.n then r18= -42.54;run;/*REPLACE UNDEFINED -VE VALUES WITH 5TH PERCENTILE*/
OPTIONS PS=60;
proc REG;
/*FULLSET REDUCED SINCE [A]PC5_2,3 BOTH LINEAR COMBINATIONS OF OTHER PC'S AND */
/*[B] STEPWISE MODEL SHOWED NO SIGNIFICANCE FOR MANY RATIOS-REMOVED TO REDUCE*/
/* ELIMINATION OF CASES DUE TO MISSING VALUES*/

model R18=PC1-PC5 PC2_1-PC2_3 PC3_1-PC3_3 PC4_1-PC4_3 PC5_1
R2 R4-R7 R14 R15 RCD13 RC19_1-RC19_4 RC20_1-RC20_4 RC21_1-RC21_4 PHATFULL PHATFLG1
       /selection = stepwise
        slentry=0.20
        slstay= 0.17
        details; RUN;

                 Stepwise Procedure for Dependent Variable R18

Step10    Variable PC2 Entered        R-square = 0.27080562    C[p] =  0.45197285

                      DF         Sum of Squares       Mean Square          F    Prob>F

        Regression    10         73063.97944656     7306.39794466       6.13    0.0001
        Error        165        196738.32619616     1192.35349210
        Total        175        269802.30564273

                   Parameter           Standard           Type II
        Variable    Estimate              Error    Sum of Squares          F    Prob>F

        INTERCEP  -5.43912059        7.32514861      657.39973247       0.55    0.4588
        PC2        1.18016458        0.78405163     2701.47437889       2.27    0.1342
        R4         3.43035735        1.14178653    10762.51894090       9.03    0.0031
        R5         0.04067632        0.01574679     7956.17729508       6.67    0.0107
        R6         0.12998540        0.04356892    10613.06165676       8.90    0.0033
        R7         0.18406472        0.05860813    11760.62694384       9.86    0.0020
        R15        2.10228139        1.14758195     4001.46757719       3.36    0.0688
        RC20_3    12.80331208        7.70065493     3296.05435434       2.76    0.0983
        RC21_1   -23.33363171       10.79583691     5570.02411556       4.67    0.0321
```

RC21_2	-21.72121906	7.07421407	11241.31256541	9.43	0.0025
PHATFULL	-21.03391096	9.71094919	5593.99052888	4.69	0.0317

All variables left in the model are significant at the 0.1700 level.
No other variable met the 0.2000 significance level for entry into the model.

Summary of Stepwise Procedure for Dependent Variable R18

Step	Variable Entered	Variable Removed	Number In	Partial R**2	Model R**2	C[p]	F	Prob>F	Label
1	R6		1	0.0850	0.0850	21.7999	16.1716	0.0001	NET INCOME/TOTAL ASSETS
2	R15		2	0.0485	0.1335	13.5336	9.6771	0.0022	CASH FLOW FROM OPERATIONS/TOTAL CUR.LIAB
3	RC21_2		3	0.0301	0.1636	9.1622	6.1857	0.0138	SALES/NET PLANT 5-25% VALUES
4	R4		4	0.0188	0.1824	7.1701	3.9421	0.0487	QUICK RATIO-ACID TEST
5	R7		5	0.0145	0.1970	6.0884	3.0801	0.0811	TOTAL LIABILITIES/TOTAL ASSETS
6	R5		6	0.0292	0.2262	1.8973	6.3838	0.0124	RETAINED EARNINGS/TOTAL ASSETS
7	PHATFULL		7	0.0135	0.2397	1.0442	2.9764	0.0863	ESTIMATED RISK OF FAILURE FULL MODEL
8	RC21_1		8	0.0090	0.2486	1.1466	1.9912	0.1601	SALES/NET PLANT LOWEST VALUES
9	RC20_3		9	0.0122	0.2608	0.5728	2.7287	0.1004	SALES/INVENTORY 75TH-95TH PERCENTILE
10	PC2		10	0.0100	0.2708	0.4520	2.2657	0.1342	COST OF CAPITAL BORROWING FACTOR

Appendix P

3SLS Analysis for Simultaneous Equations Estimation: Failure Risk and Working Capital/Total Assets and Interest Coverage after Tax

[SAS Extract]

```
LIBNAME SERVICE "C:\MYSASDIR";
DATA ;SET SERVICE.PREDF;
MISSING N P;
if r18=.p then r18=27.15; /*REPLACE UNDEFINED +VE R18[ZERO
DENOMS]WITH 95TH PERCENTILE*/
if r18=.n then r18= -42.54;run;/*REPLACE UNDEFINED -VE WITH 5TH
PERCENTILE*/
RUN;

OPTION PS=60;
OPTION LINESIZE=80;
PROC MODEL BLOCK ; /*CHECK NO. OF INSTRUMENTS MUST BE >=NO. OF
PARAMETERS ESTIMATED IN ANY EQUATION*/
EXOGENOUS R7 R6 R4 R5 RC20_3 RC21_1 RC21_2 RC21_4 RCD18 R15 PC1 PC2
PC3 PC5 PC4 PC2_1 PC5_1 ;
ENDOGENOUS PHATFULL;
/* EQN 1:CHAPTER 6 MODEL MINUS R7*/
/*AND INCLUDING R7 IN EQN 2 FOR R2 SINCE HIGH PAIRWISE CORR*/

PHATFULL = 1/[1 + EXP[-INT1 - B1*PC3 -C1*R2 -D1*PC5_1 - F1*RC21_1 -
G1*RC21_4 - H1*PC5 - I1*PC4 - J1*PC2_1 -K1*RCD18 - L1*R15]];/*11
PARAMETERS*/

/* EQN 2: */

R2=INT + E*R7 + M*R6 + N*PHATFULL + B*PC3 + O*PC1;/*6 PARAMETERS*/

/*EQN 3:*/

R18 = INT2 + M2*R6 + L2*R15 + P*RC21_2 + Q*R4 + E2*R7  + R*R5
 + C2*PHATFULL + F2*RC21_1 + S*RC20_3 + J2*PC2;

FIT PHATFULL R2 R18 /3SLS DETAILS OUT=PREDFSIM OUTACTUAL OUTPREDICT
INSTRUMENTS _EXOG_;

LABEL BANK="OUTCOME Y VARIABLE BINARY 0/1"
 R2="WORKING CAPITAL/TOTAL ASSETS"
 R6="NET INCOME/TOTAL ASSETS"
 R7="TOTAL LIABILITIES/TOTAL ASSETS"
 R15="CASH FLOW FROM OPERATIONS/TOTAL CUR.LIAB"
 PC1="LEVEL OF ACTIVITY/DEMAND FACTOR"
 PC2="COST OF CAPITAL BORROWING FACTOR"
 PC2_1="COST OF CAPITAL BORROWING FACTOR LAG1"
 PC3="LABOUR MARKET TIGHTNESS FACTOR"
 PC5="EXPENDITURE FACTOR"
 PC5_1="EXPENDITURE FACTOR LAG1"
 PC4="CONSTRUCTION ACTIVITY FACTOR"
```

```
 PC4_1="CONSTRUCTION ACTIVITY FACTOR LAG1"
 RCD13="CASH FLOW FROM OPERATIONS/SALES"
 RCD18="INTEREST COV.AFTER TAX >0 /NO INTEREST"
 R18="INTEREST COVERAGE AFTER TAX"
 R4="QUICK RATIO-ACID TEST"
 R5="RETAINED EARNINGS/TOTAL ASSETS"
 RC20_3="SALES/INVENTORY 75TH-95TH PERCENTILE"
 RC21_1="SALES/NET PLANT LOWEST VALUES"
 RC21_2="SALES/NET PLANT 5-25% VALUES"
 RC21_4="SALES/NET PLANT HIGH VALUES"
 PHATFULL="ESTIMATE OF FAILURE RISK FULL MODEL"
 PHATFLG1="ESTIMATE OF LAGGGED RISK ONE PERIOD";
RUN;
```

```
                                      Model Summary

                                 Model Variables         20
                                   Endogenous             1
                                   Exogenous             17
                                 Parameters              28
                                 Equations                3

                                 Number of Statements     3

Model Variables: R7 R6 R4 R5 RC20_3 RC21_1 RC21_2 RC21_4 RCD18 R15
                 PC1 PC2 PC3 PC5 PC4 PC2_1 PC5_1 PHATFULL R2 R18

Parameters: INT1 B1 C1 D1 F1 G1 H1 I1 J1 K1 L1 INT E M N B O INT2 M2
            L2 P Q E2 R C2 F2 S J2

Equations: PHATFULL R2 R18

                           Model Structure Analysis
              [Based on Assignments to Endogenous Model Variables]

Exogenous Variables: R7 R6 R4 R5 RC20_3 RC21_1 RC21_2 RC21_4 RCD18
                     R15 PC1 PC2 PC3 PC5 PC4 PC2_1 PC5_1

Endogenous Variables: PHATFULL R2 R18

NOTE: The System Consists of 1 Recursive Equations and 1
Simultaneous Blocks.
                           Block Structure of the System
                              Block 1: PHATFULL R2
                           Dependency Structure of the System

Block 1 Depends On: R7 R6 RC21_1 RC21_4 RCD18 R15 PC1 PC3 PC5 PC4
                    PC2_1 PC5_1
       R18      Depends On: Block 1 All_Exogenous

                           The 3 Equations to Estimate are:
PHATFULL = F[ INT1, B1, C1, D1, F1, G1, H1, I1, J1, K1, L1 ]
R2       = F[ INT[1], E[R7], M[R6], N[PHATFULL], B[PC3], O[PC1] ]
R18      = F[ INT2[1], M2[R6], L2[R15], P[RC21_2], Q[R4], E2[R7],
           R[R5], C2[PHATFULL], F2[RC21_1], S[RC20_3], J2[PC2] ]

Instruments: 1 R7 R6 R4 R5 RC20_3 RC21_1 RC21_2 RC21_4
             RCD18 R15 PC1 PC2 PC3 PC5 PC4 PC2_1 PC5_1

                                2SLS Estimation Summary

                             Parameters Estimated       28
                             Unique Instruments         18
```

Nonlinear 2SLS Summary of Residual Errors

Equation	DF Model	DF Error	SSE	MSE	Root MSE	R-Square	Adj R-Sq
PHATFULL	11	224	6.58521	0.02940	0.17146	0.7034	0.6902
R2	6	229	199855	872.72783	29.54197	0.9323	0.9309
R18	11	224	240085	1071.8	32.73846	0.2831	0.2511

Nonlinear 2SLS Parameter Estimates

Parameter	Estimate	Approx. Std Err	'T' Ratio	Approx. Prob>|T|
INT1	0.184650	0.15935	1.16	0.2478
B1	0.807328	0.16448	4.91	0.0001
C1	0.00106434	0.0006594	1.61	0.1079
D1	-0.734355	0.15197	-4.83	0.0001
F1	-2.175588	0.44128	-4.93	0.0001
G1	1.401390	0.25929	5.40	0.0001
H1	-0.688603	0.20398	-3.38	0.0009
I1	0.333400	0.11265	2.96	0.0034
J1	0.437285	0.11532	3.79	0.0002
K1	-0.857651	0.15465	-5.55	0.0001
L1	-0.062513	0.03178	-1.97	0.0504
INT	69.412231	4.78139	14.52	0.0001
E	-0.776267	0.01602	-48.46	0.0001
M	0.103577	0.03497	2.96	0.0034
N	-16.049382	9.97585	-1.61	0.1090
B	1.620378	0.84039	1.93	0.0551
O	1.115681	0.56487	1.98	0.0495
INT2	-7.038631	6.62413	-1.06	0.2891
M2	0.170120	0.03973	4.28	0.0001
L2	2.403631	1.03976	2.31	0.0217
P	-17.720740	5.97474	-2.97	0.0033
Q	3.435907	1.03867	3.31	0.0011
E2	0.200377	0.05257	3.81	0.0002
R	0.042619	0.01417	3.01	0.0029
C2	-22.905197	10.54481	-2.17	0.0309
F2	-23.328022	8.77857	-2.66	0.0084
S	12.194026	6.50882	1.87	0.0623
J2	1.321278	0.63587	2.08	0.0389

Number of Observations		Statistics for System	
Used	235	Objective	137.4966
Missing	1	Objective*N	32312

Nonlinear 3SLS Summary of Residual Errors

Equation	DF Model	DF Error	SSE	MSE	Root MSE	R-Square	Adj R-Sq
PHATFULL	11	224	6.68700	0.02985	0.17278	0.6988	0.6854
R2	6	229	213475	932.20603	30.53205	0.9277	0.9261
R18	11	224	240346	1073.0	32.75627	0.2823	0.2503

Nonlinear 3SLS Parameter Estimates

Parameter	Estimate	Approx. Std Err	'T' Ratio	Approx. Prob>|T|
INT1	0.098496	0.13644	0.72	0.4711
B1	0.733593	0.12756	5.75	0.0001
C1	0.00103854	0.0005917	1.76	0.0806
D1	-0.651793	0.11670	-5.59	0.0001
F1	-2.163156	0.38908	-5.56	0.0001
G1	1.353222	0.21317	6.35	0.0001
H1	-0.597036	0.17020	-3.51	0.0005
I1	0.320924	0.09279	3.46	0.0006
J1	0.382023	0.08727	4.38	0.0001
K1	-0.735960	0.12844	-5.73	0.0001
L1	-0.080794	0.02764	-2.92	0.0038
INT	65.465557	4.66120	14.04	0.0001
E	-0.763605	0.01536	-49.73	0.0001
M	0.149287	0.02866	5.21	0.0001
N	-8.265984	9.64291	-0.86	0.3922
B	1.154176	0.82619	1.40	0.1638
O	1.260905	0.53680	2.35	0.0197
INT2	-6.735497	6.61511	-1.02	0.3097
M2	0.164624	0.03964	4.15	0.0001
L2	2.389833	1.03828	2.30	0.0223
P	-17.334460	5.96065	-2.91	0.0040
Q	3.378581	1.03630	3.26	0.0013
E2	0.199905	0.05245	3.81	0.0002
R	0.042986	0.01414	3.04	0.0026
C2	-23.712621	10.54011	-2.25	0.0254
F2	-23.628803	8.76536	-2.70	0.0076
S	12.415964	6.49369	1.91	0.0572
J2	1.313767	0.63456	2.07	0.0396

Number of Observations		Statistics for System	
Used	235	Objective	0.3702
Missing	1	Objective*N	87.0018

Bibliography

Aitkin, M.A. (1974), 'Simultaneous inference and choice of variable subsets in multiple regression', *Technometrics*, Vol. 16, pp. 221-227.

Ahn, B.S., Cho, S.S. and Kim, C.Y. (2000), 'The Integrated Methodology of Rough Set Theory and Artificial Neural Network for Business Failure Prediction', *Expert Systems with Applications*, Vol.18, pp. 65-74.

Alam, P., Booth, D., Lee, K. and Thodarson, T. (2000), 'The Use of Fuzzy Clustering and Self-Organizing Neural Networks for Identifying Potentially Failing Banks: An Experimental Study', *Expert Systems with Applications*, Vol. 18, pp. 185-199.

Altman, E. (1968), 'Financial Ratios, Discriminant Analysis and the Prediction of Corporate Bankruptcy', *Journal of Finance*, September, pp. 589-609.

______ (1971), *Corporate Bankruptcy in America*, (Lexington, Heath Inc.).

______ (1983), *Corporate Financial Distress*, (John Wiley & Sons).

______ Haldeman, R., and Narayan, P., (1977), 'Zeta Analysis', Journal *of Banking and Finance*, June, pp.29-54.

Amemiya, T. (1981), 'Qualitative response Models: A Survey', *The Journal of Economic Literature*, December, pp.1483-1536.

Anderson, T. and Rubin, H. (1950), Estimation of the Parameters of a Single Equation in a Complete System of Stochastic Equations', *Ann.Math.Statist.*, Vol. 20, pp.46-63.

Ang, J.S. and Chua, J.H. (1980), 'Coalitions, the Me-first Rule, and the Liquidation Decision', *Bell Journal of Economics*, pp.1355-1359.

Aziz, A., Emanuel, D.C. and Lawson, G.H. (1988), 'Bankruptcy prediction - An investigation of cash flow based models', *Journal of Management Studies*, Vol. 25(5), September, pp. 419-437.

Baestaens, D.E., Van Den Bergh, W.M. and Wood, D. (1994), *Neural Network Solutions for Trading in Financial Markets*, London, Pitman Publishing.

Ball, R. and Foster, G. (1982), 'Corporate financial reporting: a methodological review of empirical research', *Journal of Accounting Research*, Vol. 20 (Supplement), Spring, pp. 161-234.

Beaver, W.H. (1966), 'Financial Ratios as Predictors of Failure', *Journal of Accounting Research*, (Supplement), pp. 71-111.

Blum, M. (1974),'Failing Company Discriminant Analysis', *Journal of Accounting Research*, Vol. 12(1), Spring, pp. 1-25.

Bowden, R.J. and Turkington, D.A. (1984), *Instrumental Variables* (Cambridge University Press, New York).

Bowen, R.M., Burgstahler, D. and Daley, L.A. (1987), 'The Incremental Information Content of Accrual Versus Cash Flows', *The Accounting Review*, Vol. 62, pp. 723-747.

Bradley, R.A., and Gart, J.J. (1962), 'The asymptotic properties of ML estimators when sampling from associated populations', *Biometrika*, Vol. 49, pp. 205-214.

Bulow, J., and Shoven, J., (1978), 'The Bankruptcy Decision', *The Bell Journal of Economics*, Vol.9 (2), Autumn, pp. 437-456.

Cadden, D., (1991), 'Neural Networks and the Mathematics of Chaos – An Investigation of these Methodologies as Accurate Predictions of Corporate Bankruptcy', *The First International Conference on Artificial Intelligence Applications On Wall Street*, New York, IEEE Computer Society Press.

Casey, C. and Bartczak, N. (1984), 'Cash Flow – It's not the Bottom Line', *Harvard Business Review*, July-August, pp. 61-66.

_____ (1985), 'Using operating Cash Flow Data to Predict Financial Distress: Some Extensions', Journal *of Accounting Research*, Spring, pp. 384-401.

Casey, C., McGee, V. and Stickney, C. (1986), 'Discriminating Between Reorganized and Liquidated Firms in Bankruptcy', *The Accounting Review*, Vol. LXI (2), April.

Chen, K. and Shimerda, T. (1981), 'An Empirical Analysis of Useful Financial Ratios', *Financial Management*, Vol. 10(1), Spring, pp. 51-60.

Chen, Y., Weston, J.F. and Altman, E.I. (1995), 'Financial Distress and Restructuring Models, *Financial Management*, Vol. 42(2), Summer, pp. 57-75.

Coates P.K. and Fant L.F., (1992), 'A Neural Network Approach to Forecasting Financial Distress', *The Journal of Business Forecasting*, Winter, pp. 9-12.

Collins, E., Ghosh, S. and Scofield, C. (1989), 'An Application of Multiple Neural Network Learning System to Emulation of Mortgage Underwriting Judgements', *Working paper* (Nestor Inc., 1 Richmond Square, Providence, R.I.).

Cox, D.R. (1970), *Analysis of Binary Data* (Methuen & Co. Ltd., London).

______ (1972), 'Regression Models and Life Tables (with discussion)', *Journal of the Royal Statistical Society*, B, Vol. 34, pp. 187-220.

Crapp, H. and Stevenson, M. (1987), 'Development of a Method to Assess the Relevant Variables and the probability of Financial Distress', *Australian Journal of Management*, Vol. 12(2), December, pp. 221-236.

Cybinski, P.J. (1995), 'A Discrete-Valued Risk Function for Modelling Financial Distress in Private Australian Companies', *Accounting and Finance*, Vol. 35(2), November, pp. 17-32.

Cybinski, P.J. (1996), 'The Role of Internal and External Environments in Service Industry Firm Failures', *The Proceedings*, *Western Decision Sciences Conference*, Seattle, Washington, April 2.

Cybinski, P.J. (2000), 'The Path to Failure: Where are Bankruptcy Studies at Now', *Journal of Business and Management*, 7(1): 11-39.

Deakin, E.B. (1972), 'A Discriminant Analysis of Predictors of Business Failure', *Journal of Accounting Research*, Spring, pp. 167-179.

Deakin, E.B. (1976), 'Distributions of Financial Accounting Ratios: Some Empirical Evidence', *The Accounting Review*, January, pp. 90-96.

De-Bodt, E., Cottrell, M. and Levasseur, M. (1995), 'Les Reseaux de Neurones en Finance: Principes et Revue de la Litterature. (Neural networks in Finance: A Survey. With English Summary)', *Finance*, Vol. 16(1), June, pp. 25-91.

Dharan, B.G. and Lev, B. (1993), 'The Valuation Consequence of Accounting Changes: A Multi-year Examination', *Journal of Accounting, Auditing and Finance*, Vol. 8(4), pp. 475-494.

Dmitras, A.I., Zanakis, S.H. and Zopounidis, C. (1996), 'A Survey of Business Failures with an Emphasis on Prediction Methods and Industrial Applications', *European Journal of Operational Research*, Vol. 90, pp. 487-513.

Dutta, S. and Hekhar, S. (1988), 'Bond-Rating: A Non-Conservative Application of Neural Networks', *Proceedings of the IEEE International Conference on Neural Networks*, Vol. II, San Diego, Ca., pp. 443-450.

Eddey, P.G., Partington, G.H. and Stevenson, M. (1989), 'Predicting the Probability and Timing of Takeover Success: A Report on Work in Progress', Paper delivered to the *Australasian Finance and Banking Conference*, University of New South Wales, December.

Edmister, R.O. (1972), 'An Empirical Test of Financial Ratio Analysis for Small Business Failure Prediction', *Journal of Financial and Quantitative Analysis*, March, pp. 1477-1493.

Efron, B., (1975), 'The Efficiency of Logistic Regression Compared to Normal Discriminant Analysis', *Journal of the American Statistical Association*, Vol. 70, pp.892-898.

______ (1979), 'Bootstrap methods: Another Look at the Jack-knife', *Annals of Statistics*, Vol. 7(1), January, pp. 1-26.

______ (1982), 'The Jack-knife, the Bootstrap, and Other Resampling Plans', *SIAM Monograph*, No. 38, Society for Industrial and Applied Mathematics.

______ (1983), 'Estimating the Error Rate of a Prediction Rule: Improvement on Cross-Validation', *Journal of the American Statistical Association*, Vol. 78(382), June, pp. 316-331.

Eisenbeis, R., and Avery, R., (1972), *Discriminant Analysis and Classification Procedures: Theory and Applications* (Lexington D.C. Heath).

Eisenbeis, R.A. (1977), 'Pitfalls in the Application of Discriminant Analysis in Business, Finance, and Economics', *Journal of Finance*, June, pp. 875-900.

Emory, C.W. and Cooper, D.R. (1991), *Business Research Methods* 4th ed. (Irwin, Homewood, IL).

Etheridge, H.L. and Sriram, R.S. (1993), 'Chaos Theory and Nonlinear Dynamics: An Emerging Theory with Implications for Accounting Research', *Journal of Accounting Literature*, Vol.12, pp. 67-100.

Etheridge, H.L., Sriram, R.S. and Hsu, K.H.Y. (2000), 'A Comparison of Selected Artificial Neural Networks that Help Auditors Evaluate Client Viability', *Decision Sciences*, Vol. 31(2), pp. 531-550.

Feinberg, S. (1977), *The Analysis of Cross-Classified Categorical Data*, 2nd ed. (MIT Press. Mass).

Feller, W. (1968), *An Introduction to Probability Theory and its Applications* (Wiley, New York).

Fisher, T.C. and Martel, J. (1995), 'The Creditors' Financial Reorganisation Decision: New Evidence from Canadian Data', *Journal of Law, Economics and Organisation*, Vol. 11, pp. 112-126.

Flagg, J.C., Giroux, G.A. Wiggins, C.E. (1991), 'Predicting Corporate Bankruptcy Using Failing Firms', *Review of Financial Economics*, Vol. 1(1), Fall, pp. 67-78.

Fletcher, D and Goss, E. (1993), 'Forecasting with Neural Networks: An application using bankruptcy data', *Information and Management*, March, Vol. 24(3) pp. 159-167.

Fogelson, F. (1978), 'The Impact of Changes in Accounting Principles on Restrictive Covenants in Credit Agreements and Indentures', *Business Lawyer*, January, pp. 69-87.

Forster, J., (1980), 'Modelling Short-Run Labour Market Behaviour: Twenty-Nine Cities in the North-Eastern USA 1964-1973', *Unpublished PhD thesis*, McMaster University, Hamilton, Canada.

Forster, J. and Ryan, C. (1989), 'The First Labour Market Decision: Leaving School in Australia', *Labour and Industry*, Vol. 6 (2), pp. 168-187.

Foster, G. (1986), *Financial Statement Analysis* (Prentice-Hall, Englewood Cliffs, N.J.).

Frecka, T.J. and Hopwood, W.S. (1983), 'The Effects of Outliers on the Cross-Sectional Distributional Properties of Financial Ratios', *The Accounting Review*, January, pp. 115-128.

Frydman, H., Altman, E.I. and Kao, D.L. (1985), 'Introducing Recursive Partitioning for Financial Classification: The Case of Financial Distress', *The Journal of Finance*, Vol.40 (1) pp. 269-291.

Furnival, G.M. and Wilson, R.W. (1974), 'Regression by Leaps and Bounds', *Technometrics*, Vol. 16, pp. 499-511.

Gahlon, J.M. and Vigeland, R.L. (1988), 'Early Warning Signs of Bankruptcy Using Cash Flow Analysis', *The Journal of Commercial Bank Lending*, pp.4-15.

Garavaglia, S. (1991), 'An Application of a Counter-Propagation Neural Network: Simulating the Standard and Poor's Corporate Bond Rating System', *The First International Conference on Artificial Intelligence Applications On Wall Street*, New York, IEEE Computer Society Press.

Geisst, C. (1997), *Wall Street: A History*, Oxford University Press, New York & Oxford.

Gentry, J.A., Newbold, P. and Whitford, D.T. (1985a), 'Classifying Bankrupt Firms with Funds Flow Components', *Journal of Accounting Research*, Spring, pp. 146-160.

______ (1985b), 'Predicting Bankruptcy: If Cash Flow's Not the Bottom Line, What is?', *Financial Analysts Journal*, Sept-Oct, pp. 47-56.

Gertner, R. and Scharfstein, D. (1991), 'A Theory of Workouts and the Effects of Reorganisation Law', *The Journal of Finance*, Vol. 46, pp. 1189-1222.

Gilbert, L.R., Menon, K. and Schwartz, K.B. (1990), 'Predicting Bankruptcy for Firms in Financial Distress', *Journal of Business Finance and Accounting*, Vol. 17(1), (Spring), pp. 161-171.

Gleick, J. (1987), *Chaos: Making a New Science* (Viking Penguin: New York).

Glorfield, L., Pendley, J. and Hardgrave, B. (1997), Evaluating Financial Distress: A Comparison of Four Inductive Decision Models, in the *Proceedings, 28th Annual Meeting of the Decision Sciences Institute*, Nov. 22-25, San Diego, pp. 358-360.

Goldberger, A.L. (1990), 'Nonlinear Dynamics, Fractals and Chaos: Applications to Cardiac Electrophysiology', *Annals of Biomedical Engineering*, Vol. 18, pp. 195-198.

Goldberger, A.S. (1964), *Econometric Theory* (Wiley).

Gombola, M.J. and Ketz, J. (1983), 'Note on Cash Flow and Classification Patterns of Financial Ratios', *The Accounting Review*, January, pp.105-114.

Gombola, M.J., *et al* (1983), 'Cash Flow as a Predictor of Failure', Working paper, *Pennsylvania State University*, July, 1983.

Goss, E.P. and Ramchandani, H. (1995), 'Comparing Classification Accuracy of Neural Networks, Binary Logit Regression and Discriminant Analysis for the Insolvency Prediction of Life Insurers', *Journal of Economics and Finance*, Vol. 19(3), pp. 1-18.

Haavelmo, T. (1943), 'The Statistical Implications of a System of Simultaneous Equations', *Econometrica*, Vol. 11(1), pp. 30-58.

Hamer, M.M. (1983), 'Failure Prediction: Sensitivity of Classification Accuracy to Alternative Statistical Methods and Variable Sets', *Journal of Accounting and Public Policy*, Vol.2, pp. 289-307.

Halperin, M., Blackwelder, C. and Verter, J.I. (1971), 'Estimation of the Multivariate Logistic Risk Function: A comparison of the Discriminant Function and Maximum Likelihood Approaches', *Journal of Chronic Diseases*, Vol. 24, pp. 125-158.

Hecht-Nielsen, R. (1989), *Neurocomputing* (Addison-Wesley Co., New York).

Hill, N.T., Perry, S.E. and Andes, S. (1996), 'Evaluating Firms in Financial Distress: An Event History Analysis', *Journal of Applied Business Research*, Vol. 12(3), (Summer), pp. 60-71.

Healy, D.J. (1987), 'Multivariate CUSUM Procedures', *Technometrics*, Vol. 29, pp. 409-412.

Holland, J.H. (1975), *Adaptation in Natural and Artificial Systems*, University of Michigan Press.

Hong, S.C. (1983), 'A Bankruptcy Outcome: Model and Empirical Test', *Working paper*, University of California at Berkeley, March.

Hopwood, W., McKeown, J. and Mutchler, J. (1994),'A Re-examination of Auditor Versus Model Accuracy Within the Context of the Going Concern Opinion Decision', *Contemporary Accounting Research*, Spring, pp. 409-431.

Hotchkiss, E.S. (1995), 'Postbankruptcy Performance and Management Turnover', *The Journal of Finance*, Vol. 50, pp.3-21.

Houghton, K. and Woodliff, D. (1987), 'Financial Ratios: The Prediction of Corporate "Success" and Failure', *Journal of Business Finance and Accounting*, Vol. 14(4), pp.537-554.

Izan, H.Y., (1984), 'Corporate Distress in Australia', *Journal of Banking and Finance*, Vol. 8, pp. 303-320.

Johnson, C.G. (1970) 'Ratio Analysis and the Prediction of Firm Failure', *Journal of Finance*, December, pp. 1166-1168.

Johnston, J., (1972) *Econometric Methods*, 2nd ed., (McGraw Hill).

Jones, F.L. (1987), 'Current Techniques in Bankruptcy Prediction', *Journal of Accounting Literature*, Vol. 6, pp. 131-164.

Joy, M.O. and Tollefson (1975), 'On the Financial Applications of Discriminant Analysis', *Journal of Finance and Quantitative Analysis*, December, pp. 723-739.

Judge, G.G., Griffiths, W.E., Hill, R.C., Lutkepohl, H. and Lee, T. (1985), *The Theory and Practice of Econometrics*, 2nd ed., (Wiley, New York).

Kane, G., Richardson, F. and Graybeal, P. (1996), 'Recession-Induced Stress and the Prediction of Corporate Failure', *Contemporary Accounting Research*, Vol.13 (2), Fall, pp. 631-650.

Kane, G.D., Richardson, F.M. and Meade, N.L. (1998), 'Rank Transformations and the Predictions of Corporate Failure', *Contemporary Accounting Research*, Vol.15 (2), Summer, pp. 145-166.

Karels, G.V. and Prakash A.J. (1987), 'Multivariate Normality and Forecasting of Business Bankruptcy', *Journal of Business Finance and Accounting*, Vol. 14(4), Winter, pp. 573-593.

Kassab, J., McLeay, S. and Shani, N. (1991), 'Forecasting Bankruptcy: Failure Prediction or Survival Analysis?', Paper presented at *The Annual Congress of the European Accounting Association*, Maastricht, The Netherlands.

Kelejian, H.H. and Oates, W.E. (1989) *Introduction to Econometrics: Principles and Applications*, 3rd ed., (Harper and Row, New York).

Kennedy, D., Lakonishok, J. and Shaw, W.H. (1993), 'Accommodating Outliers and Nonlinearity in Decision Models,' *Journal of Accounting, Auditing and Finance*, Vol. 7(2), Spring, pp. 161-193.

Ketz, J.E., and Kochanek, R.F., (1982), 'Cash Flow: Assessing a Company's Real Financial Health', *Financial Executive*, July, pp. 34-40.

Kim, J. and Mueller, C.W. (1978), 'Factor Analysis Statistical Methods and Practical Issues', Sage University Paper Series on *Quantitative Applications in the Social Sciences*, 07-014, Beverly Hills and London: Sage Publications.

Kimoto, T. and Asakawa, K. (1990), 'Stock Market Prediction System with Modular neural networks', *Proceedings of the International Joint Conference on Neural Networks*, Vol. 1, June, pp. 1-6.

Koh, H.C. and Tan, S.S. (1999), 'A Neural Network Approach to the Prediction of Going Concern Status', *Accounting and Business Research*, Vol. 29(3), pp. 211-216.

Kohonen, T. (1988), 'An Introduction to Neural Computing', *Neural Networks*, Vol. 1, pp. 3-16.

Koster, A., Sondak, N. and Bourbia, W. (1990), 'A Business Application of Artificial Neural Network Systems', *The Journal of Computer Information Systems*, Vol. 31(2), Winter, 1990-1991, pp. 3-9.

Koza, J.R. (1992), *Genetic Programming: On the Programming of Computers by Means of Natural Selection*, Massachusetts Institute of Technology.

Kuhn, T.S. (1962), *The Structure of Scientific Revolutions*, University of Chicago Press, Chicago, Illinois.

Lachenbruch, P.A. (1975), *Discriminant Analysis*, (Hafner Press).

Largay, J.A. and Stickney, C.P. (1980), 'Cash Flows, Ratio Analysis and the W.T.Grant Company Bankruptcy', *Financial Analysts Journal*, July-August, pp. 51-54.

Lau, A.H.L. (1987) 'A Five-State Financial distress Prediction Model', *Journal of Accounting Research*, Vol. 25(1) (Spring), pp. 127-138.

Lee, T. (1982),'Laker Airways- The Cash Flow Truth', *Accountancy*, pp.115-116.

Lee, C. (1985), 'Stochastic Properties of Cross-sectional Financial Data', *Journal of Accounting Research*, Vol. 23, Spring, pp.213-227.

Lee, K.C., Han, I. and Kwon, Y. (1996), 'Hybrid Neural Network Models for Bankruptcy Predictions', *Decision Support Systems*, Vol.18 (1), September, pp.63-72.

Lenard, M.J., Alam, P. and Madey, G.R. (1995), 'The Application of Neural Networks and a Qualitative response Model to the Auditor's Going Concern Uncertainty Decision', *Decision Sciences*, Vol. 26, March/April, pp. 209-227.

Lenard, M.J., Alam, P. and Booth, D. (2000), 'An Analysis of Fuzzy Clustering and a Hybrid Model of the Auditor's Going Concern Assessment', *Decision Sciences*, Vol. 31(4), pp. 861-883.

Lev, B. (1974), *Financial Statement Analysis: A New Approach*, (Prentice Hall, Inc. Englewood Cliffs N.J.)

Levy, A. (1991), 'A Pareto Optimal Condition for Bankruptcy and the Role of Variations in Aggregate Variables', *The University of Woolongong Department of Economics Working Paper Series*, 91-9.

______ (1994), 'Continuation and Liquidation Timing: A Pareto Optimal Approach', *The University of Woolongong Department of Economics Working Paper Series*, 94-2.

Levy, A. and Bar-Niv, R. (1987), 'Macroeconomic Aspects of Firm Bankruptcy Analysis', *Journal of Macroeconomics*, Vol.9 (3), (Summer), pp. 407-415.

Lilien, S., Mellman, M. and Pastena, V. (1988), 'Accounting Changes: Successful versus Unsuccessful Firms', *The Accounting Review*, Vol. LXIII (4), pp. 642-656.

Lincoln, M.G. (1984), 'An Empirical Study of the Usefulness of Accounting Ratios to Describe Levels of Insolvency Risk', *Journal of Banking and Finance*, Vol. 8, pp. 321-340.

Lindsay, D.H. and Campbell, A. (1996), 'A Chaos Approach to Bankruptcy prediction', *Journal of Applied Business Research*, Vol. 12(4), pp. 1-9.

Lo, A.W. (1986), 'Logit Versus Discriminant Analysis: A Specification Test and Application to Corporate Bankruptcies', *Journal of Econometrics*, Vol. 31 pp. 151-178.

Lorenz, E.N., (1963), 'Deterministic Periodic Flow', Journal *of Atmospheric Sciences*, Vol. 20, pp. 130-141.

Luoma, M. and Laitinen, E.K. (1991), 'Survival Analysis as a Tool for Company Failure Prediction', *Omega* Vol. 19(6), pp. 673–678.

McFadden, D. (1973), 'Conditional Logit Analysis of Qualitative Choice Behaviour', in *Frontiers of Econometrics*, ed. P. Zaremka, (N.Y., Academic Press).

McFadden, D. (1976), 'A Comment on Discriminant Analysis 'versus' Logit Analysis', *Annals of Economic and Social Measurement*, Vol. 5, pp. 511-523.

McKee, T.E, (2000), 'Developing a Bankruptcy Prediction Model via Rough Sets Theory', *International Journal of Intelligent Systems in Accounting, Finance and Management*, Vol. 9, pp. 159–173.

McKee, T.E. and Lensberg, T. (1999), 'Using a Genetic Algorithm to Obtain a Causally Ordered Model From a Rough Sets Derived Bankruptcy Prediction Model', papers of *The International Symposium of Audit Research*, University of Southern California, 28 pp.

______ (2002), 'Genetic programming and rough sets: A hybrid approach to bankruptcy classification', *European Journal of Operations Research*, Vol. 138(2), pp. 436-451.

McNamara, R.P., Cocks N.J. and Hamilton, D.F. (1988), 'Predicting Private Company Failure' *Journal of Accounting and Finance* (November), Vol. 28(2), pp. 53-64.

Manski, C.F. and Lerman, S.R. (1977), 'The Estimation of Choice Probabilities from Choice Based Samples', *Econometrika*, Vol. 45(8), pp. 1977-1988.

Marais, M.L., Patell, J.M. and Wolfson, M.A. (1984), 'The Experimental Design of Classification Models; An Application of Recursive Partitioning and Bootstrapping to Commercial Bank Loan Classifications', *Journal of Accounting Research*, Vol. 22 (Supplement), pp. 87-114.

Marschak, J. (1950), 'Statistical Inference in Economics', in T.C. Koopmans, ed., *Statistical Inference in Dynamic Economic Models*, pp. 1-50 (Wiley, New York).

Martin, D. (1977), 'Early Warning of Bank Failure', *Journal of Banking and Finance*, Vol. 1, pp. 249-276.

Matolcsy, Z.P. Stevenson, M.J. and Castagna, A.D. (1993), 'The Distributional Characteristics of Financial Ratios Over Time', University of Technology, Sydney, *Faculty of Business Working Paper Series*, 19 May.

Mensah, Y.M. (1984), 'An Examination of the Stationarity of Multivariate bankruptcy Prediction Models: A Methodological Study', *Journal of Accounting Research*, Vol. 22 (1), Spring, pp. 380-395.

Moore, R.K. (1990), Predicting Bankruptcy of Texas Firms by Combining General Economic Data of Texas, National Economic Data, and Financial Data of Firms', *Southwest Journal of Business and Economics*, Vol. 7(2), pp. 24-30.

Nash, M., Anstis, M. and Bradbury, M. (1989), 'Testing Corporate Model Prediction Accuracy', *Australian Journal of Management*, Vol. 14(2), pp. 211-221.

Neftci, S.N. (1982), 'Optimal Prediction of Cyclical Downturns', *Journal of Economic Dynamics and Control*, Vol. 6, pp. 225-241.

Nelder, J.A. and Wedderburn, R.W.M. (1972), 'Generalized Linear Models', *Journal of the Royal Statistical Society A*, Vol. 135, pp. 370-384.

Norton, C. and Smith, R. (1979), 'A Comparison of General Price-Level and Historical Cost Financial Statements in the Prediction of Bankruptcy', *The Accounting Review*, January, pp. 72-87.

Odom, M. and Sharda, R. (1990), 'A Neural Network Model for Bankruptcy Prediction', Proceedings *of the International Joint Conference on Neural Networks*, Vol. II, pp. 63-68.

Ogg*, P.J. (1988), 'Quantitative Aspects of Modelling Financial Distress', Working Paper delivered to *The Inaugural Australasian Finance and Banking Conference*, University of New South Wales, (December).

Ogg*, P.J. and Forster J. (1991), 'Methodological Issues Related to the Empirical Analysis of Company Failures: A Research Plan'. Working Paper, *Accounting Seminar Series,* Faculty of Commerce and Business Administration, University of British Columbia, Vancouver, Canada, October.

Ohlsen, J. (1980), 'Financial Ratios and the Probabilistic Prediction of Bankruptcy', *Journal of Accounting Research*, Spring, pp. 109-131.

O'Leary, D.E. (1998), 'Using Neural Networks to Predict Corporate Failure', *International Journal of Intelligent Systems in Accounting Finance and Management*, Vol. 7(3), pp. 187-197.

Palepu K.G. (1986), 'Predicting Takeover Targets: A methodological and Empirical Analysis', *Journal of Accounting and Economics*, Vol. 8, pp. 3-35.

Partington, G.H., Peat, M. and Stevenson, M.J. (1991), 'Predicting the Probability and Timing of Corporate Financial Distress: Preliminary Results for the Australian Sector', *SABE Working Paper:* 91/10, University College of North Wales, Bangor, U.K.

Pawlak, Z. (1982), 'Rough sets', *International Journal of Information and Computer Sciences*, Vol. 11, pp. 341–356.

Peters, E.E. (1991), *Chaos and Order in the Capital Markets* (John Wiley & Sons Inc., New York).

Pinches, G., Mingo, K. and Caruthers, J. (1973), 'The Stability of Financial Patterns in Industrial Organization', *Journal of Finance*, May, pp. 389-396.

Platt, H.D. and Platt, M.B. (1990), 'Development of a Class of Stable Predictive Variables: The Case of Bankruptcy Prediction', *Journal of Business Finance and Accounting*, Vol. 17(1), Spring, pp. 31-51.

Pregibon, D. (1981), 'Logistic regression Diagnostics', *Annals of Statistics*, Vol. 9, pp. 705-724.

Press, S.J. and Wilson, S. (1978), 'Choosing Between Logistic Regression and Discriminant Analysis', *Journal of the American Statistical Association* (December), Vol. 73, pp. 699-705.

Pindyck, R.S. and Rubinfeld, D.L. (1981), *Econometric Models and Economic Forecasts*, 2nd ed. (New York, McGraw-Hill Inc).

Richardson, F. and Davidson, L. (1983), 'An Exploration into Bankruptcy Discriminant Model Sensitivity', *Journal of Business Finance and Accounting*, Vol. 10, Summer, pp.195-207.

Richardson, F.M., Kane, G.D. and Lobingier, P. (1998), 'The Impact of Recession on the Prediction of Corporate Failure', *Journal of Business Finance and Accounting*, Vol. 25(1-2), pp. 167-186.

Rose, P.S., Andrews, W.T. and Giroux, G.A., (1982), 'Predicting Business Failure: A Macroeconomic Perspective', *Journal of Accounting, Auditing and Finance*, Vol. 6, Fall, pp. 20-31.

---

* *Nee. Cybinski, P.J.*

Rose, P.S. and Giroux (1984), 'Predicting Corporate Bankruptcy: An Analytical and Empirical Evaluation', Review of Business and Economic Research, Vol.19, pp. 1-12.

Santomero, A. and Vinso, J. (1977), 'Estimating the Probability of Failure for Commercial Banks and the Banking System', *Journal of Banking and Finance*, October, pp.185-205.

SAS Institute Inc. (1993), *SAS/ETS User's Guide, Version 6*, Second Edition, (SAS Institute Inc., Cary, NC.)

Scott, J. (1981), 'The Probability of Bankruptcy: A Comparison of Empirical Predictions and Theoretical Models', *Journal of Banking and Finance*, September, pp. 317-344.

Schwartz, K.B. (1982), 'Accounting Changes by Corporations Facing Possible Insolvency', *Journal of Accounting, Auditing and Finance*, pp. 33-43.

Sharma, D.S. (1997), 'Cash Flows & Distress Analysis: A Review and Critique of the Literature', *Working Paper*, School of Accounting, Banking & Finance, Griffith University.

Shumway, R.H. (1988), *Applied Statistical Time Series Analysis*, (Englewood Cliffs, N.J., Prentice Hall).

Siegel, P.H., de Korvin A. and Omer K. (eds.), (1995), *Applications of Fuzzy Sets and the Theory of Evidence to Accounting*, (Greenwich, CT, JAI Press).

Standard and Poor (1991), *COMPUSTAT® PC-PLUS (North America) CDROM Database*, Standard & Poor's Compustat Services, Inc.

Taffler, R.J. (1984), 'Empirical Methods for the Monitoring of U.K. Corporations', *Journal of Banking and Finance*, June, pp. 199-227.

Taffler, R.J. and Abassi, B. (1984), 'Country Risk: A Model for Predicting Debt Servicing Problems in Developing Countries', *J.R.Statist.Soc.A*, Vol. 147(4), pp. 541-568.

Theodossiou, P.T. (1993), 'Predicting Shifts in the Mean of a Multivariate Time Series Process: An Application in Predicting Business Failures', *Journal of the American Statistical Association*, Vol. 88(422), pp. 441-449.

Udo, G. (1993), 'Neural Network Performance on the Bankruptcy Classification Problem', *Computers and Industrial Engineering*, Vol. 25, September, pp. 377-380.

Utans, J. and Moody, J. (1991), 'Selecting Neural network Architectures via the Prediction Risk: Application to Corporate Bond Rating Prediction', *Proceedings: First International Conference on Artificial Intelligence Applications on Wall Street*, (IEEE Computer Society Press, Los Alamitos, CA.).

Vinso, J. (1979) 'A Determination of the Risk of Ruin', *Journal of Financial and Quantitative Analysis*, March, pp. 77-100.

Viscione, J.A. (1985),'Assessing Financial Distress', *The Journal of Commercial Bank Lending*, pp. 39-45.

Ward, T. (1995), 'Using Information from the Statement of Cash Flows to Predict Insolvency', *Journal of Commercial Bank Lending*, Vol.7 (7), pp. 29-36.

Watson, C.J. (1990), 'Multivariate Distributional Properties, Outliers, and Transformation of Financial Ratios', *The Accounting Review*, Vol. 65(3), July, pp. 682-695.

Wecker, W. (1979) 'Prediction of Turning Points', *Journal of Business*, Vol. 52, pp. 35-50.

Weisberg. S. (1985), *Applied Linear Regression*, (John Wiley & Sons, Inc., USA).

Weston, F.J. and Brigham, E.F. (1975), *Managerial Finance*, 5th ed. (Holt, Rinehart and Winston, New York.)

White, G.I., Sondhi, A.C. and Fried, D. (1994), *The Analysis and Use of Financial Statements* (John Wiley & Sons, Inc., New York).

White, M. (1980) 'Public Policy Toward Bankruptcy: Me-First and Other Priority Rules', *The Bell Journal of Economics*, Autumn, pp.550-564.

______ (1981) 'Economics of Bankruptcy: Liquidation and Reorganization', *Working Paper*, New York University, (August).

______ (1984, revised 1989, 1991), 'Bankruptcy Liquidation and Reorganization', in D.Logue, Ed., *Handbook of Modern Finance*, (Warren, Gorham and Lamont, New York).

______ (1989), 'The Corporate Bankruptcy Decision', *Journal of Economic Perspectives*, Vol. 3(2), pp. 129-151.

______ (1994), 'Corporate Bankruptcy as a Filtering Device: Chapter 11 Reorganisations and Out-of-Court Debt Restructurings', *Journal of Law, Economics and Organizations*, Vol.10, pp. 268-295.

Wilcox, J. (1971), 'A Simple Theory of Financial Ratios as Predictors of Failure', *Journal of Accounting Research*, Autumn, pp. 389-395.

______ (1973), 'A Prediction of Business Failure Using Accounting Data', Empirical Research in Accounting: Selected Studies, *Journal of Accounting Research* Vol.11 (Supplement), pp. 163-179.

______ (1976), 'The Gambler's Ruin Approach to Business Risk', *Sloan Management Review*, Fall.

Wilson, R.L. and Sharda, R. (1994), 'Bankruptcy Prediction Using Neural Networks', *Decision Support Systems*, Vol. 11(5), June, pp. 545-557.

Wolf, A., Swift, J., Swinney, H. and Vastano, J. (1985), 'Determining Lyapunov Exponents from a Time Series', *Physica D*, Vol. 16, pp. 285-317.

Wood, D. and Piesse, J. (1987), 'Information Value of MDA Based Financial Indicators', *Journal of Business Finance and Accounting*, Winter, pp. 27-38.

Yorke, J.A. (1976), 'Simple Mathematical Models with Very Complicated Dynamics', *Nature*, Vol. 261, pp. 459-467.

Zavgren, C.V. (1983), 'The Prediction of Corporate Failure: The State of the Art', *Journal of Accounting Literature*, Spring, pp. 1-38.

Zavgren, C.V. (1985), 'Assessing the Vulnerability to Failure of American Industrial Firms: A Logistic Analysis', *Journal of Business Finance and Accounting*, Spring, pp. 19-45.

Zavgren, C.V. and Friedman, G.E. (1988), 'Are Bankruptcy Prediction Models Worthwhile? An Application in Securities Analysis', *Management International Review*, Vol. 28(1), pp. 34-43.

Zmijewski, M.D. (1984), 'Methodological issues related to the estimation of financial distress prediction models', *Journal of Accounting Research*, Vol. 22 (Supplement), pp. 59-86.

Index

For Product Safety Concerns and Information please contact our EU
representative GPSR@taylorandfrancis.com Taylor & Francis Verlag GmbH,
Kaufingerstraße 24, 80331 München, Germany

Printed and bound by CPI Group (UK) Ltd, Croydon, CR0 4YY
08/05/2025
01864376-0001